THE ALCHEMY FIRE MURDER

A Mary Wandwalker Mystery

By
Susan Rowland

 CHIRON PUBLICATIONS • ASHEVILLE, NORTH CAROLINA

© 2023 by Chiron Publications. All rights reserved. No part of this publication may be reproduced, stored in a retrieval system, or transmitted, in any form by any means, electronic, mechanical, photocopying, recording, or otherwise, without the prior written permission of the publisher, Chiron Publications, P.O. Box 19690, Asheville, N.C. 28815-1690.

www.ChironPublications.com

Interior and cover design by Danijela Mijailovic
Printed primarily in the United States of America.

ISBN 978-1-68503-129-9 paperback
ISBN 978-1-68503-130-5 hardcover
ISBN 978-1-68503-131-2 electronic
ISBN 978-1-68503-132-9 limited edition paperback

Library of Congress Cataloging-in-Publication Data

Names: Rowland, Susan, 1962- author.

Title: The alchemy fire murder : a Mary Wandwalker mystery / by Susan Rowland.

Description: Asheville, North Carolina : Chiron Publications, [2023] | Summary: "Former Archivist Mary Wandwalker hates bringing bad news. Nevertheless, she confirms to her alma mater that their prized medieval alchemy scroll, is, in fact, a seventeenth century copy. She learns that the original vanished to colonial Connecticut with alchemist, Robert Le More. Later the genuine scroll surfaces in Los Angeles. Given that the authentic artifact is needed for her Oxford College to survive, retrieving it is essential. Mary agrees to get the real scroll back as part of a commission for her three-person Enquiry Agency. However, tragedy strikes in Los Angeles. Before Mary can legally obtain the scroll, a young man is murdered, and the treasure stolen. Murder and theft are complicated by the disappearance in the UK of a witch mysteriously connected to the scroll. While Mary's colleague, Caroline, risks her sanity to go undercover in a dodgy mental hospital, her lover, Anna resorts to desperate measures. These, and Anna's silence over blackmail, threaten the survival of the Agency. Mary teams up with the victim's brother to track the killer, and the real alchemy scroll. Solving crimes on two continents will involve a rogue pharmaceutical corporation, Janet the witch, the Holywell Retreat Center near Oxford, plus the trafficked women they support, a graduate school in California, and a life-threatening mountain-consuming wildfire. Can these inexperienced detectives triumph over corrupt professors and racist attempts to rewrite history? Can they remake their fragile family? Will the extraordinary story of Robert Le More prove a source of hope for today?"-- Provided by publisher.

Identifiers: LCCN 2023001570 (print) | LCCN 2023001571 (ebook) | ISBN 9781685031305 (hardcover) | ISBN 9781685031329 (limited edition paperback) | ISBN 9781685031299 (paperback) | ISBN 9781685031312 (ebook)

Subjects: LCSH: Women archivists--Fiction. | Murder--Fiction. | Detective and mystery fiction.

Classification: LCC PS3618.O8815 A79 2023 (print) | LCC PS3618.O8815 (ebook) | DDC 813/.6--dc23/eng/20230228

LC record available at https://lccn.loc.gov/2023001570

LC ebook record available at https://lccn.loc.gov/2023001571

FOR JOEL WEISHAUS,
BELOVED.

**The Mary Wandwalker
Mystery Series by Susan Rowland:**

#1 - *The Sacred Well Murders*

#2 - *The Alchemy Fire Murder*

ACKNOWLEDGEMENTS
AND HISTORICAL NOTES

I would like first to thank my brilliant critique group, the mystery writers, Gay Toltl Kinman and Meredith Taylor. It is not their fault I am stubborn.

Also, I am grateful for support and patience of kind family and friends, in particular Cathy Rowland, John Rowland, the extended tribe, and all who know me at Pacifica Graduate Institute, and Greenwich University, London.

Huge thanks to Christine Saunders, Leslie Gardner, Evan Davis and Guillaume Batz, Claire Dyson, Ailsa Camm, Caroline Barker and Ailsa Montagu, Kathryn Le Grice, Ida Covi, Roula-Maria Dib, Lori Pye, and Jacqueline Feather and many more who contributed tea and sympathy, not to mention wine and cakes. Special thanks also to the Jungian Society for Scholarly Studies for encouragement.

This is a work of fiction, and no character is based on a real person, nor did any of the events depicted take place.

However, the career of my Francis Andrew Ransome, seventeenth century alchemist, dispenser of medicines, and Governor of colonial Connecticut, does resemble that of the historical John Winthrop Jnr. He really did become an alchemist member of the British Royal Society in London before setting sail for the colony with a barrel full of alchemy manuscripts. He did not, I hasten to add, steal an alchemy manuscript from an Oxford college. See reading list below for W. Woodward's wonderful source on his life and the precious unfulfilled

v

possibility that some colonists arrived in New England with a spirituality compatible with indigenous Americans.

Similarly, St Julian's College Oxford, exists on the spot occupied today by St Edmund's Hall, and borrows elements of its origin. Rather than a male archbishop though, I chose to imagine a college founded by a woman theologian renowned for positing a feminine and maternal side of God. Julian of Norwich is my exception to imagined historical figures (1343-1416). She lived walled up as an Anchorite and is the author of *Revelations of Divine Love,* the first known work in English by a woman scholar.

The Alchemy Fire Murder gives her an interest in alchemy that is neither historical nor incompatible with her theology. I also have her corresponding with an Oxford mason convulsed with grief. Together they decide to build a residence for students that will be named for Mother Julian. To support the spiritual and physical health of the students, she sends the gift of an alchemy scroll received from an Islamic scholar.

As mentioned in the story, alchemy travelled to medieval and renaissance Europe largely through Islam and before that from Africa. India and China also have rich alchemy traditions. What today may appear as a complex and confusing mixture of chemistry, theology, philosophy, and art, continues to influence modern culture from Shakespeare to surrealism to depth psychology and transdisciplinarity.

My fictional alchemy scroll bears a slight resemblance to *The Ripley Scroll*, named after Canon George Ripley (1415-1490), of which twenty-three copies exist, some in the Bodleian Library in Oxford. Coincidently or not, The Huntington Library in Pasadena, near Los Angeles, also has a copy.

FURTHER READING

Norwich, Julian of. (2022) *Revelations of Divine Love by Julian of Norwich.* Oxford World Classics.

Shaw, V. and Unknown (2018) *The Ripley Scroll: A Facsimile of the Pursuit for the Philosopher's Stone.* Erebus Society.

Woodward, W. W. (2010) *Prospero's America: John Winthrop Jnr., Alchemy, and the Creation of New England Culture, 1606-1676.* University of North Carolina Press.

CONTENTS

PROLOGUE: OXFORD 1399, January
PRIMA MATERIA OR
MOTHER JULIAN'S GIFT

They came early. When the knocking began, the household was yawning and laying fires in Master Giles's new Hall for students. Muttering a curse, the maid fumbled with the key. Perhaps she was gagging on the sewage liquefying in the rain, and the new door stuck. Wrenching it open, she was taken aback to see two women in stained cloaks of rough hessian. The old one, with a milky palsied eye, wielded a big stick. She stopped mid-bang.

"Where's Master Giles, the Mason?" she demanded.

"Beggars go to the kitchen!" snapped the servant. "God forgive you for abusing the master's charity. This Hall isn't taking students yet. We await a precious gift, Master says."

"Our Lady forgive *you* for insulting Mother Julian's emissaries. Fetch your Master. We bring the treasure that consecrates this heap of stones. Make way, woman."

The servant folded her arms. The old woman raised her voice to pierce the interior.

"Master Giles, come forth." She stamped her stick, ignoring the mud splash.

"Master Giles, of dumb rock and clay no more. Bless your Hall with the Mother's Alchemy Scroll."

She raised her voice to a shout. "Let this Hall be sanctified. Inspired by God, let the Alchemy Scroll…"

Her companion shot out a coal-colored hand to the old woman's arm, stopping the flow. The servant stared at her for the first time. She gasped.

1

"You... you're from..." The word lost; she recalled a dark-skinned, brightly robed man who sold a rare manuscript to Master Giles. The Master was strange that way, spending his gold on books.

"I was born in Morocco, in Africa, that is," said the young woman with a small smile. She had kind eyes, decided the servant. "My name is Sister Mary Jacob of the new Convent of the Holy Well. My companion goes by Lilies of the Field. Did your Master not tell you? He wrote to the Mother that the Hall is ready to receive her sacred gift. After delivering the Scroll, we go to the farm to begin the new convent."

"You're nuns?" The woman stepped back as if to invite the women inside. Doubt froze her. "Never seen nuns like you. And the Master works in stone. He builds colleges, not wattle and daub pig sties. This Hall he is finishing is the first... first..."

Sensing movement behind, she turned. The man who waved her aside had a red beard with bushy hair threaded with white. His green robe flapped as if he had lost weight, and there was strain around his mouth and eyes. While scrutinizing the arrivals, the man completed the maid's description.

"The first dedicated lodging for students in the University. Paid for by myself and Mother Julian of Norwich, the Anchorite."

Both women nodded. He continued: "If I heard aright, then you bear her divine Alchemy Scroll, her gift to protect the students who will live here. She can never leave her cell, walled up as she is. God protect her."

The astonished maid dropped a curtsy to Master Giles, then bobbed in the direction of the visitors before scuttling away. The big man beckoned his guests inside. Shaking water drops from their headscarves and cloaks, the nuns inspected the newly plastered room. Its chapel-like proportions pleased even Sister Lilies. Arched windows gleamed with an expensive skin of glass. In between hung woven wall hangings. Beside the scrubbed hearth, a kneeling manservant struggled with the fire. Damp logs, thought Master Giles.

Uncertain how to welcome visitors from the famous Anchorite, Master Giles hesitated, seeking a polite greeting. Before he could speak, the younger woman walked over to the tapestry on the farthest wall. Donated by Master Giles, it depicted a scene specified by Mother Julian. The whitest wool depicted tiny houses in a wooded valley. These stood for the new convent, the silent and secret twin of this student Hall in Oxford.

Watched by her fierce companion, the dark woman put her face inches from the fine weave, detecting in it a whiff of sheep. She brushed her fingertips over the depicted convent, then the desert mountain that filled the top half of the landscape. Master Giles felt a prickling of sparks down his spine.

A thump, the sound of cracking wood, and the hearth opposite spurted with gold flames. Their gleam colored the walls below the silvering rain on the windows. Master Giles blinked. His Hall was no longer an empty dormitory in a wild wet city. He recalled the secret kept from his men: the Hall's alignment with the spring moon at equinox. He gulped.

The walls are alive. Just as the Mother said, *the arrival of the Alchemy Scroll brings the Hall to the protection of God, a shelter for souls.*

He caught the fierce satisfaction in Sister Lilies's one blue eye.

"Forgive my people," he said to both women. He bowed again to the scowl of the old woman. "We expected you at the noon hour, and then in the habits of the new order."

"No habits," snapped the old one, taking the stool near the fire. She was not done. "Given the incomparable value of the Mother's gift, Master Giles, we travel as poor women. Did you hear our names? I am Sister Lilies, a copyist. This is Sister Mary Jacob, starwatcher and herbalist."

The man bit his lip. He could contain himself no longer.

"Let me see it, Sisters. In God's mercy, I beg you. Let me see Mother Julian's Alchemy Scroll before it is locked away."

3

Master Giles's plea made the women pause. His clasped hands were white at the knuckles. They exchanged glances.

"Will it cure the plague?" he burst out.

His manservant stopped poking the flames. The look he gave his Master was one of sorrow.

The younger nun got to her feet. "Master Giles." Her voice was gentle. "Master Giles, the rain and stench of Oxford are overpowering. Might we ask for water to wash and somewhere for our cloaks to dry?"

"Of course," he said at once. "My apologies, you must break your fast with us. Bring the ham, the best wine, and that round of cheese," he directed to the manservant. His gruff voice sounded crushed.

"I sent our packhorses to your stables," said the old woman, weariness in her tone. "Our man knows which box holds the casket."

Master Giles shut his eyes for a second. When they opened, it was as if a flint had sparked in each.

"Let me show you where the students will dine," he said. "When you have eaten your fill, I will beg your indulgence to unwrap the Alchemy Scroll. The table is longer than the one in the Bishop's Palace."

"Let your maidservant scrub the oak to the whiteness of the grain," said Sister Lilies. "Set your best wax candles in the window sconces and put fresh rushes on the floor. Then, yes, Master Giles, you shall see the Alchemy Scroll before we secure it in this Hall."

*****

It took until the church bells rang eleven times to prepare the room to the satisfaction of Sister Lilies. Master Giles knew he should be outside cuffing his apprentices while they finished the garden wall. Yet he could not tear himself away.

He hunched at one end of the table to reflect on his correspondence with Mother Julian. Her first message addressed him as Oxford's famous builder of colleges. She dreamed of benefiting poor scholars and required a stonemason of equal vision. He, on the other hand, was a burned-out shell of a man. Despair incinerated any interest in new projects.

Three years before the Black Death had swallowed much of Oxford in one stinking summer. Its greedy jaws took his sweet-lipped wife and tiny boy. Defying the priest who directed him to the plague pit outside the city wall, Master Giles himself dug the grave for their pus-filled bodies. No earthly delight remained for the stonemason.

"Your devoted servant," he wrote to Mother Julian, scratching out and replacing the letters many times until he'd carved them deep into the vellum. After a few months, Mother Julian spoke of her longing to make divine love visible in stone. Such work was restorative to the soul if the vision was shared. Part-funding and then constructing Mother Julian's Hall for Poor Scholars would rekindle Master Giles's spirit, she assured him.

So, the renowned builder, whose college chapels glittered delicate and durable as petrified forests, now faithfully followed another's instructions, and a woman at that. Her words soothed him as he directed his men or handled the chisel himself. It worked. Every mortared block or window polished warmed his soiled heart. Now he watched in silent prayer as Sister Mary Jacob unrolled the last layer of fine linen around the Scroll.

"Mother Julian's Alchemy Scroll is longer than your table, so we will show a section at a time."

He nodded and stood up. He did not dare to speak.

The next hours were the strangest of Master Giles's life. Neither before nor after did he ever encounter such astounding beauty in gold and silver leaf, nor such extraordinary beasts, more monstrous and elegant than travelers' tales. Never again would he encounter glass instruments dreamed up by necromancers. With tubes and round bellies, the flasks bubbled in green, gold, and red. One seethed and flashed, as if giving birth to a star.

Black and scarlet writing surrounded long teeth and tusks, ran up the ribs of snakes, and poured from the mouth of a mermaid. The script was in no language he'd ever seen. The two nuns shook their heads when he pointed a trembling finger.

"Look at the dragon, the fire in its mouth and burning on the mountains," whispered Sister Mary Jacob, not taking her eyes from the Scroll. Her words broke the waxen seal of the mason's awe.

"Sisters, that woman has a serpent tail. The green lion swallows the sun. Four elements become a castle with a fountain that spouts blood and fire. Why does the dragon breathe his smoke into the bath? Why is that naked king also a naked queen? Where be those lands where the mountains are consumed by fire?"

Master Giles spoke louder and louder. Tears poured from his eyes. Unsteady on his feet, he staggered to the bench by the wall and sat, covering his eyes with the backs of his hands.

"Master Giles, are you well?" The old woman asked sternly.

"I cannot read this sheet of dancing flames," he said. "It scorches my eyes."

"You begin to understand the sacred trust of the Mother's gift," said Sister Lilies.

"My sister will rewind the Scroll. Together we will secure the casket in the special room. Let me hear from your lips what the Alchemy Scroll means for Mother Julian's new Hall for Poor Scholars."

Giles looked up, his face wet. He rose to his feet, telling himself it was foolish to be afraid of the old nun.

Sister Lilies pursed her lips. "The Mother says to pray for less fire and more patient earth in my humors," she muttered.

Giles's expression cleared.

"The Alchemy Scroll works on the heart," he said. "It plants words as I plant stones. The Scroll-maker is my brother. He paints the mysteries of God while I, guided by the Mother, built the new Hall as a door to heaven," he said. His rapt thoughts took him beyond his visitors.

"Now I see why the Alchemy Scroll cannot leave the Hall. It is part of its fabric, a protection. Its holiness means it cannot be touched by naked palms. That is why the Mother wrote it will only be shown to one sick unto death."

He swallowed. "The Mother said it had curative powers. I had hoped... the plague?"

"No," said the uncompromising Sister Lilies. "The Alchemy Scroll is no cure for the sinful body with its pus and decay. Rather it teaches the soul to turn to God."

They heard a cough. Sister Mary Jacob stood at the door. "Alchemists are known for being physicians and makers of medicines. There are colors and herbs in the Scroll that we do not know." She added quietly, "Mother Julian believes that the Alchemy Scroll is medicinal for the body as well as the soul. That is why we Sisters of the Holy Well are the Key Keepers. We hold some of the Scroll's secrets."

Master Giles looked at her, dazed.

"By God's breath, I will obey Mother Julian's commands," he said. "I will tell no one of the visions the Scroll contains."

"You must keep silent," said Sister Lilles. Anxiety flushed her. "Seal up your prayers lest the Alchemy Scroll be burned by priests." She wet her lips, prepared to say more.

However, Sister Mary Jacob intervened.

"When the time comes to open Mother Julian's Scroll, the Hall will send for the Sisters of the Holy Well." She paused. "This is Mother's last instruction to you. We guard the key," she said slowly. "It will be passed down from Sister to novitiate. By the tongue, not the book."

*****

Their business concluded; the nuns made haste from the city. Sister Lilies did not like streets crammed with gowned young men. Many sought to impress the Church by their zeal in rooting out anything strange, occult, or held by women.

The final stage of the nuns' journey took them to their new home. To protect the women, the convent would be discreetly bound to the new Hall. Prayer, Hall, Scroll, and Convent spanned a secret symmetry to which one woman in every generation would hold the key.

The nuns reached the new Convent farm before the stiffness in Sister Lilies's knees became too painful. In the weeks that followed, the women labored. Snow fell late that winter, so the new lambs had to be kept in the kitchen. Planting for food as well as medicine had to be delayed. Even so, they dispensed remedies, together with salves and poultices for cracked bones to the county poor. The nuns found serenity in preparing the new Convent. Soon enough the sun would suck new shoots from the soil.

Late one night, the two Sisters sat over tallow lamps. After leafing through her copies of herbal recipes, Sister Lilies showed her sketches of beasts from the Alchemy Scroll.

"Our ink is low," remarked Sister Mary Jacob. "Amongst other things. We need supplies from Oxford. You should add colors to your Alchemy Scroll drawings. Some tinctures we saw back at Mother Julian's Hall are unknown, even to me. Nonetheless, I will try the Apothecary on the High Street. Your bones ache in these damp months, so wait for me here."

"Be careful," said Sister Lilies. "If they guess what we are copying, they'll call us witches."

"They already call us witches," replied Sister Mary Jacob, with a slight smile. She gave her companion a goodnight kiss on the cheek and left.

PART ONE
MASSA CONFUSA

CHAPTER 1
A PRESENT DAY SUMMONS

Winter persisted into early March across southern England. After two hours sitting patiently on a train, Mary Wandwalker saw trees as skeletons on either side of the tracks. Undaunted by the thickening clouds, she repeated to herself the essential nature of her journey.

I'm off to secure the Agency's first real job, a new life to rattle old bones. It's an adventure. I must impress, and I will, she thought. Never mind I hate the very idea of my old College; so much depends on this appointment. For forty years I guarded England's secrets. Now I'm going to make a few of my own.

The old train wheezed and shuddered. Her toes hurt with the cold. She'd unbuttoned her heavy lavender coat before a tinny voice announced that the heating was off until Oxford. Braking suddenly at Didcot Parkway, the train shuffled into a palpable silence. Oh oh, thought Mary. They never switch the engine off on a halt. Not a good sign.

She was impatient for the last push to the city of colleges and spires. Despite avoiding St. Julian's College for thirty-nine years, she was not the sort of person who failed to keep appointments. Even though I'd rather be heading to any other college, she grouched, gazing through the window beyond which the wind blew something gritty. Are those snowflakes? I don't believe it. In seconds, the platform was obscured by what looked like swirling white fur.

Miss Wandwalker ran her fingers through bobbed hair, now all colors from forbidding grey clouds to strands of silver.

11

She relished irony. Even the weather does not want me to go to my Oxford College. I'm going anyway, she promised herself, clenching gloved hands.

"A crisis," the youngish Dame Eleanor of St. Julian's College had said, "needing the utmost discretion. St. Julian's needs you, Miss Wandwalker."

It was a summons she could not ignore since the dramatic changes in her life. Abruptly dismissed after a lifetime managing an Archive in London, Miss Wandwalker began a venture without experience, without training, or, she now realized, without sufficient starting capital. Her Depth Enquiry Agency website gallantly proclaimed: "We dig deep into secrets that the police have no time for. Discretion is our priority."

Together with two unlikely co-workers, the never married Mary set her heart on making the fledgling business into an extended family, or its nearest substitute. Stuck on a freezing train in a wild snowstorm, Mary quailed at the fate of fledgling birds whose parents had unwisely decided to nest.

"Your Enquiry Agency is a sort of family business?" queried Mary's former boss, Mr. Jeffreys, a skeptic. "Because you have no family. Oh dear, Miss Wandwalker, what have you got yourself into?"

"You think we're incapable?" Mary's chin was up.

"I think *you*, Miss Wandwalker, can do anything you put your mind to. I know your steel from our long association at the Archive. Your son's widow and his former girlfriend however…" He left the rest unspoken.

You don't know Caroline and Anna, thought Mary. You don't even know *me*.

St. Julian's College wanted, nay demanded, her presence. Mr. Jeffreys was on the College Board, Mary recalled. Most likely he'd recommended them. When she mentioned this, Caroline said that Mr. Jeffreys and she seemed incapable of leaving each other alone. Mary did not dignify such nonsense with further remark.

The old train remained suspiciously quiet. Condensation on the windows began to sprout frost leaves. Even the last family, with their grizzling toddler and noisy crisp packets, abandoned hope and the carriage. With relief, Mary heard the door slam, followed by wrangling as they disappeared into the storm.

In the hush, she reviewed the phone call from St. Julian's. The woman's California drawl held an arrogance undercut by something else. Anxiety, Mary concluded. Interesting. After proclaiming a crisis at St. Julian's, the voice continued:

"Miss Wandwalker, the College has a problem. An incalculable loss... threatens our very survival. Must be treated with utmost discretion, secrecy. We can't go to the police. My sources recommend you, your Depth Enquiry Agency. As an alumnus I know we can count on you."

Certainly not was Mary's reply, bitten back. If she went with her gut, she would switch off her phone and throw it into a drawer. She would then disappoint two pairs of hopeful eyes, one green and trusting, the other, black and fierce. Mary could not fail Caroline and Anna. After all, she had promised her dead son she would take care of them. The Dame was still speaking.

"I've set up a meeting for us later this morning. My office in the Principal's Lodge. I take it you remember where that is."

There was no help for it. Mary pulled herself together. Putting her phone on speaker, she set her coffee machine to distill a dark brew with a fiery heart.

"Dame Eleanor," she said with forced calm. "What's this all about? My... *our* Agency is highly specialized and er... busy." The minus symbol on the Agency bank account made her pause.

"I've checked up on you," came the frustrating voice. "Shall we say 11 a.m., to give you time to get here? Ask at the Porter's Lodge for directions."

"We'll *say* twelve noon," said Mary, firmly, "I have business I to take care of first."

This was not true. Having secured the last word, she realized that it was a cheap victory. She did not want to go, but she did not have a choice.

13

Did this woman know the financial straits of the Agency? With only one client so far, and that a low-paying charity, they were desperate for more cases. Long ago, Mary had sworn off St. Julian's, yet Caroline and Anna depended on her.

Theoretically equal partners, Mary was in no illusion about who needed to be the public face of the Agency. With chronically depressed Caroline clinging to hope for their future, and Anna... well, Anna was Anna: an unpredictable, perhaps even dangerous young woman, who was just what their Agency was designed to contain.

Anyway, both Anna and Caroline were away on a missing person case. Some therapist calling herself a witch had vanished en route to hospital. At least it was in Oxfordshire, so Mary could rendezvous with Caroline and Anna in the city.

"My sources...," Dame Eleanor had said. Sources? Now Mary recalled a crucial detail about their client with the missing person. Online sources about the Holywell Retreat Center mentioned an historic connection to St. Julian's College. Mary had sent Caroline and Anna with instructions to report back. With any luck, the old woman had merely wandered off. But the irony grated.

In fact, Caroline phoned the news that the case of the missing therapist was proving complicated.

"You know, her vanishing could be connected with St. Julian's," she said doubtfully.

"*What?*"

"Well, I'm not sure about that. But listen, Mary, Anna says this is more than a missing person. She's sure the old woman is in danger."

"It's a Retreat Center. How dangerous can that be?"

Mary was being disingenuous. She knew that Holywell housed and treated victims of sex trafficking. Yet the missing woman was an elderly resident, one of the counselors, not a traumatized teenager.

Rumor had it that the Holywell women were witches. Mary discounted the rumor. Surely the reputation for esoteric spirituality and herbal medicine did not go that far? Holywell chose the Depth Enquiry Agency, the email said, because they knew that Anna was a trafficking survivor.

Survivor, thought Mary. Anna was nothing if not that.

Now, en route to a second and possibly lucrative client, it was so cold that even Mary's frustration froze. The train did nothing while snow settled on the deserted platform. The white stuff covered crushed paper cups from the Expresso Bar, discarded tickets, and a few biscuit wrappers.

Mary was about to dash to the café for a hot drink when the lights went out and the sign twitched to CLOSED. She stamped her feet to get blood back while fretting about arriving late. It would put the Agency, *her*, at a disadvantage. She had to *do* something. Grabbing her bag, Mary stepped out of the carriage, ignoring the wind that gripped her throat.

"Excuse me, when is this train departing?"

The uniformed guard was muttering into a radio. He barely looked up, his exposed cheek raw under a cap.

"You on the 10:50 to Oxford ma'am? It's canceled. The snow." His accent was pure Birmingham.

"Canceled? That's no good. I'm due in Oxford in forty minutes. I have an appointment at one of the Colleges."

"The points are frozen, see?" said the man with an irritating lack of urgency. "They reckon they'll have them working in time for the 2:15. Maybe..." He stopped, catching sight of Mary's expression. Her grey eyes glittered.

"I need a taxi. Immediately. And Southern Rail will pay for it." The guard took a step back. Mary glared on.

"Taxi? Yes, ma'am! Let me call one for you now. I'll escort you through the ticket barrier. Just this way, please."

15

CHAPTER 2
ST. JULIAN'S COLLEGE HAS A PROBLEM

With mixed feelings that jelled in the cold, Mary clambered from the taxi at the medieval gate of St. Julian's. Careful of the snow under her unsuitable shoes, she ignored the porter holding his hands to a red-barred electric fire and strode to the Principal's Lodge. Every stone and arch loomed at her, calling in voices she could not let herself remember.

She had been a deliriously happy student at St. Julian's College, until the unexpected death of her fiancé. Now forty years later, Mary crunched through the quad concentrating on the blue-tinged shadows. That wet on her cheeks must be the snow melting as Mary wrenched open the elaborate door rarely used by students. She slammed it shut behind her, as if she could split off her memories to perish in the skin-searing cold.

At least the Lodge was hospitably warm. Despite wood paneling from the seventeenth century, it possessed excellent insulation and twentieth-century heating. Mary took the ornate stairs followed by a corridor studded with portraits of past principals. Arriving at a door carved with Tudor roses, she knocked.

After the usual greetings, the Principal made sure Mary noticed the valuable antiques that confirmed her status. Trying too hard? wondered Mary. The woman seemed to be hesitating.

"Your name intrigues me," said Dame Eleanor Martinez, an expensively dressed woman in her late thirties. Her condescension made Mary grit her teeth. As if no one had ever

17

commented on it before. "Wandwalker, so unusual. Is it from Latin?"

"Old English," said Mary shortly. "Means 'wind-talker' I'm told." She did not add that Anna claimed that Wind Talkers were ancient women who spoke to the gods.

"I was headhunted from California Catholic University," explained Dame Eleanor, pouring thin coffee. "Dame is a courtesy title because the position is usually 'Master.'" She gave a tiny smile. "I'm a feminist theologian, although feminism doesn't mean anything anymore."

Mary bristled. Surely the woman did not believe that women had achieved equality. She lived in Oxford, after all. The Dame continued.

"St. Julian's Board wanted my research on Mother Julian. As a former student, you'll know all about her gift of the *Alchemy Scroll*." The Dame sounded cautious even when emphasizing her last two words.

Mary stared at the much younger woman. What was she on about? In her late thirties, the sharp-eyed Dame appeared to have difficulty making up her mind. A toss of her silk scarf drew attention to her expensive clothes, including a red cashmere sweater. Anna could name the designer, Mary guessed. The woman's artfully streaked brown hair complimented her olive skin. Only strain lines around mouth and eyes betrayed anxiety.

Theologians have changed, thought Mary. Memories surfaced of a bald man in a cape scuttling through a windswept quad. So, why mention the Alchemy Scroll? Everyone knew about it, even though it was rarely accessed.

"Naturally, I know St. Julian's has an Alchemy Scroll that goes back to Julian of Norwich. However, I've never seen it," Mary said, sipping her bitter brew. She decided to ignore the hunger pangs sharpened by the cold. "Hasn't it been here since the college's foundation? I didn't think anyone was allowed to study it."

She put down her cup. Why did Dame Eleanor keep looking toward the door?

18

"Ever since the *Hall*'s foundation," corrected Dame Eleanor. "Exceptions are made for a few scholars. In fact, you could say that sums up our problem."

Instantly, Mary had questions, but Dame Eleanor was reluctant to leave teaching mode.

"Julian of Norwich endowed a Hall for poor students with an Oxford stonemason. It was the first purpose-built student residence, opening in spring 1399. Of course, Mother Julian's Alchemy Scroll is older. Our *St Julian's* did not become a college until 1657."

This must be her regular college speech. Mary had had enough. She became brisk.

"And now there's a problem. With the Scroll, I assume. How can The Agency help?"

"We want you to look at the Scroll, first."

"We?"

"Ah, yes, you came highly recommended. He'll be here any moment. Meanwhile, my assistant can fetch the Alchemy Scroll. It comes in a sort of casket."

A few minutes later, the carroty haired young man Mary had glimpsed in the outer office entered with a wooden box. When he placed it on the desk, Mary saw carvings of the sun and moon. Carrot top nodded at Dame Eleanor and ducked out. Mary got to her feet, curiosity warring with her resistance to anything that involved St Julian's.

A heavy tread creaking the wooden stairs announced Dame Eleanor's unnamed "he." As the large man entered, Mary's cheeks flamed again. She turned her head away, pointedly snubbing the Black-British man who brushed drops of melted snow off a charcoal coat. Ignoring Mary in turn, he removed his outer garments to reveal a suit of dazzling pearl grey.

Mary sighed, noticing how Mr. Jeffreys, her old boss at the London Archives, filled the room. It was he who had the effrontery to suggest that getting fired was really a great opportunity. A chance for a new kind of life, to find your own ground, he'd said. Mary burned at the memory.

To her scowl, he smiled. "Ah yes, Miss Wandwalker. No surprise to see you here. You'll remember our very first meeting in the quad here at St. Julian's."

Mary's jaw dropped. In all their years working together, he had never alluded to the incident. Nor had she.

In her first term at St. Julian's, one midnight Mary woke to drunken roaring below her window. With a shock she identified racist taunts. She remembered that St. Julian's had admitted one of the university's first black students, a quiet young man now in his third year reading law. The crack of knuckle against jaw drew her to the window.

Where were the college porters? This must be the infamous all-white, elite Rugby Club she'd heard about. She wanted to pretend it wasn't happening, when she made out a figure being dragged toward the middle of the lawn. Forgetting shoes, she ran downstairs in bare feet. Yanking open the outer door, she yelled and then heard the thump of thick boots as the drunks made their getaway.

When Mary stepped onto the damp grass, she saw a lonely figure sitting in the eighteenth-century fountain where the revelers had tossed him. In the silver lamplight, something sticky dripped from his nose. Mary ran over and held out her hand. After a pause, Jeffreys took hold and stepped carefully from the water onto the lawn, slippery now with his blood.

In the surreal moment, they exchanged no words. She wiped his nose, which was bleeding from an encounter with a bronze spout shaped as the mouth of a dolphin. For the rest of that term, one sleeve of her nightgown had a brown stain that would not wash out.

Eight months later, Jeffreys graduated with a First and entered the Civil Service fast-track. Perhaps he did not forget Mary. When she hit hard times, it was his signature on the letter inviting her for an interview at the Archive.

Forty years later, Jeffreys "let her go." Today, in Dame Eleanor's study he grinned at the mixed emotions on Mary's face. She had not forgiven him.

"Of course, you know each other," said Dame Eleanor absently. Her attention concentrated on the box as if she was afraid of what was inside, Mary thought. The Dame nipped to her desk, unlocked a drawer, and extracted a long iron key blackened with age. The key opened the Alchemy Scroll's casket, whereupon the Dame reverently extracted an object wrapped in layers of cloth.

There was a sweet metallic smell. Oilskin? No, incense, thought Mary. Without meaning to, she moved closer. A pair of leather gloves appeared in front of Mary, and she put them on.

Snowflakes patted the window like tiny ghost-white hands. Dame Eleanor switched on another lamp. Mr. Jeffreys moved to stand with his back to the window, as if protecting the Scroll from the snow. Mary delicately unrolled about six inches. For less than a minute she stared. Very gently she put her gloved finger and thumb to grip the Scroll edge. She frowned, then stood very straight, giving the impression of a taller woman.

"It's a fake," said Mary. Her two companions let out identical breaths. Both had severe expressions.

"How do you know?" said Dame Eleanor. She was not surprised, Mary saw.

"The paper," said Mary, staring down at the Scroll. She could hardly believe what she was saying. "I mean it *is* paper. I never saw the Alchemy Scroll, but we were told it was vellum. Paper was rare until the end of the medieval period. This paper is thicker than usual. A wash has been applied to resemble vellum."

"Congratulations, Miss Wandwalker," said Mr. Jeffreys ironically. "You've just sealed the fate of your old college. St. Julian's will be bankrupt in less than a month."

Mary reeled. "Bankrupt? Surely not. The St. Julian's Scroll was never that valuable. Aren't there are other copies in Europe? Isn't there an older version of this Alchemy Scroll in the Vatican's sealed archive? And anyway," she said addressing Mr. Jeffreys, "alchemy was debunked. No one ever turned lead into gold. Alchemy was for charlatans."

21

"Ah," began Mr. Jeffreys. "Our rational Miss Wandwalker adheres to the popular view that alchemy was only about metallurgy and gold. How undiscerning of you."

Mary's cheeks blazed. "What are you talking about?" she snapped. She could see the Dame clasping her hands. Why were they so upset about a missing medieval Scroll? Mr. Jeffreys enlightened her.

"Quite apart from the fact that alchemy proves to be a form of what we today call psychology — the alchemists projected themselves into the work — without realizing it, of course — the St. Julian's Alchemy Scroll is, *was,* unique in being the sole copy in vellum."

He sighed and gave Mary his most earnest expression.

"You see, Miss Wandwalker, it no longer matters that the Alchemy Scroll at St. Julian's is not the oldest amongst the seven versions in libraries across Europe. Vellum absorbs and retains. Paints, potions, and essences last for centuries soaked into parchment or vellum while paper decays." Mr. Jeffreys banged a fist on a chair back, a sure sign of frustration to Mary.

"Gross exaggeration," said Mary, stung. She knew all about paper. "When I was in the Archive…"

Dame Eleanor intervened. "Mr. Jeffreys is upset about the College's position," she said in a soothing voice. "His point about the Scroll is that we are talking about unique mixtures of vegetable and mineral substances, some only recently identified. Vellum retains minute amounts of rare compounds where paper does not."

Mary opened her mouth and shut it again. She nodded at Dame Eleanor to continue.

"You see," said Dame Eleanor, waving Mary over to a table with a tray of coffee and biscuits, "back then alchemists made medicines. You could call them the research chemists of early pharma." She spoke with intensity, willing Mary to understand.

"Not just what they mixed in their labs; *alchemy manuscripts were medicinal too. Today we would understand them as uniting psychology, science, theology, and visual art with substances absorbed by scent and skin.*"

22

Mary took a breath and slowly nodded. She did not understand alchemy, but she could see that the Dame and Mr. Jeffreys were upset. She could see the Dame gauging her response before continuing.

"Paper alchemy texts lose potency. Vellum preserves the secret compounds. For our Alchemy Scroll, St. Julian's records suggest unknown tinctures with extraordinary powers. And so…" Dame Eleanor sighed.

"And so," continued Mr. Jeffreys in a harsher tone, "when the College fell into debt, its mortgages were bought up by Mer-Corp, an American Bank with a huge pharma division. They demanded the Alchemy Scroll as collateral in return for a rate of interest that the College could afford. To them, collateral included access by one of their experts."

"That was before we found out about the copy," confirmed Dame Eleanor, gloomily, pressing a button for her assistant. She held up a hand for silence until the young man had disappeared with the false scroll. Mary sat down and pulled off the gloves, white leather, she noticed, lying them next to her empty coffee cup.

"You understand the problem, Miss Wandwalker," said the Dame after the door had clicked shut. "The College's finances depend on the loan secured against the Alchemy Scroll, the *real* Scroll."

Mr. Jeffreys interrupted. "Forget your skepticism about alchemy, Miss Wandwalker, and listen carefully. This problem is bigger than you can imagine."

Mary wanted to snap back and leave the stuffy office. But what about the survival of the Agency? And, yes, she supposed she did care about the longevity of St Julian's.

"Well, Miss Wandwalker," Dame Eleanor continued. "I won't bore you with battles in academia that I don't follow myself. You are right, of course, that science from the eighteenth century on has rejected alchemy. But given the crises of *this* century, alchemy is being reevaluated, and not only as early psychology." She glanced at Mr. Jeffreys, he nodded.

"Today it appears that alchemy combines what we might call Eastern and Western medicine. After all, there was an alchemy in China and India, as well as Africa. European alchemy came from the East through Islam. Mother Julian's Scroll is just one example."

The Dame paused for another glance at a frowning Mr. Jeffreys.

"Go on, spell it out," he finally said.

The Dame took a deep breath. "Most unfortunately for St. Julian's, our mortgage holder Mer-Corp's chemists suspect that the original vellum Scroll contains ingredients for a new antibiotic or antiviral."

Mary Wandwalker sat up. It did not take the recent pandemic for her to realize that such a new drug would be supremely precious, in money as well as lives.

"I see," she murmured. "Just the possibility of that kind of new drug would make the St. Julian's Alchemy Scroll priceless." She added an afterthought: "As if it really could make gold."

The Dame nodded. "Everyone knows our Scroll has never left the College. The Alchemy Scroll is the foundation of St. Julian's. We got the money from Mer-Corp on the Bursar's valuation of the original, not least because his Ph.D. student has been studying it."

Mr. Jeffreys snorted his opinion of the Bursar.

"Not fair, Mr. Jeffreys," said the Dame, wearily. "You know he's a chemist, not an historian nor an expert in manuscript authenticity. We wouldn't let him take samples from the Scroll until... well until Mer-Corp said they needed proof of provenance. Now they've announced they're sending their own expert."

Dame Eleanor poured herself a glass of water from a carafe on her desk. Her hand shook. "If we don't find the original Alchemy Scroll, the College will be ruined." She suddenly looked older. "I was appointed to sort out the financial mess in this historically poor College. Now I find I could be sealing St. Julian's fate."

CHAPTER 3
WHO STOLE THE ALCHEMY SCROLL?

Mary prided herself on being a practical woman. She refused to dwell on the unthinkable, such as the closure of her Oxford College.

"Right. The problem, as I see it, is how to recover the Alchemy Scroll given by Mother Julian. Tell me how the medieval Scroll got switched?"

The younger woman turned to Mr. Jeffreys. "You're sure we can trust Miss Wandwalker's discretion? So far only I, you, the Bursar, and his postgrad know the situation with the missing Scroll."

Mary bristled. Perhaps she could swing out of the College gates with head held high. She'd be invisible in the falling snow. Certainly, she'd had enough of Mr. Jeffreys's mysterious authority. The man by the window grinned.

"Calm down, Mary. I'm on the Board of St. Julian's, that's all. I recommended you because I know you are the ideal person when it comes to… er… lost manuscripts. I care enough about this college; *my* college," he repeated with emphasis, "to see it gets the very best." He smiled blandly at Dame Eleanor. She relaxed and managed a thoughtful nod at Mary.

Mary did not believe for a moment that Mr. Jeffreys had told all he knew. Yet she was intrigued by the Alchemy Scroll. Also, she reflected, her new Agency possessed a similarity to St. Julian's College: debts of existential proportions. She turned to the Dame, whose lipsticked mouth was cracked with worry lines.

25

"So, if the Scroll never leaves..." she began, not sure of the question she wanted to ask. "It has a special basement. You only get to go inside if...if..."

"If there comes a time of '*grete sicknesse, then the scholer shal holde ye Scroll with a naked hand so that by the gras of oure lady he shal be made whole*,'" quoted the Dame from the Founders' Charter.

"The Alchemy Scroll originated in Persia, sent by an unknown Islamic scholar to Mother Julian. You know," she said, warming to her own research subject. "She dedicated her life to the feminine in the divine. In the medieval period, just imagine. To her, God was a forgiving mother, so different from the punishing rhetoric of the Church."

Dame Eleanor's enthusiasm was hard to stem. "Alchemy depicts a conjunction of spiritual feminine and masculine to make what they called the *panacea*, a cure for diseases, including the mind; what we now call psychosomatic. Obviously, the Scroll invoked the placebo effect."

She waved her hands. "Only in the nineteenth century did they discontinue the practice of allowing sick students to hold the Scroll. No good against tuberculosis, they said."

Mary tried to conceal her impatience. Just how had her College lost its greatest treasure?

"We need you to get it back," said Dame Eleanor, glaring at Mary. "We *must* have it back for the expert valuation in two weeks, or the college will default on its loans. Mer-Corp will foreclose."

"Two weeks..." exclaimed Mary. "Can't you postpone?"

"Unfortunately, not," said Dame Eleanor, a bit shamefaced. "The initial assessments by our Bursar, Godric St. John, worked fine when the loan was offered. Now they're sending a real alchemy scholar, a Professor Macdonald. The College has... er taken on too many...unusual commitments."

There was something the Dame did not want to talk about. Mary reviewed the story so far. Jeffreys turned back to the window, as if fascinated by the snow.

26

"The copy," Mary began. "That must take expertise, and… of course precise knowledge of the Alchemy Scroll. You don't put it on display. Tell me you haven't published it on the web?"

"Certainly not," said the Dame, shocked. "The Founders Charter speaks of divine secrets. Publishing it would subject us to a nightmare of conspiracy theories." Seeing Mary about to ask a question, the Dame continued.

"Miss Wandwalker, the Alchemy Scroll is in no known language. No one has been able to decipher it, not even Mother Julian, who wrote some annotations. Her notes add to the priceless nature of the manuscript."

Mary leaned forward. "So, the next step is to narrow down who had the opportunity to copy it and leave the fake."

A choking sound came from Mr. Jeffreys. One cheek was illuminated by the bluish radiance from the falling snow. Mary frowned at him. Was he *laughing*? He grinned as if she were his prize pupil.

"Miss Wandwalker, you've forgotten to ask *when* the Alchemy Scroll was stolen."

Turning from him with dignity, Mary pasted on a charming smile for Dame Eleanor.

"I should have said right away." The Dame sighed. "It's not a recent theft. We've narrowed it down using chemical analysis and the help of the Ph.D. student. The Scroll was substituted in 1658 between 22nd March and 28th November."

Mary sat back, stunned. "St. Julian's Alchemy Scroll has been a copy since *the seventeenth century.* No wonder…"

"No wonder it wasn't effective against TB a hundred and fifty years ago," agreed Dame Eleanor drily. "Although it did some good during the great influenza outbreak of 1739, when the Thames froze. Placebo, of course. You see, we know who took the real Scroll."

"You *know* who stole it?"

Mary did not like feeling forced to catch up. "So, you must have the location."

27

"Not exactly. Just probably," said the Dame. She was too tense, Mary saw. "And we do need you to go get it. Mr. Jeffreys thinks you could negotiate for us. With… the current holders… if they really do have it." She seemed to see something in Mary's face because she heaved a sigh.

"Look, Miss Wandwalker, I know I've not explained it well. It's all so overwhelming, you see. The Bursar, Professor Godric St. John, says that if we do not have the real Alchemy Scroll when Macdonald arrives, then Mer-Corp will destroy the College. They'll sell the mortgages to foreign real estate investors."

Noting Mary's expression, she added, "convert the College buildings into fancy apartments. No more St. Julian's." She looked bleak. "This Government won't step in. I'm just a theologian, not a financial wizard."

Despite the woman's worldly poise, Mary smelled fear. She'd missed one obvious question. Now there was another.

"I see. Tell me, who took the Scroll?"

There was a silence while Dame Eleanor gulped more water.

"His name is, was, Francis Andrew Ransome. Back then he was a well-known alchemist in London, part of the secret circle that became the Royal Society. After substituting the Scroll, he emigrated to America and became the Governor of the new colony of Connecticut."

"America? A Governor?" Mary was startled again. "You're sure?"

The Dame bristled. "We've been working on this nonstop," she reproved. "It all fits, Miss Wandwalker. In 1658, just after St. Julian's Hall became a College of Oxford University, Ransome arrived to consult the Alchemy Scroll. Our records show he was drawn by its divine potency and medicinal recipes. On subsequent visits, he brought an artist friend to copy pages for him to take to the New World, or so he said."

"Ah," said Mary.

28

The Dame threw up her hands. "The artist went by the name, Le More, Robert Le More. He and Ransome sailed for America on 29th November of that year." The Dame paused, dwelling on the learned thief. "Godric St. John's research student put together a timeline by examining college records."

Fascinated, Mary forgot about Mr. Jeffreys blocking the window, watching her. Now he intervened. "Your Agency could have been set up for this. You've been advertising the kind of in-depth services — on a missing person, say — that the police cannot do. Now here is real depth, the deep past."

He was enjoying her dilemma, Mary could tell. She was not mollified.

Dame Eleanor turned up the lamp on her desk. It shone yellow on her sculpted hair.

"Francis Ransome had the reputation of being a kind of Prospero: magically dispelling winter storms in the Atlantic; that sort of thing. We know, or think we know, that he took the Alchemy Scroll to the town he founded to house his alchemical foundry, New Portsmouth. Fortunately, public legal documents in the early colony have been put online."

She paused and licked her lips. Mary leaned to catch the Dame's lowered tones.

"We found his last Will and Testament, Miss Wandwalker. The will mentions a magical and astrological manuscript of great rarity. In fact, a scribble on the margin says it is "borrowed from Oxford," if you can believe it. Magic and astrology mean alchemy, I'm told. Governor Ransome was one of those alchemists who concocted and prescribed medicines. Before 1700, he was famous for his alchemy remedies. No doubt the reason he took the Scroll."

"Because of its reputation for medicinal properties? And left a copy behind?" Mary tried to envisage the extraordinary theft.

"It's a wonderful reproduction," said Dame Eleanor apologetically. "A work of art, really. Le More included Mother Julian's annotations in old ink. We can tell how perfect the copy is from a few medieval sketches. So, we know that the version Ransome left us has the same extraordinary creatures, gold leaf, unknown language, symbols, paintings of glass retorts, alchemy furnaces, and so on. If it hadn't been for Godric St. John testing the tiniest sample for his research — ironically on a grant from Mer-Corp."

Dame Eleanor's shoulders slumped. She glanced at Mr. Jeffreys for support. He nodded.

"It seems that our Scroll, the Le More reproduction, contains compounds from plants only found in the Americas. One was tobacco, or was it yam? At any rate, from imports to England only available after the 1620s."

"From the early settlers," said Mary. "Getting back to the manuscript in Ransome's will...?" she prompted. She was starting to see why she had been recommended.

Again, Dame Eleanor looked doubtful. Mary sat up straighter. She summoned the earnest figure of Caroline and the slightly menacing one of Anna.

A cough came from the large man at the window, and the Dame continued, wearily.

"Although Ransome's descendants stayed in New England, they sold the contents of his study to The Los Angeles Museum of Early Manuscripts — 'early' means here early in the history of America, you realize. Along with books, letters, charters, and household accounts are three sealed chests."

She smiled grimly. "We need you to open them, Miss Wandwalker. Find the real Alchemy Scroll, and then negotiate its return to St. Julian's with absolutely no publicity." She folded her hands.

Mary gazed at her prospective client. She would not be rushed. Mere months ago, Mr. Jeffreys thrust her into what promised to be lonely retirement. Instead, she'd cashed in her assets, obtained a mortgage on a run-down house in Surrey, and set up the Depth Enquiry Agency with her two extraordinary associates, as Mr. Jeffreys called them.

"So, Miss Wandwalker, will you take the case?" It was Jeffreys, not the Dame. Mary waited for as long as she dared and then nodded.

"We will email you our standard contract and rates," she said.

Dame Eleanor did not hide her relief. "The College is very grateful, Miss Wandwalker. Mr. Jeffreys says I need not meet your associates." The Dame raised her eyebrows at Jeffreys, who coughed again.

"Extraordinary women," he murmured. His eyes met Mary's. Oh yes, they were extraordinary, all right.

Mary had a flash of Caroline, her dark cloud of depression capable of blazing insight and empathy. And Anna, whose will to survive made her a formidable internet hacker. She even calls herself a cyberwitch. If the three of them could tune their skills, the world would thrum indeed. Lulled by the hot room, Mary's head drooped.

"Miss Wandwalker?" The Dame looked from her to the door.

Stung awake, Mary seized the initiative. "I have a few more questions."

"Naturally. Professor St. John will brief you. We have a contact at the Los Angeles Museum for you. He's an alum of our degree in History and Curatorial Studies, Dennis Patrick Murphy. When I remembered that D.P.'s parents were on sabbatical in California, we secured an internship in the very museum that holds the Ransome Bequest. Reports on D.P. are favorable. He will meet you at the Museum. You'll travel to Los Angeles after I've briefed the Director."

"We've purchased your flight to LAX for the day after tomorrow," added Mr. Jeffreys.

Mary nodded. She belatedly realized she ought to have taken out her notebook. Never mind, her memory was excellent.

Dame Eleanor could not let her go without reiterating her chief worry. "Miss Wandwalker, we must, we absolutely *must* insist upon complete discretion. If there is a whisper, on a Facebook page, or Twitter, or anything… The College would be destroyed. It's not just Mer-Corp foreclosing, although that would be bad enough. We have hundreds of years of reputation based on Mother Julian's *actual* manuscript."

She was wringing her hands, Mary noted. People do that? Mary looked down, preparing a cutting rejoinder.

"And there's more…" said Mr. Jeffreys softly. Mary felt rather than heard the sigh from the other woman.

"Oh, yes, there's more," she said with reluctance. "You see; the College has a…a connection with a local Retreat Center, called Holywell. The truth is… well, we've lost a witch."

Mary's head shot up: "A *witch?*"

Holywell, where therapists call themselves witches. I knew it, Mary groaned inwardly. Holywell is where Caroline and Anna have gone. Our Agency is already involved.

CHAPTER 4
WHAT HAS BEEN SPLIT
MUST BE REUNITED

By ten o'clock the next morning, Mary's hand was tired from making notes in Professor Godric St. John's study. So far, the briefing on the Alchemy Scroll dwelt on the professor's astonishing discoveries rather than the Alchemy Scroll's fate in America. Perched on a wingback chair while the St. Julian's chemist expounded, Mary became uncomfortable and keen to escape.

Godric St John ignored Mary wriggling her back. Refusing a bed in College the night before had backfired since the only affordable Bed and Breakfast might as well have stuffed its mattress with straw. That's what they did in Mother Julian's time, she reflected.

"*What has been split must be reunited,*" Professor Godric St. John declaimed, addressing his formidable bookcases.

Another male for whom older women are invisible, Mary had earlier concluded. Supposed to be discussing the replacement Alchemy Scroll, St. John kept harping on the original.

"What has been split must be reunited," he repeated. "You see, a great reunion is foundational to alchemy. Alchemy reunites spirit and matter with extraordinary possibilities. Ironic, is it not, Miss Wandwalker, given our predicament with the missing Scroll? We at St. Julian split from our precious treasure for centuries, and we did not know."

"Um ye...es, could you tell me more about how you found out?" reminded Mary. "That the Alchemy Scroll you have is seventeenth century and not the one from Mother Julian?"

St John winced, staring down at the quad. The Bursar's white curls resembled the wigs of frockcoated, unsmiling men in the college portraits. There was an undeniable crystalline smell about his dusty person. His skin looks freeze-dried on either side of that sharp nose, decided Mary.

St. John bowed graciously at the passing students below. None of them looked up, Mary noticed. She surreptitiously checked her phone. Anna and Caroline should be arriving soon from Holywell. Mary wanted all three of them to press the Professor of Chemistry about the fake Scroll. Caroline and Anna have... different instincts, she said to herself. Also, there was the matter of the Alchemy Scroll's connection to the missing witch that Dame Eleanor mentioned.

This emphasis on witchcraft is unnecessary, thought Mary; distasteful even. The resident women at the Retreat Center are qualified counselors with doing regular therapy. Who cares if they do a few spells in their spare time?

Seeing St. John pointing like a hunting dog at inferior life forms, Mary decided to offer him his favorite subject: himself.

"It was your expertise, I believe," she began.

No, you can do better, Mary.

"Your *groundbreaking* research that uncovered a secret hidden for over three centuries. What a phenomenal achievement."

Too much? Apparently not. Godric St. John swiveled in her direction and allowed her a supercilious smile. She's met that preening manner before when she was an archivist. As he prepared to describe his brilliant deductions, there was a rapping on the door. Mary sprang to her feet.

"That will be my fellow operatives," she said, wondering how to prepare him for Caroline and Anna.

"I think not," said Godric with irritating assurance.

34

Mary forced a smile and sat back down. Her host trotted to the door and returned with a skinny young man in jeans and an old camel hair coat, holding his head at an awkward angle. Mary also noted how the blue rims of his glasses contrasted with his brown skin and shiny black hair.

"Miss Wandwalker, my Ph.D. student, Ravi Patel," announced St John. "He's working with me to find new pharmaceuticals. Since his doctorate explores alchemical compounds, he's assisting me with the Alchemy Scroll."

"Oh, you're Miss Wandwalker." The young man blinked at her as if she was under a microscope. That awkward bend in his neck must be from all these low medieval doors, thought Mary. Patel took a step toward her, glasses glinting as they caught lamplight.

"You're going to get the real Alchemy Scroll back for us. I... that is we... need it for the next stage in our research."

"I hope I can retrieve it," said Mary with caution. "Um... what's your research again?"

"Alchemy's potential use in modern medicine," said the young man, warming up. He kept glancing at St. John as if asking permission to speak.

"You see, back then the alchemists were doctors, or what we would call pharmacists. They invented all sorts of medicines that were later simply poured away, the recipes burned as rubbish. Now we're finding the most astonishing compounds..."

St. John hissed, and Patel's jaw dropped. "So sorry, Professor," he blabbed.

The young man's cheeks were fired with a feverish flush. "Professor St. John got me a scholarship to work on St. Julian's Alchemy Scroll. When we get the real one back, I'm going to strip away its secrets."

Repelled by this desire to crack open the Scroll like an egg, Mary prepared to be severe. Could the historical significance of the Alchemy Scroll survive such corrosive attentions?

35

"Surely the language has never been identified?" she queried remembering details from yesterday. "Aren't the illustrations a mystery? I've been hearing of strange beasts, magical colors."

Ravi Patel exchanged a smug expression with his supervisor. Mary envisioned Patel collecting samples from the vellum. Surely not actually *scraping away* at the paints and inks. What about Mother Julian's Founder's Charter insisting that the Alchemy Scroll be preserved as a precious and health-benefiting holy relic?

"Mr. Patel will accompany you to America to retrieve the *real* Alchemy Scroll," stated Godric St. John into the air between Mary and his student.

"Absolutely not!" exclaimed Mary. "My agency... *our* agency," she corrected, hearing movement on the stairs, "is independent. We do not collaborate with outsiders."

St. John choked, and Patel turned scarlet. Before either could utter a word, there was a knock on the door, followed by a banging that shook the picture next to it. Mary leapt to open it and usher in Caroline and Anna. Directing them to the sofa, she ignored the scattered hardback books minus their dustjackets. The chilled women sat down, but there the resemblance ended.

Anna, in her twenties, swung her long raven hair, which seemed to emit sparks. Patel's eyes fastened on her green satin trousers below a close-fitting black jacket. Mary devoutly hoped that Anna's designer clothes came from her past life as the consort of a criminal. High fashion was Anna's disguise. She hid behind her beauty and impersonated the dress codes of wealth. The young woman surveyed the two men while giving nothing away about herself.

Sitting quietly beside her was her lover. In her forties, Caroline's curly hair had faded from copper and needed a trim. She was the one who scooped up the books and arranged them on a side table before unbuttoning a slate-colored raincoat that had seen better days. Dressed in jeans and at least two sweaters, Caroline kept her green eyes upon Mary. Caroline hated meeting new people.

"Godric St. John and Ravi Patel," said Mary, tired of titles, "these are my associates, Anna Vronsky," the young woman inclined her head, "and Caroline Jones. They've been to the Holywell Retreat Centre to enquire about your missing person," she said. At the mention of Holywell, both men started. Godric St. John recovered first.

"We try not to have too much contact with that… Holywell. The missing woman is *their* business. Your job is to recover our Alchemy Scroll."

"At least for now," broke in Ravi Patel. He glanced apologetically at his superior. "The Professor knows we need help from the Key Keeper once we get the real manuscript. That's the woman who has disappeared."

"The Key Keeper, did you say? The Key Keeper is the missing therapist? That suggests a connection to the Alchemy Scroll."

Mary already knew this interesting fact. Caroline had been on the phone that morning, although she'd not been able to explain the Key Keeper's mysterious function regarding the Alchemy Scroll. "I believe Dame Eleanor is in touch with Holywell. We are to find *both* the Alchemy Scroll and the Key Keeper."

Mary watched Ravi and St. John digest the news. Ravi got even redder. St. John banged his fists, then made his face bland. Mary knew mutinous sparks when she saw them. Right then she decided that these two were keeping something back. She was about to demand cooperation when Caroline surprised her.

"Why do you want the Key Keeper to help you?" Caroline asked, puzzled.

Mary coughed. This was fascinating. First, the student contradicts the Professor and now silent Caroline speaks up. For the first time in their relationship, she realized that Caroline's dowdiness was also a disguise. She liked to hide from notice, but that was not all she was. Anna, on the other hand, was provoked.

37

"The witch that holds the Key to the Scroll will not give it to *you*." Her frown included both men. She bit her blood-red lipstick. Patel took a step back before answering.

"She must give us her secrets. We're working on a major pharmaceutical breakthrough. The Key Keeper knows…"

This time a strangled sound from St. John was enough to stop Ravi. Just how indiscreet was he about to be? wondered Mary, looking at Anna's incendiary scowl.

"Certainly, the therapist can't help anyone if she's vanished," she broke in, dryly.

"Her name's Janet Swinford," said Caroline earnestly. She addressed Mary. "She was due to be admitted to Oxford's John Whitcliffe Hospital nine days ago: the closed psychiatric ward. Now she's gone. No one knows where."

Mary knew why Caroline was disturbed. A locked mental ward was a fate that Caroline had narrowly escaped herself with her chronic clinical depression.

Anna glued suspicious black eyes to Godric and Ravi while she slid a green gloved hand over Caroline's cold fingers. Caroline always lost her gloves, remembered Mary.

Fortunately, Anna's delicate build belied unusual strength and ferocity. Trafficked as a child, she had only recently begun to adapt to life outside organized crime. Her contributions to the Agency included talents honed outside the law. Her tone to Godric St. John verged on menace.

"I will find the Key-Keeping witch," came her slightly foreign accent. "I will keep this promise just as you will keep your promise to the seven women at Holywell."

Ravi Patel bumped his head on the roof beam, confused. He was about to speak when Godric St. John condescended to address Anna.

"Miss er… Vronsky, you are referring, I presume, to those illegal immigrants, the girls at the Holywell Retreat Center, run by… those Wiccan women. If I had my way, they would be sent back where they came from. I have made my position clear to Dame Eleanor and the Board."

He folded his arms as if that ended the matter. He doesn't know Anna, thought Mary. Forestalling her associate, Mary spoke decisively.

"Professor St. John, Holywell will remain part of this Agency's commission. We're going to search for the Key Keeper as well as retrieve the Alchemy Scroll for St. Julian's." She paused then continued.

"Moreover, we understand — and support," she added significantly, "Holywell's role in upholding St. Julian's Founders Charter." She ignored his snort. "Dame Eleanor told me about the Retreat Centre's vision of Mother's Julian's theology," she continued, "that the poorest students today are those completely cut off from education, like formerly trafficked women. Holywell is providing a home for them until they can become your students."

Godric St. John's expression was pure vinegar. Mary remained undaunted.

"By gaining higher education, these women will return to their communities as future leaders. They will cease to be victims."

"Full scholarships! Foolish nonsense," muttered the older man. His eyes gravitated to Anna. Men did stare at her, women, too. Mary wondered how St. John felt about women students in general. Although the college had been coed for twenty years, the Bursar struck her as a man who looked back fondly to when Oxford colleges were all-male preserves.

Their position on Dame Eleanor's experiment made clear, Mary wanted to leave. However, to get Caroline and Anna's assessment of St. John, she needed him talking. Let him expound on the Alchemy Scroll, let slip what it really meant to him. Time to get this precious peacock to display his feathers.

Mary smiled with deceptive sweetness.

"Professor St. John, my colleagues cannot wait to hear about the amazing discovery of the Alchemy Scroll substitution. Could you go over it for them? It would be such a treat."

Caroline hid a smile. Anna plastered on an expression that Mary called part ingenue, part contract killer.

The silver hound ran a manicured hand over his tight curls.

"Delighted, Miss Wandwalker. Perhaps you ladies would care to join me at High Table luncheon? I can finish my briefing over a passable Sole Meuniere."

"Ump," Mary trod on Caroline's foot as they got up, knowing she disliked formal meals. She graciously accepted for them. Mary guessed Anna had already scoured the room for portable valuables. On the phone, she'd waxed gleefully on the College's weak security.

Following the men down the spiral staircase, Mary knew that whatever the ceremony put on by St. Julian's High Table (where the dons had a dedicated chef), lunch would differ markedly from dinner that evening. For they were to dine at Holywell with the counselor-witches of Oxfordshire.

CHAPTER 5
A MIXING OF BITTER SUBSTANCES

The three women endured rather than enjoyed the formal High Table lunch at St. Julian's while Godric St. John discoursed about the Alchemy Scroll. Two hours of St. John's pomposity left Caroline exhausted, and Anna riled. Mary was sardonically entertained.

On leaving, Mary reflected that when Anna was angry, it was a good idea to give her something to focus on.

"You drive us to Holywell, Anna," she said, "since you know the route and Oxford traffic is so intimidating."

Anna gave the briefest of nods.

Dodging around puddles of melted snow, the three women nipped through the arch of the Porter's Lodge. Striding ahead, Anna, who rarely wore a hat, tossed her midnight hair in the milder wind. An eagle's wing, Caroline had called it, in admiration. Mary sighed. She and Caroline followed Anna to Oxford's multistory car park, that rare blot on the city of towers, gargoyles, and spires.

"Anna got fired up by what St. John said before lunch." Caroline spoke in an undertone to Mary, eager to explain her lover. Mary understood but let Caroline talk. "You remember how horrible he was about trafficked girls becoming students at St. Julian's. Anna never talks about being trafficked herself, but meeting those poor young women, working with them... well it's like..."

"Sisters?" said Mary, wanting to understand as they passed the iron gates of another college.

41

"Seeing herself again, her younger self." amended Caroline. "It's like those girls stepped out of her past. She's tried so hard to lock it away."

"Ah," said Mary, a little lost. Anna was so blazingly intense. To Mary's secret relief Anna had wanted Caroline with her at Holywell.

The multistory car lot resembled a dungeon. Their secondhand car was dirty with snow melt. Anna backed out with an unnecessary crunch of the gears. Caroline began a few remarks about Holywell. She said she wanted to prepare Mary for the special atmosphere. After all, the Retreat Center was highly unusual in having existed in some form since the foundation of St. Julian's Hall in the Middle Ages. That explains why it combines mainstream counseling with a unique spiritual framework. To the female practitioners, the Earth is a divine goddess.

"You see, Mary, even though the resident women are proper therapists, trained and registered, they also take what they call 'the craft' very seriously. Spells and rituals are their kind of alchemy, nourishing the soul and keeping inner fires alight."

Caroline leaned forward from the back seat. Correctly identifying Mary's expression, she winced.

"No, Mary, don't be all boring and skeptical. Witchcraft is part of what Holywell is. To them, it is living Mother Julian's visions of the divine as maternal. Just imagine. Locked in her cell, Julian gets sick, she faints. Then come the visions. God reveals himself as *herself.* God is a divine Mother very like the ancient religion of the Earth Goddess at Holywell. The Alchemy Scroll has the same idea in visual form. *St. Julian's holds the Scroll, but the witches truly live it.* "

Caroline's whole face was alight. Mary mentally chewed on Caroline's words. They touched her. She did not know how. Caroline had not finished.

"Given the climate emergency, seeing the divine in Mother Earth is important, essential even. Today we lose the radical quality of Mother Julian's theology. The witches see this project with the trafficked women and St. Julian's as a kind of spiritual rebirth...."

Caroline's gentle tones continued after Anna banged on the horn to force their small silver car into a chain of supermarket delivery trucks.

Appearing gratified by Mary's attention, Caroline continued. "For years, Holywell has prioritized therapy, not magic," she explained. "Although today's therapists believe that magic and alchemy were part of the Center from its founding, the occult side to Holywell remained hidden until the 1960s. They hung on for ten years after the repeal of the Anti-Witchcraft Act of 1735. Only then did they let people into the secret of the craft."

Mary listened to Caroline's history, conflating it with the emails, texts, and phone calls since Anna and Caroline had driven off. Drawing on years of archivist skills, Mary evaluated, blended, and cross-referenced sources with long-honed skills. The picture gleaned of Holywell was of an institution remarkable for its longevity and its unorthodoxy when it came to the occult, ecology, and psychotherapy.

Caroline filled in the details of the current project of seven young women rescued from a London brothel. Snatched from extreme poverty in their home countries to be sold repeatedly across Europe, the teenagers ended up as modern slaves. They broke inside. Holywell supported these traumatized young women through a much-publicized trial.

After their captors received long prison sentences, the counselors worked to heal the teenagers' deep mental as well as physical scars. To give them a real future, the Key Keeper, Janet Swinford, proposed using their ancient connection to St. Julian's College.

"No one knows what the Key Keeper does with the Alchemy Scroll," Caroline said to Mary's raised eyebrows. "It's a secret the other women respect. Only handed down from one Key Keeper to the next."

"No one at St. Julian's knows either," reflected Mary. "But they are worried about her disappearance. Dame Eleanor is quite unnerved by it. How did you say she vanished, Caroline?"

"En route to hospital," sighed Caroline, continuing.

To begin with, no one worried, Caroline explained. Janet's periodic stays in the John Whitcliffe Psychiatric Ward were part of Holywell's busy routine. After a couple of days, the Holywell Retreat manager, Dorothy Chamberlyn, rang to see how Janet fared. Horrified to learn she'd never arrived, Dorothy was about to call the police when she received a frantic message from St. Julian's: "Tell no one about the missing Key Keeper of the Alchemy Scroll."

The message hinted at danger to Janet Swinford if it got out that the Key Keeper was AWOL. Let her hide in her private cave if that is what she needs. Wanting to believe that Janet could look after herself, while disgusted by the College's priorities, Dorothy consulted the Holywell witches. They suggested trying twenty-first century scrying. She googled "discreet enquires" and found the Agency website.

During Anna and Caroline's fact-finding visit, it was Caroline who found herself in long conversations with Dorothy. In the well-scrubbed kitchen, they lingered over mugs of cocoa late into the night.

Caroline grew enthusiastic about updating the historic link between Holywell and St. Julian's, a College named for a woman whose life incarnated the holiness of the feminine. Unfortunately, those nighttime discussions about the trafficked girls took a toll on Caroline's fragile health.

Mary knew the rest of the story. Caroline lost too much sleep, bad for her chronic depression. Spotting charcoal moons under her eyes, Anna found her lover spooning instant coffee from a jar simply to get out of bed. Ruthlessly, she made her swallow the "for-emergencies-only" stash of anti-anxiety pills. For two days Caroline slept for 22 hours. Even when awake, she barely registered the charms and incense offered by the concerned counselors.

44

Much later, Mary was able to piece together Anna's observations during that early stay at Holywell. Her attention never wavered from the young clients. To begin with, the trafficked women aroused her suspicion. She knew what survival meant for vulnerable prostitutes. The strategies were not nice; they were not altruistic. Anna scrutinized their gestures, tracked their thoughts, and assessed their desires.

Like a cat, Anna was only superficially domesticated, Mary later reflected. She sprayed listening devices like a feline marking territory and then buried them like dead mice. Ignoring curious glances directed at herself, Anna caught the signs of a shameful secret. By the time she drove Mary and Caroline toward Holywell, the memory of those covert exchanges had stoked her rage. Something was going on with those teenagers; she would find it out.

Driving with deadly determination, Anna's silence concealed furious planning. For at the most recent communal meal at Holywell she'd set a trap. Mentioning the search for the Key Keeper, she'd spotted a twitch of Leni's mouth, answered by a flicker from Olga.

Mary knew that to Anna, secrecy was ingrained. She didn't know how to share her suspicions with Caroline and Mary. At this moment Anna feared neither woman would trust her on body language.

From the back of the car, Caroline had one more startling fact about Janet Swinford, the Key Keeper. Dorothy had told her that before the disappearance, the woman announced it was time to initiate her successor.

"At the next full moon," Janet proclaimed at one of the communal rituals, or so Dorothy said. In Caroline's imagination, Janet's northern accent got stronger with her Key Keeper duties. Mary did not know what to say. Initiating Key Keepers for Alchemy Scrolls had nothing to do with the Agency's contract. Later she would realize how mistaken was that assumption.

Meanwhile, Anna was driving as if she ruled the road, in Mary's opinion. What could be bothering her about Holywell?

45

She opened her mouth to berate Anna, then stopped as they shot past a policeman on a motorbike. Mary saw the helmeted cop swivel toward their vehicle, spot something in Anna's profile, and fall back.

Mary swallowed. Before she could find words for Anna, she was distracted by a new glass and brick complex just off the Ring Road. As an historic city of spires and towers, Mary knew that Oxford forbade skyscrapers. They got one anyway. Only it had been turned horizontal and squashed onto a nineteenth century factory. "Palmer's Perfect Potions" could still be read in fading letters.

"What on earth is that?" said Mary, trying to ease the tension in the car. Anna put her foot down as the car swerved around a white van before taking the turn for Abingdon. Mary had the sensation of only two wheels fully gripping the road.

"Aaannna. Drive sensibly for goodness' sake."

Caroline moaned as held her head.

"Sorry," muttered Anna. She slowed the car from fast to not so furious. "That factory. It belonged to that old professor, St. John. Only that's not his real name. He used to be Godric Palmer. After inheriting the building and land, he sold everything to an American drug company called Mer-Corp, seven years ago."

"Anna thinks he gave money to St. Julian's to get the Fellowship," said Caroline softly.

"Oh," said Mary, understanding. "Good research, Anna. However, his work must have something going for it," she continued. "After all, he discovered their Alchemy Scroll is a fake."

Anna grunted. For her the roads were a war zone.

As Mer-Corp was the name of the corporation that held St. Julian's mortgages, Mary took out a notebook and wrote it down. Anna scorned Mary's archaic technology, but she liked the feel of a biro indenting the paper. She was an archive person after all.

"Could he be lying?" said Caroline. "St. John, I mean." Her voice cracked; she must have one of her headaches. Mary worried about her. Holywell strained on her fragile health, and now they were going back.

"I saw the Alchemy Scroll," Mary explained. The one at St. Julian's is definitely a seventeenth century paper copy rather than medieval vellum. Also, I don't think Godric St. John would want to lie. He sees the loss of the real Alchemy Scroll as a crisis. He and his student want it for their work. To St. John, this is personal, not simply about an expert coming to check it out."

Anna bit her lip, making no comment.

"Ah," said Mary, pulling a vibrating phone from her coat pocket. "Email about the air ticket to L.A.," she explained. "I go to find the real Scroll the day after tomorrow; gives us a chance to work together on the missing Key Keeper."

Neither of her companions responded. The sky darkened to scorched earth above the busy road south.

Their aging vehicle had just enough room for the three of them plus suitcases. Anna swung down a country road that seemed bereft of markings. It was easy to miss the weathered sign: "To Holywell Retreat Centre." Not for nothing did the Center promise privacy and quiet. Gears ground noisily as Anna slowed down, a little. The road narrowed into a single lane and started to dip.

Mary noticed a change in the rural landscape, all wet with melted snow and ice. Slate roofs rose out of the damp turf. They looked like farm buildings. On either side of the lane the fields were dotted with sheep. New lambs huddled under their mothers' bellies. With the chill afternoon the black clouds threatened to burst. Too mild for more snow, raindrops splattered on the windscreen as the road divided between converted barns and a Tudor house with ornate brick chimneys.

Mary's stomach lurched at the first sight of Holywell. Above the carved front door, the old brickwork showed a crack forking upward. In the dim light it darkened like a vein. Holywell looked vulnerable. Mary's thoughts went to the missing resident. Had the woman taken something essential when she disappeared?

PART TWO
SOLUTIO

CHAPTER 6
HOLYWELL'S VULNERABLE CLIENTS

As they approached the house, Caroline explained to Mary and Anna what Dorothy Chamberlyn, Holywell manager, had told her. In the beginning, relations were good between St. Julian's Hall and its secret sister. In pre-Protestant decades, gold flowed to Holywell, where alchemical and magical rites remained secret. Pious largesse from St. Julian's in the early 1500s allowed the Sisters to redesign their main house after an unfortunate meeting between lightning and thatch.

Mary nodded absently, preoccupied with her sense of foreboding. The three women had arrived within minutes of the rain. Energized, Caroline sat up. She swallowed some pills with a swig of water from a bottle in her handbag, keen to introduce Holywell to Mary.

"You know it was so dangerous for the Holy Well sisters after King Henry abolished the monasteries. Doubly dangerous, I mean. As alchemists, spell-makers, and as Catholic nuns. The Hall had to protect them."

Danger. This got Mary's attention.

"Henry made all of England Protestant," continued Caroline. "Many monks and nuns ended up as beggars. To stay on their land, the Holywell women claimed to be farmers. They declared themselves tenants of St. Julian's."

Caroline was flushed. The burning of heretics and witches touched her intimately. "It took centuries before the actual well could reclaim its reputation for healing without the women

51

being accused of evil magic. They all could have, *would* have, been burned at the stake."

Mary was concerned about Caroline's agitation. She gave her a half smile as they unloaded their bags. There was a cough. Anna folded her arms.

"What is it, Anna?"

She muttered. "The girls know about Janet."

"Of course, they do," said Caroline eagerly. "We were there when they were told. The counselors don't keep secrets; that's all part of the therapy."

Anna looked exasperated. "Noooo, Caroline. The girls *know*... at least one or two. They know what happened to Janet. I think they sold her..."

Anna stopped at Caroline's gasp and Mary's shock. "Well, all right, not exactly *sold* her. They sold her out, got paid for information about her. I was watching them; I saw."

"And you didn't think to say anything before?" Mary was skeptical about Anna's suspicions.

"No evidence. They'll deny it. I'll need to get into their phones..."

Caroline was opening and shutting her mouth. "So, you can't be sure...I mean I can't believe..." she stopped at Anna's set face. "Darling, I..." Mary had to act decisively.

"We've arrived, and our job is to find the missing woman. Anna, you keep on with the girls; it's a lead. Caroline and I will concentrate on the counselors. Before bed tonight we'll exchange information. We have a plan."

"Right," said Caroline, not looking at Anna. Anna said nothing. She made the car roar as she took it to the parking area at the back of the house.

"A tricky situation," Mary muttered. She kept her eyes on Caroline, who was pressing the bell marked "Reception, please ring and enter."

*****

52

Forty minutes later, Mary had the chance to observe the inhabitants of Holywell over big pots of tea and plates of homemade scones. Youth distinguished the "clients" (trafficked women) from the mostly middle-aged "residents" (counselors). Mary's gaze lingered on the woman in charge, Dorothy, who was pouring tea from a huge urn. The woman's hollow-cheeked calm made Mary curious.

Meanwhile, Caroline hugged and chatted indiscriminately; while Anna, ignoring good manners, melded with a wooden beam in the corner, her body radiating predator energy.

Anna's stance recalled to Mary an article about abuse victims concentrating their bodily senses to extraordinary levels. Was this what she was seeing with Anna? Following some invisible current, Mary saw her close in on a girl scuttling across the room to grab the hand of another young woman. Mary saw Anna's mouth flicker. It was not a smile.

No, Mary decided, I'm not getting involved with Anna's suspicions before I've had a chance to meet Janet Swinford's colleagues. I must make up my own mind about this missing person case. She scanned the busy lounge dotted with worn sofas in various shades of blue. They blended with a floor of scrubbed flagstones that looked very old.

Everywhere there were women. Teenage clients kept passing cigarettes, eyes darting nervously at the older women. Every so often they dashed out of the French doors to light cigarettes with a passion that spoke of darker addictions. Some of them had been crying. They wore similar sweatshirts with assorted faded logos. Mary caught a glimpse of scars poking out from long sleeves. Mary was handed a cup of tea by a thin African girl. With a jolt, Mary realized what the scars meant. How many of these girls had self-harmed?

"Thank you, Sarah," said Dorothy, coming over to Mary. The manager's cropped hair was warmed by a henna rinse. She looked comfortable in her jeans. Mary had heard about her kindness to Caroline in the infirmary. She's trying to beam warmth and humor to the whole room, Mary thought.

Nevertheless, a current of anxiety permeated. "Sarah," said Dorothy again, and the girl turned back. "No news of Janet, I'm afraid."

The girl's expression turned bleak. She ran for the French doors with her cigarette already half lit.

"Our youngsters are distressed by the disappearance of Janet," said Dorothy, to Mary's unspoken question. "Of course, they began by saying they never spoke to her," she sighed. "Then two admitted helping her in the garden. Voluntarily," she'd added drily. "Sarah was originally trafficked from the Congo, then sold in Europe. You'll know that all seven come from the same brothel in London."

Mary nodded, encouraging Dorothy to keep going with her story. More systematic questioning could wait. She knew that Caroline's chronic depression was not the same as Janet's bipolar disorder. Even so, living with Caroline's occasional crashes made her feel on the edge of quicksand. Janet sounded worse. Dorothy went on.

"Two of our women were seized as refugees fleeing Syria. Their English isn't too good; they couldn't understand Janet. She's from the north, you know. But Virginia is the one really upset. You wouldn't think it because she's the one I believe when she said she never spoke to Janet. She never talks, well, to... to anyone. When the word 'kidnapped' came up at breakfast, she fainted. So traumatized is she by being gang raped after being snatched that she cannot remember her past."

Mary gulped. She turned back to the nervous girl, she noticed earlier. "Olga," said Dorothy automatically. With greasy hair drooping on protruding shoulders, Olga, like most of the others, was excruciatingly thin. She held her tea as if the cup was made of lead. Oblivious of Mary and Dorothy, she stared ahead between tiny sips of the hot brown liquid. Mary shivered.

"This has got to stop," said Dorothy to Mary. "You can see how stressed they are. We can't go on like this. This morning I phoned the police about Janet's absence. Ah, so you've had the utmost secrecy talk from St. Julian's," she said to Mary's expression. "Poppycock. Here at Holywell people come first." She sighed.

"Are the police searching for Janet?" enquired Mary. At this point she would be glad if the task of the Agency could be scaled back to the missing Alchemy Scroll."

"No," said Dorothy. She was clearly annoyed as well as worried. "The Inspector talked about scarce resources. He said that Janet, being bipolar, had probably gone somewhere to be alone. Therefore, we need you, the Depth Enquiry Agency. Find Janet for us, Miss Wandwalker, please."

Dorothy's hands shook. Her cup and saucer rattled. She put them on the coffee table before anyone else, except for Mary, noticed.

"Miss Chamberlyn, you know we're also commissioned by St. Julian's," she said stoutly. "We will find Ms. Swinford; she is part of the story of the Alchemy Scroll."

"Call me Dorothy, please. Yes, I had a very odd telephone conversation with Dame Eleanor about the Alchemy Scroll. I'm sure she was wondering whether to divulge a secret and thought better of it. That's fine by us. Key Keeping is what Holywell does for St. Julian's. We want Janet back. Find her and then we can get on giving these girls new lives. For that too, St. Julian's has a part to play."

Mary had her doubts about counseling by witches, but it was not her place to say so. Mary was good at knowing her place.

She looked over at Caroline, slumped on a sofa and gloomily eating a scone heaped with cream and jam. Stuffing in the last mouthful, Caroline stole a glance at Anna, now moving towards Olga.

"Ah, yes, Olga," said Dorothy, following Mary's gaze. "She misses Leni, of course."

"Misses Leni?" asked Mary. "I thought all seven were billeted here."

"Officially that's true," said Dorothy. "But Leni speaks the best English, so she is our brave one, the first out in the world. She's started work at St. Julian's. They're letting her live in."

"They've given her a job?" said Mary. Then she remembered Anna's warning. "A job offered before or after Janet vanished?"

"The next day," agreed Dorothy cheerfully.

Was she willfully unsuspicious? wondered Mary.

"Leni's a cleaner, or as they call them in Oxford colleges, a scout. It's not much. The pay's atrocious, but the plan is for St. Julian's to get more and more involved with the girls' rehab. Eventually, they'll get full scholarships, free tuition, room, and board. A few will do postgraduate work and become real leaders in their communities." Dorothy spoke bracingly.

Mary looked at the five young women exhibiting various signs of discomfort: addiction scars, undernourishment, nervousness, and downright sullenness. Her cool grey eyes met Dorothy's rueful understanding.

"Yes, it's a lot to ask," agreed Dorothy. "Especially right now. Some may not make it, and we will have to find other sources of support for them. However, we agreed, all of us who practice here, that Mother Julian wants us to try. Janet too. She was one of the keenest. Janet herself has a sad history. She said it was about time that the Mother's spirit of compassion returned to St. Julian's."

Mary risked looking doubtful. Dorothy Chamberlyn laughed and got up.

"I am *so* glad to meet you, Miss Wandwalker. You are just as Anna and Caroline said you would be."

She gracefully exited the room, but not before touching the shoulders of the young women with a whisper for each. They brightened like dying embers. Olga had already slipped out of the room, pursued by Anna.

Mary was troubled. No one wants to talk to us about the Key Keeper. Yet her disappearance is really hurting, she reflected.

Dinner was a vegan stew from the Retreat Centre's garden flavored with fresh herbs and wild garlic. Janet Swinford tended

56

the Holywell vegetable garden. She'd been about to begin spring planting when she took sick.

The meal was too quiet. Caroline reached out a hand to an older woman who whispered back. Several counselors tried bright remarks, only to be met with resentful stares from several of the young women. Eventually, Dorothy shook her head at a big woman pedantically asking about English lessons. The group subsided into sounds of bowls scraping and the sawing of a loaf baked by Virginia. The counselors ignored the bread's charred outside and sawdust texture inside.

After eating, the three women of the Agency gathered for their official meeting with the counselor-witches in a room dominated by a round table big enough for everyone, with room to spare.

Anna pinched Mary's arm. "Got into Olga's phone and downloaded texts between her and Leni," she muttered in her ear. "Will unscramble the data overnight." Mary swallowed her questions. Anna was less tense away from the trafficked women. Yet Mary sensed that Anna was also not comfortable among the counselors. Cyberwitch she may be, yet Anna had been hardened into a loner.

Dorothy announced that the young women were completing the washing-up, minus for tonight only the supervision of Cherry, the cook. Afterward, they could watch TV until bed by 10 p.m.

"We begin our council," continued Dorothy, "by welcoming Miss Mary Wandwalker from The Depth Enquiry Agency," she smiled warmly, "We've asked them to find Janet, and they need our help. I do not need to say how worried we all are."

A murmur of agreement ignited the table. It died away in the chill that pervaded the room. Caroline shivered.

"You may know more than you realize," began Mary, awkwardly. The whole setup at Holywell made her feel alien.

"What d'you mean by that?" demanded a large woman. Overly defensive, noted Mary. In her late fifties with permed orange curls and a slight squint, she leaned forward to stare at the three outsiders. Now Mary noticed that the table was marked by graffiti made by coffee cups and decades of food spills. The other counselors watched in various stages of unease. Everyone waited for Mary's response.

She swallowed. Caroline stared with anxious eyes. Anna scowled to remind Mary to keep quiet about Olga and Leni.

"Well...um..."

"Cherry." The woman sniffed.

"Cherry. Well, we think... we, the Agency, think that by talking it over with you and amongst you, some tiny detail, maybe something that looked irrelevant at the time... this could..."

"Of course, it's what *we* do," exclaimed a silver-haired woman with a hawkish nose and dancing eyes. "Sort of, anyway," she amended. "I'm Naomi." She beamed around the table, and the counselors started to relax.

Dorothy intervened.

"Yes, let's give Miss Wandwalker a chance to get to know us," she said smoothly. "Anna and Caroline," she bobbed her head at them. "Good to have you back. Let me introduce our company. Cherry and Naomi, you've met. John is sitting opposite." She indicated a square-jawed woman with no hair.

"I identify as male," John said loudly, as if used to making this point. "My work is with the voices crying out to us from the wild. I'm an Earthwitch."

She stopped and resumed in a different voice. "Janet grows things. There must *be* a connection. Wherever she is. I've tried. All night I've petitioned the spirits..." As if the earth was choking her, she could not finish. The last unidentified woman, a diminutive Chinese figure, tugged John's arm.

"Slowly, slowly, my beloved; you've done everything you can, used all your spells. Don't...don't wear yourself out, dearest John." She spoke perfect unaccented English.

John bent her bare scalp and kissed the top of the speaker's dark head.

"Linda tried to help," they explained. "I've been trying and trying, but the earth will not speak Janet's name." They both took a huge breath. "Janet's gone beyond our powers."

A moan from Naomi resonated around the circle. The Holywell women were shocked. Even Dorothy was stricken.

CHAPTER 7
MARY TAKES CHARGE

When Mary did not know what else to do, she took charge. After the distress shown by the witches about Janet, she spoke briskly.

"This is where our Agency comes in. We specialize in doing what the police cannot or will not do. Investigating in *depth*. I promise, we'll find Janet."

Even as she spoke, Mary became aware that there was something else going on in the room. Anna shot her a foul glance. Mary wanted to scowl back, let Anna take over, if she knew how to talk to these people. She heard a sob from the bald woman who angrily brushed her eyes with a hand. With a jolt, Mary recognized the effects of chemotherapy. Had she been too abrupt, dismissive even? Rescue came from an unexpected source.

"Well, you were a sanitary inspector," remarked Anna to John. "Perhaps you should be looking into the shit." John grimaced. Anna had calmed her.

"Now then, Anna," said the Chinese woman. "You're feeling bad that you can't pinpoint Janet online. Just think how the rest of us feel. I've tried every finding spell in the old books that Janet keeps." She sighed and turned to Mary.

"Miss Wandwalker, Mary, I'm Linda. No one could pronounce my name when I arrived in this country. I was a mail order bride from Malaysia. I ran away, of course. John and I met in local government."

61

She laughed like a woman who often laughed. "We were the Health and Safety team inspecting Holywell for license renewal. Somehow, we never left."

A humorous murmur rose from all the counselors at this familiar anecdote. Linda defused the tension. Mary sensed that was often her role. She looked for guidance at Caroline and Anna. She wanted to signal goodwill, but how was this helping them to locate Janet?

Dorothy understood Mary's agenda.

"To summarize, Miss Wandwalker. We've tried our own methods to find our Key Keeper. When Janet did not check in from the hospital, I rang the Ward Matron. The hospital is just as confused as we are. They thought they sent a regular ambulance for Janet. But no, it was canceled. An ambulance arrived here, the paperwork was in order, paramedics put her in a wheelchair, and took her out.

"It seemed fine, but then... silence. After none of us could reach her, we met in council like this." Dorothy indicated the round table. "We decided to try a new ritual, um... a sort of group spell. It means getting out the rarely used herbs, building up the power. Unfortunately, it takes time."

"Which we don't have," said Mary. She was trying to hide her skepticism.

"Which Janet may not have," added Caroline quietly.

"Janet's often at the John Whitcliffe, you see," said Cherry. "Having her go to hospital is part of... of how things are. And we've been so busy with the girls — I mean women, sorry Dot — but to have her disappear like this... it's never happened before."

"There's one thing we haven't really tried," said Naomi, gravely. "And you won't like it, Dorothy."

Dorothy looked alarmed. "What? ... Oh no, we can't. It would destroy everything we've worked for." For the first time, she looked haunted.

"Dot, you've got to consider Janet's safety. Her life's at risk..."

Mary stepped in. "You must tell us, Dorothy. Our Agency cannot be deprived of vital information."

The other counselors knew what Naomi was getting at. John looked grim, Linda concerned, Cherry insistent. Before Dorothy could find words, Caroline spoke.

"I know what you don't want to do," she said huskily. "You don't want to go back to the trafficked women. To question them thoroughly would be contrary to your therapy, which is about trust." To Mary's surprise, Dorothy nodded.

"We offer a safe space," she said to Mary's incomprehension. "We cannot even hint at suspecting them of being involved in kidnapping."

There, it had been said: the crime and the trafficked clients of Holywell in the same sentence.

"*We* are not their counselors," Mary broke in. Anna could be on to something with Olga and Leni. Specifying their suspicions would not be politic. She glared at Caroline to keep quiet.

Dorothy was about to object again when they heard a beeping sound. Anna pulled her designer bag from the floor and extracted an unusually large phone. It was gleefully alive, shuddering in flaming colors of violet and red. Mary had never seen anything like it. It was mesmerizing.

"Wow, Anna," said Caroline, "results from your cybercraft search for Janet. It's taken days, hasn't it?"

Everyone leaned toward the glowing object on the table.

Anna grunted. Her hands flickered over the screen now divided into a grid. Mary watched, feeling foolish. It was silly to feel at such a disadvantage with these new devices. Mary gritted her teeth.

"Look," said Anna, passing the screen to Mary on her other side. Mary was touched that the phone had not been offered to Caroline first. Then she discovered why.

"Oh, no." Caroline had spotted the large letters on the screen. She leaned across Anna, grabbing the phone. She let it drop to the table. Cherry seized it first, then handed it over to Dorothy without comment.

"The Old Hospital?" said the manager looking at Mary, perplexed. "I don't know it. We have ties with most of the mental health facilities in Oxfordshire."

"What is it? Where's Janet?" the other women started asking. Naomi took the phone from Dorothy's unresisting hand.

"It says here that Janet asked to be transferred to The Old Hospital. No address. It *looks* like her signature."

"Give it here," said Linda. "Right you are, that's how she scribbles her name. Are we worried it's a forgery?"

"No way to tell without the original paper," said Mary, always the Archivist.

"No paper," said Anna quietly. "This was signed straight onto a screen."

A low moan came from somewhere. It was Caroline. Instantly, Anna was kneeling beside her with one hand on her cheek. She kissed her lover. When Anna put out her hand, John put a glass of water in it. Anna guided it to Caroline's lips. Mary grabbed Caroline's bag for her variety of pills and tranquilizers.

"No pills," said Caroline, sounding stronger. "I'm all right, really. It's the shock. I thought The Old Hospital was a legend."

"A legend?"

"Maybe I remember something…"

"Go on, Caroline."

"Is it *that* place…?"

"It's where…you know, *they* go…"

Mary held up her hand for silence.

"What is The Old Hospital?" she asked Anna, who ignored her. Caroline kept sipping. She smiled wanly at Anna. *Caroline already knows too much about The Old Hospital*, Mary realized.

"The Old Hospital's a story, an urban myth, if you like. It is where you go to die," said Caroline. "If you're a loony." She gave a half smile.

"That is chronically mentally ill like me. It's a sort of joke, black humor passed around by patients in the old asylums. Back when there were loads of mental hospitals where people might

64

stay for decades. When someone very sick got moved out, it was said they went to The Old Hospital to die." Caroline shut her eyes and shuddered. Then she opened them.

"I suppose when they shut all those asylums down... Maybe, just maybe they left one. Or sold it to a private company who kept it open. Obviously, it's not part of the National Health System."

"Perfect place to conceal someone already mentally ill," Mary concluded. There was something uncanny in the idea.

She was stunned. So were the counselors. With minimal gestures, nods, Mary saw them communicate. They were alert, united, in touch. Some decision had been made, for Dorothy stood.

"Caroline, wait," she said, gently. "We have to invite the spirits to join us."

There was a general stirring. In a few seconds, each woman was back. Dorothy was lighting the stub of an ordinary kitchen candle, then incense sticks in a bowl of white sand. Tiny spirals of smoke produced an odor of sage, followed by cinnamon and woody spices.

Cherry poured water from a silver jug into a tiny glass dish that looked very old. Were those astrological symbols engraved on the outside? Naomi, with a trembling hand, opened a small wooden box and tossed a teaspoonful of brown grains next to the three other offerings. John sat with open hands arranged on the table, while Linda turned off the overhead lamp.

The room shrank to the flickering candle and fragrant cloud. A radiant dome framed their faces. Everyone looked alike. Mary found her knees touching other taut knees. With elbows resting on the table, the circle was unbroken.

"We invite Fire, Earth, Air and Water to sustain us in our trouble," said Dorothy, as if this was an everyday event.

"Praise the goddess," whispered the counselors. Caroline too, Mary noted. Not, however, Anna, who detached her hands from Cherry and Naomi and refreshed the screen on her phone.

"Now," said Dorothy briskly. "We are protected. So is Janet, who is of this circle, wherever she may be. Caroline, tell us about this legendary hospital that might not exist."

The candlelight returned glints of copper to Caroline's hair. She was calm now. But it was Anna who spoke.

"I've found references to a 'Ye Olde Asylum' as far back as the sixteenth century. Documents have been posted by several medical archives. Some are from alchemy books. They say that the Old Asylum, or mental hospital, was *nigredo,* or darkness. It was a place to find the *prima materia,* or primal stuff, used for alchemical transformation."

She paused; then continued. "They said The Old Hospital was the earthly seat of Hell."

Mary felt her own face blanching to match Caroline's.

"We don't want a history lesson," Cherry broke in rudely. "What's this got to do with Janet?"

"Any link to alchemy might be relevant," said Mary. "Alchemy is what the St. Julian's Scroll is all about. Janet is the Key Keeper, and there is... er a problem with the Scroll."

Mary could not believe her own words. Was this the utmost discretion she'd promised Dame Eleanor? The pungent smell of incense must be confusing her. Next to her, she could feel Caroline getting ready to speak. No, she had to stop her. Go on, Mary, do it. She said nothing.

"Given Janet's disappearance, you should know the truth." Everyone's head shot to Caroline. Mary shut her eyes. *She was going to do it.*

"Around the time Janet disappeared, St. Julian's discovered that the original medieval Alchemy Scroll is gone. What they have is a copy."

"*Caroline. We promised. Discretion.*" Too late, Mary recovered her voice. Now she had to secure the support of witches she could neither understand nor control.

"Sorry, Mary," Caroline muttered. "With Janet in danger, they have a right to know."

She wasn't sorry. Mary could tell. Anna gave one of her sardonic grins, and Mary realized that she was not sorry either. Interesting.

The counselors appeared astonished. Mary scrutinized them carefully. Dorothy started banging her fist on the table. "So that's what the Dame meant," she said in a strangled voice. Then stronger, "I presume the loss is connected to the financial crisis at St. Julian's."

"How so?" asked Naomi, speaking for them all. "When exactly…"

"1658," Mary pulled out the diary where she'd written up her notes. "The expert copy was good enough to deceive until recent tests."

"How could that work?" said John, skeptically. "Oh, don't bother. Really, we only care about Janet."

Dorothy frowned at her. "Janet has a special relationship with the Alchemy Scroll; she'll care about the substitution," she said, reprovingly. Her foot was tapping nervously on the floor. Despite the healing ritual, the counselors remained jittery.

"Let's consider The Old Hospital." Caroline's determined tone drew everyone's attention. "The story gets around those of us with chronic hard-to-treat depression — that's an actual diagnosis. The Old Hospital was where you could go — and you had to agree to it — when there was no hope left. They just give you all the drugs you need to dull the pain. And then you die."

There was silence. Even the candle's flame seemed to waver. Mary shivered.

"You mean, they… the doctors *kill* the patients?" said Naomi, horrified.

"No… not deliberately," said Caroline. It's just… well, they don't worry too much about the size of doses. Too much of the depression drugs can be fatal."

"That's really terrible," said Dorothy, gravely. "If it's true. I'm surprised we've never heard about it. We all hoped Janet would change her mind about giving up as Key Keeper; but

67

whatever she wants, her home is here. Nothing changes our commitment to caring for her — and each other."

The other women murmured their assent.

"It's just a story," said Caroline, her green eyes wet. "At least that's what I thought. A kind of urban legend; not... not real."

"Yet here it is on Janet's intake form. We are supposed to believe she signed it in the untraceable ambulance," said Dorothy. "What do you think, Miss Wandwalker? Could Janet's disappearance be connected to the St. Julian's Scroll? Doesn't seem likely if the theft was in the seventeenth century."

"St Julian's doesn't care about us," sneered Cherry. "Dame Eleanor phoned you in hysterics wanting the Key Keeper. We now know it was because she'd found out about the Scroll." She addressed Mary with bitterness. "Don't worry, we won't say anything about the missing Alchemy Scroll. Holywell keeps secrets. It's what we do."

"What we're not saying," broke in Naomi, "is what we are all thinking. Janet was taken because she's the Key Keeper to the Alchemy Scroll. It's the only possible reason."

"Well," said Mary, slowly. "Look at it this way. Even though it is centuries after the substitution, finding out about the copy — and St Julian's financial peril — are new. And with Ms. Swinford being the Key Keeper... coincidences are rarely coincidences."

She did not add that Dame Eleanor had said she believed the Scroll had healing properties that could be worth millions to a corporation.

"So, you'll investigate both angles," Dorothy instructed Mary. "The Scroll and The Old Hospital, which may turn out to be connected, I see that. And," she said firmly, "I haven't forgotten about questioning the girls. That's *not* possible."

Mary nodded. She felt rather than saw Anna's intention to completely disregard those instructions, at least for Olga and Leni. Mary agreed, and Caroline would come round. This time it was the Agency communicating without speaking.

"We'll find Janet," said Caroline, earnestly.

"We'll get the Alchemy Scroll and make sure the College keeps its promise to the women," said Anna, in an unusually long utterance.

"I'll email you our contract," said Mary Wandwalker.

CHAPTER 8
LIKE TREATS LIKE

Mary insisted the three of them get some sleep before deciding their next moves. She woke early, recalling that they only had a day before her departure to Los Angeles. A plan was needed before leaving Caroline and Anna to look for the Key Keeper.

At 8 a.m., they gathered in a converted barn that Holywell used as a classroom. Its main windows looked away from Holywell House to hills where sheep ignored the fine March rain, much as they had done for centuries. Mary suggested bringing over their breakfast. With a flask of coffee almost as good as her own, she waited for an opportune moment to begin. From looks and nudges, Caroline and Anna had ideas of their own.

The fact that Anna and Caroline were waiting to talk to her did not reassure Mary at all. Anna stared moodily at a bowl of freshly peeled apple and yogurt that she was absent-mindedly spooning into her mouth. Her other hand worked the upgraded phone. Caroline chewed on a slice of toast, looking anxiously at Mary. Brushing off croissant crumbs, Mary pretended to frown at pages of notes she took from a briefcase salvaged from her Archive days.

She laid the sheets side by side and pursed her lips. Reaching for her cup, Mary was surprised to find it empty, so she rose to collect the thermos and poured most of the remaining liquid. All right, she said to herself.

"We've got to think of this case as two problems," she announced. "At least until we have evidence they are connected.

71

One is finding the original Alchemy Scroll in Los Angeles, and just as important is getting Janet Swinford back to Holywell. I do not know for sure these problems are related."

"They are," said Anna, picking up her phone.

"How do you know?" said Mary, her patience already depleting. Why was Anna so difficult?

"Darling?" added Caroline hopefully.

Anna sighed, exaggerating her cooperation. "Caroline and I talked last night. I found a girl who knows about Janet being taken." She sniffed.

Mary knew she was dismissing Dorothy's prohibition on involving the young patients.

"I heard Olga when she phoned Leni at St. Julian's. Then I showed her what I'd decoded from their phones. Olga and Leni got messages from the same burner phone. First enquiries about the Key Keeper, and her relation to the Alchemy Scroll. Then queries about Janet, offering money. Olga freaked out. She ran off until I shut her in a cupboard."

"*What*?" said Mary.

"Just for a few minutes. She's fine." Anna was dismissive. Mary gulped and turned to Caroline, who shrugged. Anna carried on regardless.

"Olga said it was all Leni's idea. She sold information about Janet, her exact diagnosis, medication, when she would leave for hospital. Everything. I wanted to slap her."

"You didn't?" Mary sounded hoarse.

"Of *course,* she didn't," said Caroline with a loving smile. Then, "Did you, darling?"

Anna did her enigmatic look. Mary sighed.

"Okay, Anna, whoever bought the information knew when to send the fake ambulance for Janet," said Mary. "The question is who? If the burner phone person really did begin with the Key Keeper and not Janet specifically…?" Mary tailed off. Anna nodded vigorously.

"Agreed. This is evidence linking the Alchemy Scroll to Janet's disappearance. Did you get a name off that burner phone?"

Anna scowled. "Not yet. Olga *said* they don't know either. Contacted anonymously; cash left in an envelope by the gate. So... so... old style." Anna sounded more shocked by the archaic payment than the actual betrayal.

"What does that mean for Janet?" asked Caroline.

"Danger," said Anna, glowering. "Because whoever took her wants her secrets about the Alchemy Scroll, secrets she won't give up."

"Because the job of the Key Keeper is keeping the secrets," said Caroline slowly. Mary frowned at both. Janet was in peril.

Caroline glanced at Mary. She was the glue that kept Mary and Anna together, she knew that. Sometimes she was the glue that kept them in the same room. Caroline swallowed her last fragment of toast, took a final swig of her tea, and sat up straight.

"I know what to do," she said.

Anna dropped her phone and glared. Mary had a bad feeling. She could guess what Caroline would say.

"To find Janet Swinford," continued Caroline, avoiding their eyes. "I'm going to check into The Old Hospital."

"No," said Anna and Mary in unison. It was what Mary had feared. She was taken aback by Anna's opposition. Perhaps she had misjudged her.

"Out of the question, Caroline," rapped Mary.

"It's the only way," said Caroline. "You know it is. Anna cannot find it on the web. Mr. Jeffreys can't either, can he?"

Mary looked stubborn. Caroline had guessed correctly that she had called her former employer. "The Old Hospital: legend certainly; findable building, no," he had said drily.

"It's all right, Mary," said Caroline, touching her hand. Caroline was gaining substance. "I'm not scared. Really. I'll have Anna to watch over me, won't I?" turning to her lover, who had folded her arms.

"You can't do it," Anna said in her uncompromising way.

73

Caroline paused. They locked eyes. Mary physically drew back. Caroline clasped her hands on the table, white knuckles beneath freckled skin.

"You're saying I'm a coward?"

Anna took a breath. "It's too...risky. Too much could go wrong." She crouched toward Caroline; hands scrunched into what could have been claws.

Caroline smiled into the jaws of the wildcat. "Not if you protect me. Nothing will go wrong. Mary must go to Los Angeles. That's what she wants; what St. Julian's wants. Mary's an archivist; she knows how to find the Alchemy Scroll, and... um, stuff. While she is doing that, we must get Janet Swinford."

Mary could see the logic of Caroline's plan. She didn't like it. Yet, how else could they find The Old Hospital? Invisible to visitors, The Old Hospital took patients. Caroline has the right medical history, Mary reflected. Janet Swinford needed rescuing. Last night the witches were adamant that she would never desert Holywell.

"Perhaps..." Mary began, diffidently, "there's a way that could keep Caroline safe..." She broke off. Anna rose to her feet. Caroline stood up too, confronting Anna.

Mary remained sitting.

The quiet morning was filled with cawing rooks. Then came a loud clatter as Anna kicked away her chair and stormed out of the room. Scorched, Mary and Caroline exchanged shaky smiles.

"It's okay. I think it's okay," said Caroline. "She'll come round. She'll calm down. It's just that... that she..."

"Loves you?" completed Mary, optimistically.

"Worries about me," said Caroline. "But she can't be the only brave one. I keep telling her that."

"No one expects you to act like Anna," said Mary, gently. She noted Caroline's flushed features. "I can't act like Anna," Mary added truthfully. "And that's a good thing."

Caroline giggled. Mary was thinking of Anna's creative approach to legality.

74

"How would you get to The Old Hospital, if, and it's a big if, we decide — as a team — to do this?"

"I've been thinking about that," said Caroline. "Our regular doctor would help. You know, Dr. Conway is always on at me to try new treatments. Suppose I told her that Anna had discovered that The Old Hospital is doing a drug trial? Anna could easily fake a website that would make it look kosher for me to sign up. Dr. Conway could begin the referral chain. You know, start the process."

Caroline looked... gallant. Yes, that's the word, thought Mary. There was more animation about her than Mary had seen for weeks. Allowing her to be an undercover agent might boost her confidence. Or it could just as easily destroy her fragile equilibrium. Mary recalled Dr. Sarah Conway, a tired black woman of her own age whose imaginative discretion Caroline was counting on.

"Dr. Conway can't just send you away..." she began, monitoring the disappointment clouding Caroline. "She can't book you into a facility that no one really knows about. Unless..." she was starting to piece together a strategy. "What would convince an overworked doctor to take a crazy risk?"

"I could tell her I was desperate."

The door swung open; Anna was back. She had their full attention.

"Leni's been arrested," she said. "She asked for me. I'm taking the car back into Oxford. She may have more information about Janet."

Caroline gave a squeak.

"Wait, Anna. Not so fast," said Mary. "Why's she been arrested? And where? What's the point of asking for you, and not Dorothy or one of the counselors? Does she know what Olga told you last night about selling information?"

Anna grabbed her leather jacket from the back of her chair. "She was arrested at St. Julian's. Leni got the cleaner job, remember? Now she's been charged with assault on a Professor. They say she was trying to steal the Alchemy Scroll."

75

Mary's jaw dropped. "That would be the fake Scroll," said Mary, playing for time. "Not the real one, although she would not know that. Just hang on, Anna. We've gotta think this through. You can't just rush off!"

"Anna, wait a minute," said Caroline. "The better to help Leni." She'd hooked Anna's attention. The young woman grunted. With reluctance, she sat down. A thought struck her, Mary saw.

"Your Mr. Jeffreys can get her out." It was a statement, not a question.

"No, he can't," retorted Mary, knowing that it was entirely useless to explain the exact status of the Government Archive that Mr. Jeffreys controlled. "We'll have to find another way."

Anna looked disgusted. The car keys were jangling in her jeans pocket.

"Tell us what happened?" said Caroline. "Is Leni hurt?"

Anna thought briefly. "They wouldn't tell me much. She attacked that slimy old man, Godric St. John. That's what Dorothy said. She's trying to find the Holywell lawyer. The assault happened after she broke into the room where they stash the Alchemy Scroll. I want to go." Anna kicked a table leg in frustration. "She's only allowed one visitor apart from her lawyer. She asked for me." Her voice had become obstinate.

"Go to her," said Caroline, glancing at Mary. "Mary and I should make a start as well."

"Not to the Old Hospital!" jumped in Anna. "I won't let you!"

There was a pause that seemed to go on for hours. Mary broke it.

"*Like treats like,*" she said in a different tone, almost meditative. She was looking out of the window.

"What's that?" said Caroline. Anna locked eyes with Mary.

"'Like treats like' is a principle from magic, alchemy even," continued Mary. "I read about it online last night. It was in those articles you emailed me." Mary nodded to Anna, acknowledging how slow she was with what Anna had assembled. The rain had

76

stopped, the sky became translucent. Yet the temperature was dropping. There would be ice tonight.

"Mother Julian wrote it in the margins of the original Scroll: 'Like treats like.'" Mary sighed. "Look, both of you. Leni asked for Anna. No doubt because you got the truth from Olga. In some way you are alike."

Mary hoped that Anna would accept this reference to her past. The young woman narrowed her eyes. Mary began again. "Caroline wants to go to The Old Hospital to find Janet Swinford, the Key Keeper." She held up her hand. "I need to go to the Museum of Early Manuscripts in Los Angeles. Like treats like."

Caroline stood up and gathered her things; she was resolute. Anna wanted to dog Caroline's every movement; yet, she also felt the pull of the trafficked woman. Perhaps, thought Mary, with sudden insight, Anna wants to help Leni *because* she lacks the empathetic skills of the Holywell counselors. After all, Anna's past lacked people who trusted her.

"Anna," said Mary, leaning over the table. "Go to Leni. See what you can find out. Get Dorothy to take you to Oxford Police Station. She'll have a car. Then catch up with Caroline. She won't even *contact* The Old Hospital before you're back."

"Given the odd status of Holywell and St. Julian's, I expect they have an arrangement with a law firm," reflected Caroline. "Mary's right. It's going to take a day or two to get the referral." Her hands clasped, this time appealing to Anna. "You'll be at The Old Hospital almost before I will. I promise."

Anna grimaced. She pulled out her phone and began working with the skill of a master craftsman in clay. Her olive fingers touched, pressed, stroked, and made weird signs on the opaque surfaces. Various beeps, tones and soft cries could be heard, then the chime of a grandfather clock. Mary had the strangest sensation of vast wheels beginning to turn.

Finally, Anna faced Mary and Caroline.

"Still can't locate that… place. I'll have to track Caroline. Back in our basement, I have something she can wear."

77

The crisis was over; Anna was back on the team. Mary concealed her relief.

"We'll meet at our house in Surrey tonight. I need to pack for Los Angeles. And tomorrow, 'Like treats like.'"

CHAPTER 9
TWO BRITS IN SNOWBOUND
LOS ANGELES

By getting an early flight from Heathrow to Los Angeles, Mary arrived at The Museum of Early Manuscripts on the same day. She had a 3 p.m. appointment with the St. Julian's intern. He had been briefed that she wanted to search the Francis Andrew Ransome bequest. Despite snow on her earlier journey to Oxford, Mary was astonished as her taxi entered the choked freeway. *Snow*, she said to herself groggily, *in Los Angeles.* The elderly Hispanic driver correctly deduced why his passenger was rubbing her eyes.

"Yeah, effing snow," he barked. His unaccented English was worn by nicotine. "Mayor's talking about closing the freeways if it keeps up. Airport bought secondhand snowplows from Minnesota. Otherwise, LAX would be closed by now. Effing climate change."

He coughed, and Mary shrank back in her seat. Unsure of his credit card machine, she fumbled for paper dollars in one of her coat pockets.

How incongruous to see Los Angeles with the same weather as Oxford, thought Mary. After a doughnut ring of chain stores and gas stations, all deserted, the taxi sped through emptying streets. Glass towers peered down from under hats of snow. Between them, Mary spotted a few nineteenth-century blocks in brick among low buildings with concrete facades that had no discernible purpose. Sidewalks, ledges, balconies, and doorways grew white fur. Gusts billowed down streets like ash.

79

I guess I don't know America at all, Mary told herself. So be careful, Mary. The Museum of Early Manuscripts nevertheless surprised her. The taxi drew up to a pleasing modernist building in classical style. Half columns bulged from the street face, while snow on the front steps looked intimidating in the waning daylight. Something about the building reminded Mary of her own Archives where she'd spent forty years. That edifice had been seventeenth century.

Unused to blizzard conditions, Mary shivered. Exiting the airport, she'd buried her hands in her pockets to search for some heat. Yes, she'd remembered her gloves, but they were only knitted, not good in this damp cold.

Incongruously, she flashed back to another city unused to snow before climate change. The London TV news had led with a red double-decker swinging half circle as it slid down a white lane dotted with parked cars. In Los Angeles, Mary's tired eyes felt scarred by whiteness.

Midnight chimed on her body clock, an ocean away. She thrust a handful of banknotes at her driver and accepted her small suitcase in return. He pulled his earflaps across unshaven cheeks and was gone in a haze of diesel exhaust. His ex-passenger stared up at the huge steel doors of the Museum. Fortunately, she could now see a track up the steps that must have been scraped recently. Even though flakes burnt her nose, she could tread reasonably safely.

"Hey, you must be the Brit, like me; the lady from my college," called a young male voice behind Mary, as she reached the door. Disoriented, she swung around to see a man leap up the steps to arrive by her side. He jiggled with a brass lion's head on the door and a panel slid open to reveal a keypad. With a few pressed buttons, the man ushered her inside.

Words tumbled from him as he started to unwrap his many bright scarves.

"Sorry I wasn't here to meet you. We thought your plane would be rerouted. When I confirmed your flight's arrival, I reckoned you'd go directly to a hotel, given the weather, and reschedule for tomorrow. Here, let me take your coat."

He stuck out an arm. "I can hang it up when we get to the office. Right, just down that staircase in the corner. All the intern offices are in the basement. However, we store uncatalogued materials on the third floor and in the attics. Makes no sense, of course. Yes, turn here, Miss Wandwalker. We're going to the third door on the right; it's open."

Tired and overstimulated, Mary let herself be guided by this engaging young man. Dimly, she recalled Dame Eleanor mentioning the St. Julian's graduate working at the Los Angeles Museum. Neither she nor Mr. Jeffreys had mentioned that he was Afro-Caribbean. And why should they? His home counties accent was identical to hers.

Early twenties, she thought, as the man talked, grinned, and pumped her hand at the same time. He was very tactile, taking her arm in a way Mary was unused to. Yet she instinctively felt comfortable as they entered a tiny office stacked with papers on every available surface, apart from the computer.

His sheepskin jacket is too big, Mary noticed. Thoroughly soaked, it even smelled of sheep. His grey trilby had been far from optimal for keeping off snow. The young man carefully placed Mary's coat on the one hanger on the door before throwing his hat and sodden coat into a corner.

Mary smiled at his stylish black jeans and cream sweater. She was charmed by the transformation from eccentric to elegant.

"Mr. um…" she began.

"Oh sorry, sorry. D.P. Murphy, really pleased to meet you," he said with another enormous grin, relaxing into the second battered armchair. "D.P. stands for Dennis Patrick, but I go by D.P."

"Mary Wandwalker," she said, conscious of sleepiness. "How did you know it was me, Mr. Murphy? And where is everyone? I thought this Museum was open to the public."

81

"Call me D.P., please. Everyone's gone home. We don't open when the weather is this bad. New policy because snow in L.A. is unheard of. Real winter scares folks round here. The traffic goes crazy, well, crazier. We closed a couple of hours ago and won't open tomorrow. You're lucky your flight landed. They may divert planes to Frisco. San Francisco."

Nonplussed, Mary realized that keeping her return ticket with a flexible date had been a good idea after all. She sniffed at the snow gods.

"How'd you know who I am?" she repeated at D.P.'s dazzling grin.

"What other person would be at our doors today?" he asked rhetorically, leaning over to press "Go" on a grimy yet reasonably new expresso machine. The smell of beans grinding cheered Mary no end. She began to see possibilities in D.P.

"And no one else is here?" she queried.

D.P. shrugged, getting up and opening his desk drawer to reveal a clean set of blue coffee cups in various sizes.

"Just me until tomorrow morning," he answered. "Espresso or cap? I went out for fresh milk."

"A cappuccino would be delightful," said Mary sedately. Even the smell helped her focus. Her cold hands pricked as the heat penetrated. "Are the Ransome artifacts kept upstairs?" she added innocently. D.P. nodded.

After serving their coffees, he threw himself back into his chair, crossing one impossibly graceful leg over the other.

"Governor Ransome's official papers are no problem," he said, swallowing his espresso in a few gulps and rebooting his machine. "We're digitizing all the documents from that century, so they've been moved to the office of the IT geek on the second floor." He paused. "The Director mentioned several calls about uncatalogued items in the Ransome bequest."

He switched his intensity from Mary to the gurgling coffee. "My boss wants to know if the Museum can be part of the Symposium you're planning. The request from The European

82

History Foundation came as a complete surprise. She hadn't heard about them."

A different kind of shiver made Mary take a large swallow. What Symposium? What European History Foundation? Dame Eleanor had said nothing about an event. Besides, St. Julian's was petrified of publicity. If anyone else knew about the Alchemy Scroll... Mary's tired brain struggled. D.P. had started speaking again.

"The phone call from St. Julian's said something about really early stuff," he began, sipping this time and studying her. "The European History Foundation asked for a medieval manuscript that Governor Ransome had brought over. Apparently, he sailed with a whole barrel of handwritten manuscripts."

"*Much* earlier," emphasized Mary. "We think he, Governor Ransome, may have um... borrowed a medieval scroll from his prior study at St. Julian's."

After Holywell, Mary thought it impossible to maintain secrecy over St. Julian's potentially catastrophic loss.

"Not *the* medieval scroll," he burst out. "Not the Alchemy Scroll, Mother Julian's founding bequest?"

Before Mary could say anything, he corrected himself. "No, of course not. The Alchemy Scroll never leaves St. Julian's; stupid of me even to think of it in connection with Francis Ransome."

"Quite," said Mary, stirring the frothy remains of her coffee with concentration.

"There's another medieval manuscript?" D.P.'s eyes shone brighter if that were possible. "That would be awesome!"

All at once, Mary's eyelids turned to stone. Must be the jet lag.

"Can we continue this in the morning, D.P.? You can tell me how you got into old manuscripts; not the kind of thing for someone like you, surely."

About to doze off, Mary jerked awake at her own words. Her throat constricted. What had she said? D.P. looked stricken.

An immense weariness entered his jawline, traveled to his cheeks, and made his eyes old.

"*I am so sorry*," she whispered.

"It doesn't matter, Miss Wandwalker. Although you should know that in medieval times Africans traded books all over Europe when most inhabitants could neither read nor write. In fact, the alchemy of Mother Julian's Scroll originally came from Africa."

He added, stiffly, "My family has been English for four generations." He placed his coffee cup and saucer on a pile of books. He was no longer looking at her or smiling.

"I am so sorry," Mary repeated. "No excuse for what I said. D.P., I'm not that person."

"Are you telling me you're a *good* person really?"

Mary swallowed; she was very awake now.

"I...um my comment was... very wrong. You're British like... like me. I didn't mean... jet lag..."

Excuses: She'd given short shrift to excuses in her time. At the Archive, she'd prided herself on fairness. She'd never wondered if she harbored racist assumptions. Well, now she knew. Mary struggled to find words. She failed.

"So, Miss Wandwalker, tomorrow you want to search for a medieval Scroll? Just to see if it's part of the bequest in our storage?" D.P.'s face was bland, polite.

"Er, yes, thank you. Just to see, of course," said Mary.

In her suitcase was a copy of St. Julian's Charter with the original deed of gift of the Scroll to the College, then St. Julian's Hall. Dame Eleanor had hoped it would be enough to negotiate the Alchemy Scroll's return. Mary was skeptical, while Mr. Jeffreys frankly discounted the notion that any Museum would simply hand over a precious artifact.

It was Mary who had come up with the idea of an exchange: the Ransome seventeenth-century copy for the original. It might work. After all, The Los Angeles Museum of Early Manuscripts had wealthy donors. They might want to avoid a scandal involving illustrious forebears. Then it would be a matter of swearing the museum's representatives to silence. She would not take the Robert Le More copy to Los Angeles, of course. Any cross-Atlantic transfer had to be done properly. Meanwhile, D.P. was just doing his job.

"I've got permission for you to see the stuff not yet catalogued," he said, standing up. "Give me your cup, and I'll take you to the attics. The Ransome chests have been stored there since their bequest to the Museum. Let's check that there's something for you to discuss with the Director tomorrow."

His tone told her that their informal conversation was over.

"Yes, er, thank you," said Mary, grabbing her coat. "When did the bequest get to this museum?" All she could do now was carry on. She trotted to keep up with his long strides.

"Governor Ransome's material came from Davinia Ransome. Last of the family, we think. She never married, dying here in L.A., in 1891. I did nineteenth-century American philanthropists for my undergraduate special topic at St. Julian's. Davinia was one of the few who was helping prostitutes and their children."

"That would suggest that Museum Studies is a postgraduate degree?" said Mary. She was self-taught, apart from specialized courses designated by Mr. Jeffreys.

"Yeah, I've started a Ph.D. at UCLA," said D.P. calmly. "They gave me transfer credit."

The iron cage in front of them proved, to Mary's relief, to be a fully functioning elevator.

D.P. regained some good humor as they ascended past stone carvings in modernist style. Weird masks reflected in the varnished floors.

Mary wanted to kick herself. Instead, she shut her eyes. Concentrating on the less embarrassing part of her conversation with D.P., she recalled his mention of others interested in Ransome's medieval manuscripts. Hadn't D.P. said something about a Symposium and a European History Foundation? Now it was doubly difficult to enquire without letting slip the exact nature of her mission for St. Julian's.

Just thinking about the Alchemy Scroll and her old college reminded Mary of Leni's arrest. That brought up Anna. Immediately, Mary plunged into anxiety about Caroline's attempt to find The Old Hospital. I should be there, she thought. I could phone, but I promised not to wake them at this appalling hour in the UK.

Following D.P. up a short flight of stairs to the museum attics, Mary almost choked, so flooded was she with longing to trust D.P. with the whole story.

CHAPTER 10
STRANGE MIXING

D.P. ushered Mary through blushing doors that reflected the discreet lighting. Mahogany, vastly expensive, Mary realized. So, this is the attic of The Los Angeles Museum of Early Manuscripts.

Expecting dirt, cobwebs, and cardboard boxes, she needed a moment to take in a space big enough for several tennis courts. Her head tilted to ornate bell lamps dangling from steel rafters. Mary then marveled at the sloping walls, which were mostly plate glass. Under windows sloppy with snow and twilight, Mary paced polished pine floors, innocent of dust. For the first time, she wondered if she should remove her damp shoes. No, I won't, she decided.

Instead, she touched D.P.'s arm. He gave a slight flinch, and Mary drew back. She was reassured by his sardonic smile. Mary cleared her throat.

"D.P., um... can I explain... can I tell you more about?"

No, it would have to wait until the morning. Sleep was about to fell her like an axe.

"I mean, I'm hoping we can talk tomorrow."

"Sure thing, Miss Wandwalker. I'll be in bright and early for your appointment with the Director. Plenty of time to chat. Now come this way."

D.P. scampered down the aisle between low partitions where wooden crates sat waiting. Each had been stamped with red numbers. Plenty of room for whole shipping containers, Mary reflected. D.P. beckoned Mary to a corner. He pointed

87

at three wooden chests without numbers. Bracketed with rusty iron, these were old, Mary knew.

She gulped. First, she had to ask a question.

"D.P., what did you say downstairs about a Symposium? And some European History outfit?"

The young man straightened up. He looked curious rather than suspicious; Mary was relieved to see.

"I didn't take the call myself. It came from Professor Cookie Mac. He's a big TV star over here."

He saw her confusion and grinned.

"Cookie Mac, of course, that's not his real name. Well, he did a show about the European settlers that came in for a lot of criticism. I never saw it, but the Director says that the TV series got him a huge research grant from some corporation researching lost medicines."

"Ah," said Mary. Big grants from a pharma corporation? Lost medicines? Sounds familiar.

"I'd love to meet Professor Cookie Mac." D.P. sighed. "Now he's working with some European History outfit on a special project. He said it would revolutionize how we see America — from when it was still a colony right up to today."

"The program couldn't have been on the BBC," said Mary, feeling foolishly British. "I would have remembered a name like Cookie Mac."

D.P. grinned, relaxed once more. His smile was infectious; Mary felt her anxiety fade under the bright lamps.

"Cookie Mac's real name's Professor Donald Cuchulain Macdonald. He goes by Cookie Mac, for TV. Now, look here."

D.P. knelt beside the chests, which each had a jumble of numbers and letters in chalk. When the young man took out his phone to check them, Mary had a sudden flash of Anna and her cybercraft. Mary realized she missed the young woman's laconic ferocity. Where were they now, her friends, her fellow operatives, her family?

*****

88

Midnight in the UK, and Caroline waited in bed in the discharge ward of one of Oxford's lesser hospitals. Thanks to Anna's online witchery, the hospital believed that she would be transported home. In fact, The Old Hospital had accepted Caroline's referral. Anna had outdone herself on forged doctors' letters and medical notes. Caroline signed everything on screen.

"The ambulance is on its way," whispered an elderly man in overalls.

Caroline had taken him for the cleaner. He shuffled back to something placed in the middle of the ward. A mop and bucket; he *was* a cleaner. Is that how it always was with The Old Hospital?

Caroline did not need to feign drowsiness. She'd been injected with a strong tranquilizer. Even so, her fingers felt in her gown pocket for her phone. Time to send a last text to Anna — and Mary, of course. They, whoever "they" were, would take away her phone.

It truly is the dead of night, she thought. "Find me soon, Anna," she typed, letting her eyelids fall.

While Caroline succumbed to Morpheus and prescription drugs, Anna sat at the wheel of the Agency car in the hospital parking lot. With thick cloud cover, the night was very dark. Only the streetlights cast trapezoid shadows from deserted vehicles. Anna had a dilemma. She hated dilemmas.

Frowning at Caroline's message, Anna flipped back to the one five minutes ago from St. Julian's. *Come to St. Julian's at once if you want to help Leni*, it read. It could take up to two hours to reach Oxford, three, if she waited until morning traffic thickened on the motorway. Could she risk ignoring St. Julian's until morning, so that she could follow Caroline to The Old Hospital? Given the discovery that no tracking device could be concealed under a hospital gown, it was the only way to keep track of her lover. Yet, it could be hours before the ambulance arrived. Between 12 and 6 a.m. had been the notification.

Unused to feeling torn, Anna banged a fist on the empty seat beside her, making the glowing phone jump. She didn't do decisions; she did action. With a stamp of her high-heeled boot, she started the car. Heading for the exit and the turn off to the M25 freeway, she missed the ambulance entering the hospital main gate.

With the highest opinion of her hacking skills, Anna assured herself that she could hunt down Caroline, Old Hospital, or no. She allowed herself a grim smile as she joined the humming traffic heading west. The silver car swallowed the miles back to the city where stone spires clustered like a grove of trees. Anna did not stop until she parked in the shadow of St. Julian's medieval walls.

*****

D.P. and Mary dug through layers of clothing full of holes and dust. Many items smelled of ammonia. Oh, urine, Mary belatedly realized. They were kneeling, rummaging in the first two Ransome chests. The third held boots and shoes on top of a collection of leather belts knotted like snakes.

Mary was about to withdraw to ease her aching back when she spotted it. Shoved into the corner under the top layer was a black metal box with a lock. D.P. followed her gasp and helped her lift it out. Although rusty, the lock looked formidable. Mary rubbed her aching ankles.

"I don't have a key," she said flatly.

"Ah," said D.P. "That's a problem." He looked sympathetic.

"I can't..."

"No, you can't," agreed Mary.

She was so tired her body had left the building. She could roll over and sleep right here. Perhaps Francis Andrew Ransome, Governor and thief, would appear to her in a dream and hand over the key. After all, he'd kept the Alchemy Scroll long enough. He must be ready to let it go.

"Look here," called D.P., as if to cheer up an elderly relative. "There's something fixed to under the lid of this chest, see?"

With gathering excitement, he pulled away the straw packing under the curved top of the chest. He tugged at something flexible. Mary was too weary to remind him that whatever it was could be brittle. Triumphant, he held an object out to her: a dirty leather pouch.

D.P.'s glowing brown eyes met her ghostly grey. She took the mysterious package. Gently, in her lap over her tweed skirt, she undid the stiff leather. Good, not fragile, a bit moldy, Mary held her breath.

Inside was a folded square of parchment the size of a small handkerchief. Together they placed it where light pooled on the floor. Exhausted as she was, Mary stirred.

"It's a list of contents," she said. "Probably all the chests had them."

"I see it, I see it." called D.P., banging his fist on his palm with excess energy. Mary wanted to smile; her lips managed a wriggle. Then she saw the entry.

"You mean this one," she pointed. Her ungloved finger shook.

"It's very faded."

"Yes, just look at it! Here, it says 'illuminated medieval scroll.' There's only one on the list."

"Gotta be what you're looking for. What's the next line? Could that word be "magick?""

"Yes, I think so," said Mary. "It's the spelling they used in Ransome's time. It says," she cleared her throat: "'Alchymical and Magickal Manuscript of St. Julian.'"

"Wow!" D.P. swiveled a full circle on the slippery floor. His grin spread. "Must be something to do with the College after all. Is this what you came for?"

"Undoubtedly," said Mary Wandwalker, putting out an arm for help in rising to her feet.

CHAPTER 11
ANNA AND LENI

Anna's meeting in St. Julian's left her angry and confused. Six hours later, she was admitted to Leni's cell. The miscreant from Holywell has spent several nights at Oxford Police Station without the support of anyone from Holywell. When Anna and Dorothy had tried to visit on the day of Leni's arrest at St. Julian's, they had been turned away.

"The Russian girl is being questioned. Her solicitor is with her, but no one else is allowed. Come back tomorrow."

"Leni *asked* for us," said Dorothy, outraged. "We want to see her now. I'm from Holywell, where she lives."

"We know all about you witches at Holywell. I'm telling you, Leni's remanded in custody. She's staying here. No visitors."

Anna vanished while Dorothy continued terse and fruitless exchanges. Anna did not like the police. Police stations knotted her stomach. Bitter years preceded her chance at a different kind of life with Caroline and Mary.

To survive her trafficking, Anna had grown up cultivating recklessness. She honed her aggression, ignored the pain, and learned to manipulate. Eventually, she clawed her way to trusted operative by turning her ferocious intelligence to the malleable realities of cyberspace.

Today, for the Agency, Anna roamed the web; it was her native land. Beside her, typical hackers were domesticated; she, truly wild. Anna crackled with sexuality and unpredictability. Those who knew her feared her lashing out.

93

It took a couple of days before Anna got to meet Leni in person. The cell door grated shut. Anna ignored the stabbing sensation in her belly and told herself to focus on the occupant. Hunched on the hard bed was an exceptionally thin girl. Anna recognized that her colorless hair had been chopped with nail scissors. Leni's tear tracks made stripes on her cheeks.

Anna wanted to run. She was not out of her depth with Leni, the trafficked girl accused of attempted theft and grave assault; she was in her depth, too far in. These were the memories she'd burned and buried.

"You're Anna. Why didn't you come before?" The voice was reedy and accented. It grated on Anna.

"Yes, I'm Anna. The police would not let me in before."

Anna shut her eyes. Surely when she opened them again, the cell would have faded away. No? All right. "Your friend Olga spoke to me about Janet, the Key Keeper. You sold her out," Anna accused.

"It was Olga," the girl said automatically. "Olga did it."

"Olga did what?" snapped Anna.

"Olga sold out Janet. She made the call. She copied the doctor's notes."

"She says it was you."

Leni did not look surprised, nor sad. Anna was disgusted.

"I'll go call Dorothy," she said, turning to the cell door.

"Noooo," came the whisper rising to a cry. Terrified eyes met Anna's implacable gaze. Leni's mouth hung open. She whimpered, "No, Dorothy mustn't know. Don't go. Please don't go! It must be you. Not anyone else. Please, please. Have you spoken to Professor St. John yet?"

She burst into tears. Anna was trapped. She wanted to shout at the girl. Instead, she gritted her teeth. There was a long pause punctuated by Leni's sniffing.

"You can't help," she finally muttered. "I was wrong. You can't help me."

Anna frowned. It wasn't true that she couldn't help. Professor St. John had already told her what she had to do to

94

save Leni. Her body revolted at the defeat in the girl. Anna had no compunction about calling them girls. Caroline, she was the one who cared, who took on their pain. It occurred to Anna that Caroline would demand an accounting of this strange encounter.

"I'll help," she said, forcing the words to populate the dead room. "I've seen Professor St. John. I'll help if I can."

"It was Olga..." began Leni again.

"Shut up about that. Tell me what you did about Janet and why you got arrested."

From a long way off, Anna saw Caroline smile. She breathed more easily. "Now sit up. Stop that whining."

Moving carefully, Anna descended onto the mattress next to Leni. The girl's voice came out in a squeak.

"It was all of us. No, it was *their* idea. D'you think if I told the police they would let me go? Not back to that College, I can't go back there...ever... I..."

Leni was gasping. Panic attack, Caroline had called it. Something about a paper bag. Anna looked around. There was nothing in the cell beyond a stinking toilet. What would Caroline do? Oh, *that*.

Anna snaked a strong arm around the heaving back. Gingerly, she touched knobby bones under the none-too-clean sweatshirt.

"There, there," Anna said. Caroline should be here. This scene would amuse Mary Wandwalker, she thought.

"Just tell me what you did," Anna commanded.

Leni edged further away, sniffing.

"We talked about stealing that scroll, the one with gold and pictures. They showed it to us on a tour of the College, special dispen... whatever. They call it the Alchemy Scroll." After the words tumbled out, Leni put a hand over her mouth.

"What," Anna was astounded. "You...who? *All* of you?"

Leni grabbed her arm as if it might explode.

"Quiet, please, please, Anna. They might be listening!"

"They who? The police? How...?"

"They have... um, how you say... beetles..."

Anna stared at her. "Bugs," she said shortly, and scanned the bare cell. "Not likely here. But good to be careful," she added, grudgingly. The girl had the right instincts. She sighed at the undernourished specimen. "Since I've talked to Professor St. John about the charges against you, you'd better tell me everything. Leave nothing out, and fast. I must go soon to help...um, a friend."

"It's because of you we did this," Leni hissed. "Now only you can save me." Anna was getting tired of the intrigue. What was she to these girls? Anna had made no promises to Dorothy or her charges.

"You see, we wanted to be like you. Strong, and free."

Anna stared. Leni hastened to explain. "So, we decided to be a gang and make lots of money. After we saw the Scroll..." Leni faltered.

A role model? Inspired by Anna's criminal career? Reluctantly, she began to see the thinking of the scared young women. After all, she'd told them it was her way out of prostitution. Anna swallowed. "Is that why you asked for me? I thought it was because St. John told you to."

"He did. When I got caught, old St. John grabbed me, and I hit out. I didn't mean to hurt him."

"So, you were defending yourself," In spite of herself, Anna found herself interested.

"Um...well, there was a bucket."

"A bucket? Plastic? Empty?"

"Metal. A mop bucket. I swung it at him. He got it...there."

"Where"?

"You know, in a man's *there*."

There was a pause. "Is he badly hurt?" enquired Anna.

"I don't think so," said Leni, doubtfully. She must be stronger than she looks, realized Anna. Trafficked women had to be.

"And so..." prompted Anna. "What happened next? Before the police arrived." She knew that before the law took over, the culprit was in most danger.

96

"After he stopped that horrible noise," said Leni, gloomily, "he said I had to get you to go and see him. You, and no one else, or he would have me charged with attempted murder. And the other girls as accomplices. He'd send us to prison. Forever."

Anna sighed. "Well, I have seen him. I can't tell you what he proposed, but there is no point in you worrying. Your part in the Alchemy Scroll is done. Do you understand?"

"Yes, Anna."

Soon after, Anna left the police station, raking her hair with her fingers to dislodge the scent of incarceration. Even so, she smelled grime and bleach on the Chanel jacket she'd purloined by altering shipment data online. However, she wasn't thinking about Leni's cell. She was remembering her nocturnal session with Godric St. John.

It was simple: blackmail. She was to steal the real alchemy scroll from, "your friend, Mary Wandwalker, once she has returned with it to this country. If you do not, Miss Vronsky, I will accuse you of criminal conspiracy with the trafficked girls at Holywell."

Anna wanted to hit him. Unlike Leni, she'd trained herself in restraint. Violence produced more trouble. Rather, what Mary would do?

"You are wondering how your Miss Wandwalker would react. She'd say I'm harmless without evidence. But you, Miss Vronsky, I checked you out. You come from a hard school. You know that with my Mer-Corp backers I have power beyond the law courts. Power to get those Holywell girls deported and your deal with the authorities revoked." St. John reeked of self-satisfaction.

Anna boiled. He was right. All she could do was listen to his hateful words.

"I want the original Alchemy Scroll, Miss Vronsky. I don't care who you are, you and your so-called *Agency*."

Godric St. John's lips pursed as if he had bitten into a spider. "I want that scroll brought to *me*," he continued. "No nonsense

97

about working for the College. You bring it to me here and tell no one. Or else."

Anna remained silent. She was revolted by the sweat on Godric St. John's forehead. She avoided the bulge that must be a protecting his wounded testicles for then she might show pleasure. After several moments, she threw him a word: "Money."

Part statement, part question, her response reassured St. John. He poured more purple-red wine in his glass, setting the decanter on the table by his wing armchair. He hadn't offered any to Anna.

"Money? Well, perhaps, Miss Vronsky. Later, much later. When I've found... when I can complete my work on the real Alchemy Scroll. For now, you work for me. Bring me Mother Julian's Scroll within two weeks, or I'll get that guttersnipe Leni prosecuted for attempted murder. She won't survive long in prison."

St. John tossed back the fragrant liquid and glanced at Anna, watching him. It was a challenge. Nothing in the man's demeanor acknowledged that Leni was a real person.

Deliberately, Anna pulled over an upholstered stool and sat. Some words were sparks that burned. She didn't think any more about Mary and Caroline.

"I am waiting for my answer, Miss Vronsky. The local police will be delighted that my memory has recovered. I can now describe the terrible blows; how that... that evil child with obvious malice aforethought..."

"I'll do it." Anna heard the words, so she must have spoken them.

"Say it?" St. John leaned forward releasing more chemical odors, his pointy chin thrust at Anna. She rose and donned her jacket.

"I'll get the Alchemy Scroll for you."

"Within two weeks. I must have it in time for... a project I am employed on."

"Sooner. I'll get it sooner." She was too revolted to look at him.

St. John leaned back, reaching again for the decanter. "My memory is clouding. Just make sure it stays that way. Shut the door on your way out, Miss Vronsky."

Anna slammed the door and stamped her boot heels down the stairs as loudly as she could. She had absolutely no idea whether she was going to give the Alchemy Scroll to Godric St. John.

PART THREE
PUTREFACTIO

CHAPTER 12
INTO DARKNESS

Caroline woke in the dark. She had been dreaming about Mary. The older woman told her to get up, it was her turn to make breakfast. This never happened in real life. Caroline's depression swerved unpredictably between insomnia and what Anna called Caroline being a bear, hibernating and sleeping twenty hours a day. Either way, they let her sleep when she could.

There was something over her mouth that tickled her nose. Looking up, Caroline saw red squiggles in the darkness. Where was she? She tried not to panic. She was tucked in a bed with tight blankets. The cover felt scratchy and too warm. Attempting to move her arms, she met something hard. She was tied to the bed. Fear flamed; she opened her mouth and gagged, gasping.

"Stop it."

The voice hissed out of the dark. Caroline stifled a scream. She could see nothing at all except the red dots. Some blinked like tiny flames.

"Stop that noise." The voice was irritated.

"Wishshsh awp..." Caroline tried to ease her mouth free. In the end, she decided to use her tongue, horribly dry already, to push at the prickly cloth. Twisting her head, she edged her mouth free of the bedcovers.

"Who's there?" she whispered.

"Never you mind," came a hoarse reply. It could be a woman or a man. "Just keep quiet. Otherwise, they'll bring more pills. It'll be dawn soon. Whatever you told them, some of us want to wake up."

103

The voice was angry, and a bit scared, Caroline realized. She must be at The Old Hospital. Looking back, she recalled a needle and then fiery serpents shooting through her veins. Then nothing, until waking... here. That's right, The Old Hospital is where they are keeping the witch with the key to the Alchemy Scroll. Anna would come for her, for her and the missing witch.

Anna, where are you? she spoke silently into the dark. *Come now. I need you; take me home.*

The darkness flickered once; the red dots burned. Caroline heard a faint bleeping. This must be a ward. The red dots are machines, probably. Why is it so dark?

"I can't move," she whispered, hoping the voice would answer. It did not sound... too dangerous, just... a bit aggressive.

Like Anna, she thought. Caroline wondered if she could hear breathing. If this was a ward, there ought to be several patients. Why couldn't she hear anything except the faint bleeps?

"I can't move," she said more loudly. She was punished and rewarded.

"Shut up."

Probably a woman, Caroline thought, and elderly.

"They've tied down your legs and arms. That's what they do until they see you won't wander at night. Just keep quiet. At first light, we might get a cup of tea. Maybe even sugar."

Caroline wanted to ask another question, and then another and another. She didn't. First light soon, it was a promise to hold onto. Perhaps she could start finding things out for herself. And she really wanted a cup of tea.

Two hours later there came a series of clicks followed by the ignition of artificial light. Caroline opened her eyes. She was in an old-fashioned ward she could dimly remember from visiting her grandmother as a child. That hospital had been scheduled to close, she recalled.

Clattering came from just beyond the door. Caroline trembled, then told herself to stop it. At once, three occupants of beds threw off their covers and heaved themselves into a sitting position. Nearest to Caroline was an old woman with long white hair dressed in a child's nightgown with blue forget-me-nots. Caroline saw brown stains down the front and tried not to gag. The woman turned to Caroline and glared at her. Last night's voice, she assumed.

She was distracted by the arrival of a trolley with a tea urn and piles of sliced white toast dripping with butter.

"Give, give," called a young man with green dreadlocks plaited incongruously against his pink scalp. Caroline saw that he had leg restraints, although his arms were free. These he held out to the women pouring tea into plastic mugs. They placed a mug and plate beside each bed. The two women, one African-looking, the other possibly Filipino, made no attempt to speak. Caroline wondered if they even spoke English.

"Give, give."

"Wait your turn." The voice came from a pile of paper files on a corner desk. When a head poked out, Caroline glimpsed a grey-faced woman in a nurse's uniform from the 1970s. She even had one of those old-fashioned caps. Dark bags weighed down her eyes below a mousy fringe. The face disappeared. Then came a metallic tapping. Caroline could not place it. Then came a flash from an old detective series she watched when she could not sleep. It was the sound of an electric typewriter.

Well, that settles the question of the internet, thought Caroline. How will Anna find me now?

A face loomed close, scented with tea and toast. Hunger and thirst ignited Caroline. The trolley was moving away. Twisting her head, Caroline glimpsed her plate and mug. She fought her restraints in a silent losing battle.

"Hey," she whispered as loud as she dared. "I can't... I can't get my tea. Help."

She strained her wrists under the pink blanket. The young black woman turned. Spotting the problem, she took an old-fashioned key from the bunch at her waist and knelt by Caroline's bed. After a grating sound, Caroline saw her scuttle after the vanishing trolley with its wobbling urn.

The patients were alone with tapping typewriter keys and the invisible nurse. Her piles of files had been stacked like fortress walls. Caroline shot a quick look at her angry neighbor who was gobbling her toast, butter dribbling down her chin.

Dragging herself to her elbows, Caroline pulled her plate onto the bed and picked up the mug of tea. It was warm, brown, and sweet. Like Anna, she sighed. What could she do now? What would Mary do?

"Go, go," came the young man again, waving his plastic plate like a frisbee. He looked happy, waving his arms. "Fly, fly," he said, making as if to throw the plate at the tiny windows. They were too high to show anything but blue clouds blanching to daylight.

"All right. Quiet now," came the sleepy voice from the paper stacks. "The meds are coming. Put it down."

Footsteps approached. A different trolley with a blonde girl looking about fourteen. Caroline realized she was not prepared for The Old Hospital after all. It was loaded with plastic boxes with protruding syringes. Caroline gulped. Adept at avoiding pills when trying not to worry her late husband, evading injections was another matter entirely.

The nurse came to Caroline's bed and looked at a chart at the end of it.

"I can't have needles. I'm allergic." It was all Caroline could think of.

The nurse stared at her, and then back at the chart.

"Your meds are not listed," she said in a harsh Midlands accent.

"No injections. I get a rash and a fever and..." Caroline could not remember any more plausible symptoms. To her relief, the nurse felt around and produced a tray of pills. She presented Caroline with three blue lozenges in a tiny cup and another one with water.

"All right, starting you on these," she muttered. "Until we get your records."

"Thank you," gasped Caroline. She threw all three pills into her throat and tossed in the water. It made her cough. She forced herself to lie down, shutting her eyes as if all was well. When the threatening trolley had gone, Caroline turned her head into the pillow and spat the pills into her hand.

She became aware of a movement near her bed. The old woman with the disgusting nightgown was kneeling next to her.

"Saw yer," she sang in a whisper. "Yer spat out them pills."

Caroline searched for a way to placate the woman, until she saw the wrinkled face rearranged into a wicked grin.

"Good on yer," she rasped. "Agnes Naismith," she banged her chest. "Do ye want to join the escape committee?" Agnes giggled, showing a few yellow teeth. "There's some of us who want out of here. One's a witch."

CHAPTER 13
AN AWFUL LOT OF BLOOD

Mary Wandwalker planned to sleep late in her hotel room high above the icy streets of Los Angeles. Kept too late at the Museum, her body craved rest while her mind was stuck in London time. Therefore, she insisted that her morning appointment with D.P. and the Museum Director, Melissa Oldcastle, be moved to 11 a.m.

Mary fell asleep again while planning a leisurely breakfast capped by telling Caroline and Anna of her triumph. The snow might cause trouble with flights, but surely, she and the Alchemy Scroll would be on the way home in a day or two.

It was not to be. She was roused by a violent banging on her door before 9. Easing her legs out of bed, she had the sensation of being hit by a brick. Ah, jet lag. Unsteadily, she made for the door. The assailant proved to be D.P.

"I've come from D.P. He said to bring you coffee."

Unsmilingly, he held out what seemed to Mary a gigantic cup with a cardboard holder. Mary took it, blinking and shook her head.

"Who? No, that can't be…"

"Oh, I'm Sam, D.P.'s brother. People say we look alike."

"Oh, yes, you do indeed. Come in. I'm afraid you've woken me up… Sam."

Sam strode to the window, opening the curtains. He wasn't interested in his brother's strange friend. Mary burnt her mouth on the boiling liquid. It could be coffee, she thought. Sam swung around.

109

"D.P. wants you at the Museum early. He wants to give you a tour of… the stuff. And he says that taxis will be scarce. What with the snow an' all. So, I'm to help you."

"Yes, of course. How kind of him. And you. Would you mind waiting outside for me, Sam?"

What with dressing, the harshness of the coffee, and the still falling snow, it was well over an hour before they approached the museum. Something wasn't right. There were police cars, three of them and an ambulance parked outside.

"Something going on," said Sam unnecessarily.

Mary caught hold of a grizzled member of the Los Angeles PD who said Ma'am a lot. When he heard about her meeting with the Brit intern and the Museum Director, he took several steps to the side and muttered into a radio. Then he insisted both Mary and Sam enter the museum to speak to "the sergeant. Right now, Ma'am."

Mary was about to demand an explanation when a dark-haired woman in a black-jeaned suit and a ponytail came down the steps and announced herself as Sergeant Beverly Rivera. Miss Wandwalker was to accompany them inside the museum *immediately.* It was a matter of a homicide.

Mary dropped her briefcase, which burst open. Her hand trembled as she knelt to gather copies of St. Julian's Charter and the Deed of Foundation Gift. With an anxious glance at the puzzled young man by her side, she motioned him to follow the cops into the museum's entrance hall.

Yellow crime-scene tape was strung across the stairs and elevator. An older man stood stiffly next to a woman in a black fur coat fastened to the chin. Both stared at Mary, at Sam too, she realized. With forbidding expressions, they approached.

"Miss Wandwalker," said the woman, in what Mary recognized as a moneyed New England accent. "I'm Melissa Oldcastle, the Museum Director."

Mary noticed that despite the snow falling, Melissa Oldcastle's dyed blonde coiffure remained perfect. Clearly, no snowflake dared disarrange a single hair. The Director put out a manicured finger and tapped Mary's arm.

"I must show you…a hum," she coughed, "the scene."

"Captain Lascelles," said the gruff voice of the man beside her. "We need …your statement about everything that happened yesterday."

The man's voice was oddly tentative for a senior police officer, at least from what Mary gathered from American cop shows she was secretly addicted to. She noticed Sergeant Rivera giving the grizzled man a worried look before the enormity of this meeting began to sink in.

"And you are?" Sergeant Rivera prompted in Sam's direction.

"Sam Murphy. My brother works here. I don't. He just asked me to bring this, that is, Miss Wandwalker, to an appointment this morning."

"When did he ask you?" pounced the Sergeant. Mary was getting a bad feeling.

"Last night 'bout seven. Where is he? I texted him en route, but he never answered. He always answers."

Sam remained nonchalant. Mary looked at him with concern.

"What's happened?" Mary's voice dried. She didn't want to know. She wanted to go home.

"You've got to come with us." Lascelles grabbed Mary's arm and made for the elevator, pulling aside the yellow tape. "Attic. Now."

His Sergeant brought up the rear, with Melissa Oldcastle and Sam. She concentrated on Sam, Mary noted. In the close quarters of the elevator, Mary could see the Captain's face properly. That livid scar on his right temple had to be from a bullet. She blinked. Was that a crater below his white hair with a neat black hole? Could the bullet still be lodged in there? That horror was a distraction from what was upstairs.

Sergeant Rivera cleared her throat, trying to get Mary's attention. Mary ignored her.

Somewhere — in her head — Mary could hear sobbing. Captain Lascelles returned her stare expressionlessly. Okay, so this is wealthy Museum Director Melissa Oldcastle, thought Mary, feverishly. She was trying to dredge up details she had Googled on the plane.

Educated at the Sorbonne and Harvard, Director Oldcastle's family money had paid to renovate the museum twenty years ago. The fur-coated woman looked beyond Mary with practiced distaste. Her skin said forty-five, but Mary knew she was closer to sixty-five.

It seemed too soon when they arrived at the attic and made for the racks holding the Ransome bequest. Everywhere were figures in white coveralls like menacing snowmen. Mary caught the echo of D.P.'s excited tones. He'd been eager as a child to open the untouched chests.

The smell hit her first: smoking iron with a sweet aftertaste. Between moving feet, she glimpsed a dark red pool. Blood, there was lots of blood. Beside it was a man's body. Even turned away, the head looked familiar. She heard a scream from somewhere behind her: a man's scream; a boy's scream. Mary thrust through the crowd. A strong arm tried to pull her back. She instinctively fought it off.

"Let me... let me see," she said fiercely. The arm dropped.

Captain Lascelles grabbed hold of Sam Murphy instead, who stood trembling all over. Mary knelt in front of the body. For a moment she was alone with her shuddering breaths and D.P.'s body.

His head had been smashed in from behind, probably by the ordinary hammer that lay next to him. Mary choked; she could hear retching behind her. Blood had poured down D.P.'s back and pooled on the floor when his body crashed down. Someone had turned him onto his side.

The grief was unexpected. Tears steamed on her cheeks as they had not done for since another death long ago. Oily with face cream, her tears dripped on her beautiful lavender coat.

Absurdly, she wanted to warm D.P.'s cold hands; they were splayed like brown stars. Out of the corner of her eye, Mary noticed his trilby up against the Ransome chest. She couldn't think about the Alchemy Scroll right now.

*****

"You must be the Brit," he'd said at the museum entrance. His youth, his friendliness, his enthusiasm, was that it? Mary's throat made a sound. He'd been so… so *innocent*.

Voices peaked behind her. Someone was saying that the Museum Director herself had found the body. Sam yelled about taking her place beside D.P. Mary got to her feet as Beverly Rivera darted to take her arm. Melissa Oldcastle stared from the door.

"Let me go, you bastard." That was Sam. Lascelles dropped his arm, and Sam knelt next to D.P.'s head. He stretched out a finger, then jumped back at the combined "Noooo" from all the police persons present. Not Lascelles though, realized Mary. He was just staring at Sam, as if puzzled about something.

"This is a crime scene, sir."

The young man ignored Beverly.

"My brother. Let me stay with my brother!" It was a primal howl. Mary shivered.

Looking up, Mary was shocked to see fear on the old cop's face. Instinctively, she met Beverly Rivera's eyes. The young woman gave a tiny nod. All was not right with Captain Lascelles. Sam retched. Sergeant Rivera took charge of moving people out.

"Sir, Mr. Murphy, come back here. I…that is, I mean Captain Lascelles, needs to talk to Miss Wandwalker. And you, sir," she said tautly. "Mr. Murphy, come with us," the Sergeant was saying. "You too, please, Captain." She touched Lascelles on the arm. "We're going to the Director's office, Miss Oldcastle's suite."

The older cop jerked as if someone had pressed a switch.

"Bring that man." He pointed at Sam.

Sam didn't move. Mary found herself slipping her hand into the young man's and helping him to his feet.

"Come on, Sam," she said. "Let's go."

After a few seconds, Sam Murphy unpeeled his eyes from the body. For the first time he really looked at the woman in the funny-colored coat with steely eyes. He nodded, and she led him toward the knot of museum employees. They preceded the cops out of the attic.

Twenty minutes later they were in the Director's office. Minus her furs, wraith thin Melissa Oldcastle reappeared in a cashmere suit. The unfortunate blood color combined with the blonde helmet of her hair gave her the appearance of a Viking.

Decked out like a stately home, her office possessed several arrangements of antique seating. Mary made for a well-upholstered chair that faced away from the window and toward the door. Anna once said always look for escape routes. How bleak, she'd thought back then. That seemed a thousand years ago.

Sam eased himself into a chair beside her. The Captain and Sergeant Rivera pulled up seats to face them, with Melissa Oldcastle to one side. Mary's hands shook. The smell of blood had followed them into the elegant room.

"Coffee," barked the Captain over his shoulder to the lobby. Melissa Oldcastle nodded. With the grace of aristocratic training, she rose and muttered some words out of the door. No one paid attention until they heard the note of surprise.

"Professor? We weren't expecting you today. There's been an… an incident."

Sam made a strangled sound.

114

CHAPTER 14
THEY CALL HIM COOKIE MAC

Mary leaned forward to scrutinize the newcomer. She felt her neck knot at the hatless man in his forties with a glowing bulbous nose. Stamping snow off expensive shoes, he then removed a tartan cloak. Must have cost a bomb, thought Mary. That's a genuine pattern probably hand-woven. The intruder turned to address the Museum Director.

"An incident? Here at the Museum? Nothing to interrupt our business, I trust," he said briskly. His New England accent had a faint Scottish lilt. Not genuine, Mary decided. Put on with money like the tartan. This he removed, revealing a 1950s-style houndstooth suit over a prosperous round belly.

Seizing the most imposing chair, he touched his thinning hair to discover it wet. He pulled out a handkerchief, flapped it like a flag, and rubbed it briefly across his head. Then he surveyed the shocked faces with a self-satisfied smirk. Repelled first by his attitude, then by his cologne, Mary began to guess his agenda. I hope he's not who I think he is, she thought.

"Thank you for joining us, sir," said Beverly Rivera, with an edge. "Just how did you hear of the, er, 'incident'?"

She shot a warning look at the Captain, who was staring into space. He's ill, realized Mary belatedly. She's babysitting him. He can't cope. Why are the Los Angeles Police allowing him to be here?

The large man deigned to notice her. "I heard you had a... a 'problem' with a dead employee: a Black intern. An officer on

115

the door told me," said the man, coolly. Then his gaze took in Sam, and he gagged.

"That *Black intern* was my brother," said the young man, trying to control himself. "People took us for twins."

Melissa Oldcastle intervened. "Professor Donald Cuchulain Macdonald is our distinguished partner in the Alchemy Project," she said faintly. Mary could see that she was not comfortable about his arrival. Nor was Mary.

"You're Cookie Mac," Mary said, warily.

"Certainly, I am," said the man, puffing up with pleasure. "Here for the Alchemy Scroll that the Museum has found. And you are?"

"Miss Mary Wandwalker, from St. Julian's College, Oxford." Mary turned to Sam. "Mr. Murphy was so kind as to escort me here."

"Exactly, Miss Wandwalker," broke in Captain Lascelles. New lines creased his badly shaven jaw. "You," he paused at Mary, "were the last person to see D.P. Murphy alive."

Mary cleared her throat. "Apart from his killer," she returned.

Captain Lascelles took a bottle of pills from his jacket and tossed a handful into his mouth. A tight-lipped Beverly Rivera got up to pour him a glass of water from a cut-glass jug. The ice cubes stuck together into a sort of white cloud. Mary jerked herself to attention. Jetlag when she needed to concentrate.

"We need a full statement, Miss Wandwalker," said Rivera quietly. "Let's begin with the bare facts. Why meet an intern in the first place?"

"He was more than that," broke in Sam. "Yeah, he arrived as an intern, but he was good with old stuff. He was going to be promoted. Wasn't he?" Sam was now addressing Melissa Oldcastle, who looked uncomfortable. "Wasn't he?"

The Museum Director gave a brusque nod. Mary caught a strange look on Cookie Mac's face. He was staring at Sam with something like revulsion.

116

Clinking at the door heralded coffee. Melissa Oldcastle waved in the secretary with the silver tray and exquisite china. Over the top, thought Mary. And why is Sergeant Rivera letting Lascelles pretend to be in charge? The cops should have separated us. Why let Cookie Mac crash the party?

"You've secured the Alchemy Scroll, of course," Cookie Mac instructed Melissa. "I insist on inspecting it. It is the centerpiece of my symposium keynote for The European History Foundation."

Ignoring his coffee, he banged the spoon on the sugar dish. "And I've found a place nearby, in California, calling itself The Alchemy School. Great place for a West Coast tryout."

Mary was intrigued as well as horrified. She was now certain that Cookie Mac was the expert expected at St. Julian's College. Mer-Corp was sending him to authenticate the real Alchemy Scroll. So why is he looking for it *here?* And why so anxious?

Melissa Oldcastle began a soothing murmur. She was interrupted by Lascelles setting down his saucer with a rattle. Cookie Mac was beginning to jar.

"Professor whatever-your-name-is, this is a homicide investigation. I'm asking the questions. Scrolls, lecture tours; all that is irrelevant."

His expression became tortured. Head trauma, thought Mary.

Again, Mary's eyes met those of the Sergeant. Again, the tiny shake of her head. Cookie Mac's red cheeks burned darker.

"*I* have nothing to add about any murder."

Lascelles looked puzzled; Rivera was scribbling notes.

Cookie Mac lumbered to his feet. "As soon as I've examined the Alchemy Scroll, I'll be on my way, officers. Miss Oldcastle, what have you done with it?"

There was a pause. Melissa Oldcastle looked at her expensive carpet. Then she stood to address the puffing professor.

"Professor Macdonald, I don't know where the Alchemy Scroll is. When I found the body, I happened to notice the empty box in the chest near D.P."

Mary let out a long shuddering breath. Sam drummed his heels. He cared for no scroll, Mary realized. Cookie Mac, on the other hand, alternated beetroot and chalk white.

"I *told* you it should never have been left..."

Cookie Mac caught sight of Mary's and Sam's faces, paused infinitesimally, then screeched, "My research *confirms* it. What you have so carelessly allowed to be stolen is the *real* medieval Scroll, not a seventeenth-century copy."

Mary felt her throat constrict. Beverly Rivera beckoned to a man by the door.

"Take Professor Macdonald's statement in the next room, Detective."

"But... but," Cookie Mac lost coherence. Pausing to glare at everyone, the professor pranced out.

"Sergeant... er...Captain, I'm afraid the Professor's right," said the Museum Director quietly. "This tragedy must have begun as a robbery. The Ransome bequest has been plundered."

"A bequest. That was what that, the Professor, was upset about?" said Lascelles, too slowly.

At his side, Rivera tapped industriously into her iPad. Then the sick man snapped: "We're warning you, Miss...um Director, we're here to investigate a murder, not fill out your insurance claim."

Trying to cover up his problems, thought Mary.

"It's not about insurance," spluttered Melissa Oldcastle. "The Alchemy Scroll is priceless. If Cookie Mac is right, then it's an important discovery. Francis Ransome's manuscripts came from England, didn't they?"

She was now looking at Mary. "That's why you had an appointment today, Miss Wandwalker. Some question about provenance?"

Mary had to signal agreement.

118

The death of D.P. is going to reveal St. Julian's secrets after all.

"Sir, we've downloaded the footage." The interruption came from a nervous young cop, moving from foot to foot.

"And?" demanded Lascelles.

"You ought to see it," said the cop. Lascelles grunted at Rivera. She whispered as they rose: "I'll come check with you, Sir."

"They must mean the cameras on the street in the front of the Museum," explained Melissa Oldcastle to no one in particular. Only she, Mary and Sam remained seated. A silent woman in uniform watched them closely.

"Of course," said Mary. She could remember when there were no sleepless electronic eyes. Sam shifted in his seat. Impatience or unease? wondered Mary. Does he have anything to hide?

"Mr. Murphy," came the captain's cracked tones from the door. Rivera and Lascelles entered differently, grim and focused on Sam. "Mr. Murphy, what time did you arrive here last night?"

Sam's astonished expression impressed Mary, if not the cops.

"Um, yesterday, no. I never came to the Museum," he said, indignation rising. "Weeks ago, yeah, I met D.P. outside. I've never been *in* here in my life. I don't do Museums... Before today," he added miserably.

"You weren't here last night? You're quite sure of that?"

Sam nodded.

Beverly showed Sam the iPad. "So, who's this arriving shortly before 10 p.m.," she asked, neutrally, "the time the Medical Examiner estimates as the time of death?"

Mary dashed behind Sam's chair, despite Beverly waving her away. On the screen, she saw a dark figure against faintly illuminated snow. He or she was probably dressed in black, but the light was too dim to be certain even of that.

119

"Not me," said Sam firmly, on surer ground. Mary could feel waves of emotion coming from Sam's body: Fear? Guilt? Grief? She could not tell.

"Captain, Sergeant, it's impossible to see who that is," she said. "He, if it is he, is hooded, and there's a scarf over the face," she said.

"If that's not you, where were you?"

"At home."

"Alone?"

Sam nodded. "D.P. texted me at seven about Miss Wandwalker here. He said he was working late on something big. We share a flat; I mean, an apartment." Sam looked older; he was beginning to realize the implications.

The cops frowned at Sam, Rivera assessing him, Lascelles through eyes that looked bloodshot.

"Why is the camera so far from the Museum entrance?" Mary asked. "And the light is very poor."

"A streetlight and the Museum's own camera were shot out a couple of days ago," said Melissa Oldcastle. She leaned forward to the iPad. "That's from further down the sidewalk. Captain, let me send someone to inventory the storage chests where D.P.... died. More treasures could be missing."

Lascelles looked blank. Rivera jumped in.

"Very well, send one of your staff, who will be accompanied by a detective."

Melissa Oldcastle strolled to a corner and began to mutter into her phone. She reminded Mary of Caroline and Anna. Mary renewed her determination to get in touch with Anna, since she could not reach Caroline at The Old Hospital.

The lingering scent of blood provoked feelings about Caroline, bad feelings. There's been a murder, she said to herself, and the Alchemy Scroll is gone. I've got to make a call. Damn whatever time it is back home.

CHAPTER 15
WHO'S LOOKING FOR
THE INVISIBLE COLLEGE?

Exhausted by the morning's revelations, Mary gazed at the outside wind and snow. If only she could get away, for a few seconds at least, from the odor of blood that tracked from where D.P.'s body curved like a bloody scythe. She glanced at Sam and saw accusation mingled with appeal. *It's not my fault*, she wanted to yell. There were too many police around to reach out to Sam, at least for now.

At her wit's end to find some peace, Mary demanded a bathroom break. "Let me have some privacy," she had begged, and then was able to take out her phone. No reply from Anna.

Even voicemail refused her, reporting with revolting complacency a full inbox.

Mary ground her teeth as she banged the volume on her ringtone. Oh, how she longed for Anna's cyberskills that she failed to understand. Nonsense, of course, to think that making her own phone louder would wake Anna in England.

"I wish," muttered Mary, turning to email. Ah, here was Anna: the subject, "The Invisible College." Research, Mary glowered in the perfumed glow of the museum's toilets. I don't need research. I need *news*. Tell me about Caroline. What's going on? Why aren't you talking? Nevertheless, she opened the email.

From Cybercrafter183@lilith to MaryWandwalker@gmail.com

121

Evidence of scrubbed databases on Francis Andrew Ransome. Some hidden alchemy sites confirm membership of the Invisible College (see wiki below). These also refer to artist friend and fellow alchemist, Robert Le More of London. Le More likely author C17th Alchemy Scroll, since letter archived in Los Angeles (your Museum) says they visited St. Julian's in right year. Authorship four other alchemy texts pos. attrib. R. Le More (British Museum eLibrary). I found traces of searches for both alchemists concentrated in the last 3 months. Trying to trace URLs but confirm US as well as UK. Soonest, Anna.

There was a pasted webpage entry below from something called WikiEsoterica:

Invisible College, The: c. 1640 – 1770. Affiliated group of alchemists and philosophers in London that became The Royal Society (estab. 1660, ongoing). Mentioned in German Rosicrucian literature. In letters in 1646 and 1647, Robert Boyle, later scientist Royal Society, refers to "our invisible college" or "our philosophical college." Royal Society devoted to acquiring knowledge through experimental investigation, also ethos of the alchemists. Three dated letters are documentary evidence: Boyle sent them to Francis Andrew Ransome in New England and to little-known alchemist, Robert Le More.

There was a second paragraph headed: Recent Studies.

Historian Cuchulain Macdonald distinguishes the Invisible College from other groups who also combined elements of theology, natural science, medicine, philosophy, alchemy, and even politics (since American colonies intimately involved with

London intellectuals). Recent reference to the Invisible College includes research chemist, Godric St. John of St. Julian's College, Oxford. See, "The Lost Chemistry of the St. Julian's Alchemy Scroll," St, John, G. *Journal Natural Philosophy and Science*, vol. 46, 2017 (Spring), pp. 27-54. See also Medieval Theology, Alchemical Groups, Goddess Studies, Feminist Spirituality, Julian of Norwich.

*****

Mary leaned against the marble wash basin. Godric St. John and Cookie Mac, or Professor Cuchulain Macdonald, to give him his real name; she was thinking furiously. One was an historian, the other a research chemist, and yet both were involved right now. They knew *of* each other, certainly, even if officially in different academic circles. Desperate for the Scroll, both of them, the original, not the copy. Could they be in it together?

Mary started as the door opened to Sergeant Beverly Rivera. "Are you all right, Miss Wandwalker?"

"Um, yes, of course," said Mary, a little flustered.

"I... um, just wanted to say... Well, you must have noticed that Captain Lascelles..."

"Is ill? Yes, I intend to make a complaint" Mary recovered. "You're not following correct procedure."

Mary wanted to get away. The sooner she could persuade the police to let her go, the sooner she could track down Caroline.

"The Captain's sick," said Rivera sharply. You saw that bullet scar in his head, didn't you?"

Mary pulled herself together. "Of course, I didn't mean..."

"Red tape," said Rivera, enigmatically. She sighed and relaxed. "Look, I know healthcare in the UK is different. In this country, this state even, it's all about the rules. The Captain is due for a big disability payout *if* the insurance company signs off." She paused and continued.

"Right now, the insurance company is stalling, and the police lawyers are on it. Meanwhile, the Captain has three weeks' service until he qualifies for a full pension. The Chief wanted him on desk duty, but this snow means everyone's on call. Los Angeles isn't made to cope with blizzards, to say the least. The snow's putting basic services at risk. the Mayor fears rolling power outages. That could lead to looting. So, I'm assigned to…" She spread her hands.

"To look after him," said Mary.

"To cover the basics until we can hand the case off to another squad," rejoined Rivera.

Cynically, Mary wondered if a woman in Lascelles' position would get this much support. Deep down, she remained furious at being dismissed from the Archive because at the extreme age of 60, she was judged too old to be retrained for the digital age. Mary bit back the memory. She mustn't get sidetracked.

"I need to return to England," she said with dignity.

"Impossible right now," said the Sergeant. "No question of it. This is a homicide."

"Yes, I know it's a homicide," replied Mary, crossly. "I *liked* that young man. He was…" Her voice vanished; she grabbed the marble behind her. Sergeant Rivera took hold of her arm.

"Come on, you're in shock. We'll get you some… some tea; and a doctor if you need one."

Rivera guided Mary back to the room and sat her next to Sam, who was staring into space. Mary noticed a chain with a green disc at the young man's throat. NA, it said. A girlfriend? No, it was just plastic. Oh, now she remembered from American TV: Narcotics Anonymous. He must have joined over here.

Mary took the box of tissues next to the empty coffee cups and gamely scrubbed her face. I never cared for makeup, she thought, seeing the pink and brown smear, along with globs of mascara.

"No doctor," she said firmly to an inquisitive Rivera. "No tea," she said, smiling. "More coffee would be good."

124

The Sergeant made a signal to a cop at the door. Lascelles had gone over to the window and was staring at the falling snow. In the open doorway, Mary could see figures gathering in the foyer. There was a figure in a creased camel coat. For some reason, it summoned the patrician shade of Godric St. John.

"Ravi," she called. "Ravi Patel! What are you doing here? Come and sit with us."

The young man entered and sat, looking away from blank-faced Lascelles. Mary noticed that Ravi's hands were white, even a bit grey at the tips.

"Did you forget gloves too?" she said.

Ravi shook his head.

"Miss...um, where's the Alchemy Scroll?" he said, lowering his voice and speaking urgently. "Have they found it yet?"

"Wandwalker," said Mary automatically. "I'm Miss Wandwalker. Did you just arrive?" An overnight flight could account for his odd demeanor. She doubted that Godric St. John would provide a first-class seat for a mere Ph.D. student.

"Yes," whispered Ravi. "The Alchemy Scroll's been stolen, hasn't it? I mean stolen by the murderer."

"Possibly," said Mary cautiously. "Nothing is certain at this stage. Who told you about the murder?"

"Twitter," said Ravi quickly. "Cops on the door confirmed a body in the attic."

"Ah, who's this?" Captain Lascelles had woken up again.

"This is Ravi Patel," said Mary. "He's a research student at St. Julian's College, Oxford, that owns, has a connection, to Francis Andrew Ransome. You know, the person whose bequest to the Museum is where the body was found."

Lascelles's eyes glazed over. Mary continued in desperation.

"It's a complicated story, Captain... and, and Sergeant Rivera. It's possible that the Scroll that... from that chest by the body, in fact, belongs in England. I was sent here to get it back."

Lascelles frowned at the threat to American property.

125

"We don't 'give back' historical stuff in this country," he said with finality.

"Nor do we in England," said Mary crisply, (thinking of Greece and the Elgin Marbles). "However, the Alchemy Scroll was stolen from Oxford. Ransome brought it to New England illegally. The Scroll is not American," she said, a bit louder.

Why would the police care about an Alchemy Scroll that had been in America since before the country existed?

"D.P. may have died protecting the Scroll," she added.

Lascelles eyes remained clouded.

Unlike her superior, Rivera was not lost. "So, this Scroll you say was stolen from England is the same one Professor Macdonald was raving about?"

Mary nodded. How much worse could this day get?

"Oh, so that's why you came to the Museum." Rivera was on firmer ground. "And you, too?" she indicated Ravi, who looked nervous. Before he could answer, she swung back to Mary, her expression sharp.

"So, you think the Alchemy Scroll is part of the murder? Rather a bold assumption for Miss Wandwalker, former London Archivist and amateur private detective?"

Bugger, thought Mary. I hate the Internet. And our site is not even ready. She lifted her chin and met Rivera's stare head-on.

"In 1658, Francis Andrew Ransome stole the Alchemy Scroll from St. Julian's college, my present employer. Ransome was a member of a transatlantic group called The Invisible College. They were alchemists, meaning they worked with matter and spirit together."

Beverly Rivera dropped the writing instrument she was using on her tablet. At the same moment, Melissa Oldcastle reentered the room, distracting Mary by the way she dropped into her chair with a gasp.

"Gone, it's gone. I'd hoped against hope that D.P. had moved the Alchemy Scroll. No chance. We have checked everywhere. It's disappeared."

126

The enormity of her discovery cracked her perfectly painted face, a work of art in Botox. She turned to Mary and held out her hands.

"The Alchemy Scroll *was there* when I opened the chests last week at the insistence of Professor Cookie Mac. We saw it; we *held* it. With leather gloves, of course."

Out of the corner of her eye, Mary saw Ravi begin tapping into his phone.

Melissa Oldcastle struggled with her loss. "Ransome's Alchemy Scroll was so... so beautiful and...and mysterious. I sensed a strange power... even though I couldn't recognize the language. Cookie, Professor Macdonald, said it was in code. He didn't have time to do a proper evaluation there and then, so I insisted it be put back where we found it so I could consult with the Trustees. We postponed because of the snow and that phone call from St Julian's in England." She paused to repeat the dreadful truth.

"The Scroll, the priceless Alchemy Scroll, is missing."

Mary was stunned that her mission here was at an end. The real Alchemy Scroll was now out of reach. What would happen to St. Julian's?

CHAPTER 16
BROTHER OF THE VICTIM

Mary did not have long to contemplate the loss of the priceless Alchemy Scroll to St. Julian's. Neither did the Museum Director. As for the police, Lascelles's features were blank while Rivera frowned into her phone. All of them experienced a shock.

"You're freakin' ghouls," yelled Sam, standing up. "My brother is dead. You don't care, any of you, about my brother. He's just a dead body. In-con-ven-ient."

He spoke the last word syllable by syllable, as if he wanted to make each word a blow. Lascelles's eyes burned, and Rivera tensed.

"Sam," said Mary, acknowledging his accusation. "We're sorry. It's not like that. Shock takes people... differently..."

She wasn't sure she believed what she was saying. She did not like the glances exchanged between Lascelles and Rivera, then between Rivera and the uniformed cop at the door.

"Mr. Murphy," said Rivera. "These officers will take you down to the station for questioning over the murder of your brother and the theft of the book."

"Scroll." That was Melissa in strangled tones.

"No!" shouted Sam.

"We know your record. We know you were after money for drugs." That was Lascelles, hand resting on gun at his belt.

"What? You can't arrest me," yelled Sam from the other side of the room. Two uniformed cops closed in. "I'm clean. D.P. was helping me. You're accusing me of murdering my own

129

brother. I'm innocent. It's those rich professors you should be looking at..."

The cops grasped the young man by his arms. Mary saw his internal struggle not to shake them off and be arrested for resisting. She rose and moved closer to them.

"Are you charging Sam?" Mary asked. "On what evidence?" She sounded even more British.

"Not charging yet, Miss Wandwalker. Not unless — or until — we have more evidence," said Rivera, "We're just taking him in for questioning."

Mary exchanged a helpless look with Sam as he let himself be bundled out of the room, still protesting. Mary was unconvinced by Sam as a suspect, but it was all happening too fast. She needed to get in touch with Anna, her mind frayed by anxiety for Caroline.

"Captain, I have an emergency at home..." she began, only to be interrupted by the Museum Director.

"I must speak to Professor Macdonald at *once*," insisted Melissa. "Where is he?"

"We let him go," answered the young woman. "He said he would check back with you on the Alchemy Scroll. He was on the phone with your assistant as he left the building."

"Then he'll know we've confirmed the Scroll is missing," said Melissa, sinking back. "Donna and I went together to look through the Ransome bequest. She'll tell him."

Melissa put her jeweled hands together, hands that revealed her age more than her face, noted Mary. The Museum Director seemed to be staring into some invisible kaleidoscope. Then she clapped her hands on her thighs and rose to march out of the room. Ah, the stride of an old money princess, thought Mary. Beverly Rivera continued to monitor her Captain.

Mary turned back to Captain Lascelles.

"You have to let me go back to England," she said conversationally. "I'm not a suspect. You can't keep me here."

"You're not?" asked Lascelles, puzzled.

Immediately, the Sergeant took over. "Too soon to be sure you're not a person of interest, Miss Wandwalker. The Chief is consulting with your boss at this very minute."

"I have no boss," said Mary stoutly. "I'm an independent Enquiry Agent. If you mean my *former* superior, Mr. Jeffreys; then yes, I expect him to vouch for me." Mary glanced at Ravi who was frantically texting.

Mary felt her own phone *buzz*. A text from Anna? How many times had she told her that she preferred actual talking?

"Caroline okay," the text said. Mary felt a stab of relief. It must be true; Anna loves Caroline. Caroline must be all right, which meant that Anna had seen her. Together they would find the witch who held the Scroll Key, and all would be well. Except it wouldn't without the actual Scroll.

Mary let a tide of exhaustion flood her overstimulated body. She flopped back and closed her eyes.

"Snow's getting worse," said a young English voice. "I can't see across the street. It's like the sky has fallen in." Mary opened one eye to see Ravi Patel at the window. "Do you think the Yanks have an Art Squad to trace stolen manuscripts — like in London?"

He spoke to Mary, but it was the Sergeant who answered.

"We'll contact the FBI They have an Art Division."

Mary was too tired to be relieved. If the FBI was involved, no one would want her to chase after the Alchemy Scroll. Back in the UK, she and Anna would extract Caroline from The Old Hospital and break out Janet Swinford. It was that simple. Soon this far too perplexing case would be over. Half completed was better than nothing at all.

She followed Ravi's gaze out to the falling snow. The weirdness of climate change, she thought. Nothing will remain unchanged. Yes, it was time to go home. Like a demon set free, the snow danced in the moaning wind.

CHAPTER 17
PURSUIT OF THE SCROLL
AND THE MURDERER

Soon it would be over, she had told herself in the grand office of Melissa Oldcastle. But it wasn't over; she wasn't on a plane heading for Heathrow. She was in bed in Los Angeles. Anna, I'm relying on you. Don't let us down. She shivered. Caroline, do it for Caroline, she muttered and fell asleep. Her plans had changed during that endless day at the Museum after D.P.'s body was found.

Captain Lascelles had thundered back into the Director's Office to find Mary insisting on her rights. She'd obtained the phone number of the British Consulate.

"What did Murphy say to you?" the Captain snarled at Mary, hands on hips. His position emphasized his gun holster. Beverly Rivera stood close, to intervene if necessary.

"D.P.? That's just what I've been telling you. And now Captain, I must…"

"Not the victim. Sam Murphy, *the suspect*. I saw you whispering earlier. What did he tell you?" The Captain's eyes were too bright.

"Nothing; nothing at all. He's upset about his brother. So was…am I."

The Captain swiveled to his Sergeant. "Supervise the search for Sam Murphy: roads, airports, everything."

"Sam's missing?" exclaimed Mary. "What happened?"

The cops paid no attention.

133

"Sir, the airports are closed. It's the snow. The storm's getting worse, and the Mayor has declared a citywide shutdown. They're closing the highways. Even LAX is suspending flights until tomorrow."

Beverly consulted her phone while keeping one eye on her erratic boss. "Just got the alerts," she concluded.

"He can't get out of the city." Lascelles's satisfaction revolted Mary.

She stood up. "Captain, WHY ARE YOU AFTER SAM?"

The Captain turned to her with an air of exaggerated patience.

"Drugs," he said. "It's always drugs. Sam Murphy has a record of dealing in your country. His family must've pulled strings to get him into California."

"Dealing what?" Mary strained for her authoritative voice where she had no authority.

"Doesn't matter."

"He was fifteen," muttered Beverly, looking into her phone. "It was eight years ago. And it was weed, marijuana."

"That's legal here, isn't it?"

"Not in High School."

"Wasn't he a juvenile? Aren't those records sealed?" Mary relied upon her secret addiction to late-night cop shows.

"Not to the LAPD," said Lascelles wolfishly.

He, not Sam, appeared gripped by some chemical stimulant, thought Mary. How hypocritical even if it was a prescription opioid.

"Once a drug dealer..." continued Lascelles. "Didn't I tell you to get the search going?" he snapped at his subordinate. She ran from the room while the Captain scowled at Mary with unfocused eyes.

Resuming her seat with dignity, she waited until Beverly Rivera reentered.

"Before I go, I'd like to speak to Director Oldcastle. It's about D.P.," she said to the harassed young woman.

134

Beverly had a swift reply. "The Captain released her to go home. Her house is in the older part of Los Angeles where the snow's causing chaos. She's closed the Museum for the next three days. That's how long the storm is supposed to last." She paused.

"Miss Wandwalker, if Sam contacts you, please let us know. He wasn't cuffed so was able to run off when the squad car would not start. Probably ice in the gears."

Mary ignored her request. An idea was taking shape.

"Sergeant, you, that is *we*, think the murderer took the Alchemy Scroll. So, if it was Sam needing money for drugs, (she sniffed) why would he risk coming here? He didn't have to draw attention to himself."

"Because he knew we'd be on to him," broke in Lascelles.

"So, what about Professor Cookie Mac? He's desperate for the Alchemy Scroll." She leaned forward into the space occupied by Lascelles's frown.

"The Professor turns up this morning to allay suspicions. Also, Ravi Patel, who has been allowed to leave, I note. He represents another professor after the Alchemy Scroll, Godric St. John. Where is Ravi, by the way?"

Mary felt bad mentioning Ravi. But Sam, she felt instinctively, had not killed his brother.

"Back at his hotel, I expect," said Lascelles, his words slurring.

"Captain, Sergeant," said Mary slowly and firmly. "With all this wonderful technology at your disposal, do you really want to take the risk…" Surely, she did not need to spell it out. Sometimes the obvious suspect was too obvious.

There was a pause while Lascelles's eyes closed. Beverly Rivera was holding her breath. Mary forced herself to stay quiet. These cops would not take suggestions easily. Especially not from an older woman, and a foreigner, the voice of long experience added.

"Rivera?" the appeal was in the Captain's tone.

"Okay, boss, leave it to me. I'm on it."

And the woman was gone again. So that's how it is, she thought. That's how it is with investigating teams who trust each other. Even when one of them could not function, the job got done. Trust is not an issue. Would their Agency ever achieve that rapport? Mary couldn't help a stab of doubt. Automatically, her hand found her phone.

"I have to call my... my friends in England." She got up, planning to use the lobby or the bathroom again.

"Don't leave," muttered the Captain, staring blankly at his iPad. "Miss... er..."

"Wandwalker. I'll just be in the lobby."

There was no reply from Caroline, which she expected. Also, nothing from Anna. Anna's voicemail was now operational, so she left a terse message.

The morning dragged as Mary watched figures clad from head to toe in white going in and out of the museum. Snowmen, thought Mary drowsily; they're snowmen wrapping up D.P., getting blood on their sleeves.

Eventually, Beverly Rivera beckoned Mary. She was not smiling exactly, but there was something more than her polite professionalism.

"Sir. Mr. Patel and Professor Macdonald both stayed last night at the Majestic Hotel, downtown. And they've both checked out. Patel's forwarding address is a fake. It's a deserted lot on the East Side. Macdonald gave another address in Los Angeles. It belongs to..." she checked her phone, "Something called 'The European History Foundation.'"

"You're staying at the Continental," she added to Mary.

She's verified my story too, noted Mary. Of course, she would. "So, Ravi did come earlier," she said. "I thought he'd arrived this morning."

"And we knew that Professor Macdonald has been in Los Angeles for a while," returned Beverly. "He's from the East Coast, a town called New Portsmouth."

"He came for the Alchemy Scroll," said Mary, significantly. "To *get* it for his Symposium!"

136

"Sir," said Beverly. "I've also checked up on Director Oldcastle's whereabouts. She didn't go straight home like she said. Her housekeeper says that no one knows where she is."

Mary coughed. Another suspect in the wind. Literally, she thought, glancing through the window. The snow was blowing in crazy circles, a banshee was attacking the museum.

"Sergeant, one last thing before I go," she said. "The missing Alchemy Scroll might have clues to new medicines. We discovered that Francis Andrew Ransome was famous throughout the Colony as an alchemist *and physician*. Ransome took the Scroll because it had a reputation for healing powers. That could make it even more valuable."

"Some old book that's been around for years?" Beverly looked stunned.

"Isn't the point what people *think* it contains?" Mary was fired up. "Right now, scholars and medical researchers work for corporations. Godric St. John and his student, Ravi Patel, are funded by Mer-Corp. Your Professor Macdonald wants it for his so-called 'European History Foundation.' God knows who funds that."

Lascelles looked up. "Did you say Mer-Corp?"

"Yes, Captain."

"Owns my Health Insurance Company."

"Oh." Mary did not know what to say. Beverley Rivera sighed.

"Don't worry. We'll look at *all* potential suspects, Miss Wandwalker."

"Except, *Sergeant*," Lascelles jerked his head at the window. He seemed too tired to go on.

"Of course, sir," reassured Beverly. "We have a public health emergency. This snow is causing multiple logistical problems. The Mayor's worried about looting. Right now, delivery trucks can't get into the city."

"Surely the storm won't last that long?" intervened Mary.

"Three days is perfectly capable of turning into a week. If people start worrying about food running out, we'll have panic, riots, even in this weather. In the meantime, sir," said Beverly. "We should track down those named by Miss Wandwalker."

There was barely a query in her final words. Lascelles nodded. His facial scar had a metallic glint in the snow-swallowed daylight.

Beverly's phone buzzed. She waved at Mary. "Go back to your hotel, Miss Wandwalker. We'll be in touch."

Mary made for the door. "I have a feeling that the FBI will want to meet you."

"I shall look forward to it, Sergeant. Good day, Captain," said Mary. She slipped out of the museum's front door and into a snow drift. The cold hit her face and neck like a brick.

Retreating to the Foyer, she waved at Beverly addressing the Crime Scene Investigators. "Erm…, Sergeant? Could one of your patrol cars give me a lift?"

Back in the hotel, her room had swum above the clouds. Mary flung herself onto the bed. Despite her best efforts, the police remained too keen to treat Sam as the main suspect for his brother's murder. She couldn't leave Los Angeles. Not until D.P.'s death had been resolved. She owed him that.

Mary groaned, turned over, and slept. Dreaming, she ran down corridors with Anna in front of her. Wait, where's Caroline? she called. The person who could have been Anna disappeared.

CHAPTER 18
STEW

The Old Hospital served the midday meal in a canteen away from the wards. It gave cleaners and nurses time to change bed linen and swish a dirty mop around the floors.

"It's stew," trilled Agnes. Delight smoothed some of the lines on her face. She dashed into the drab room pulling Caroline's arm.

A wave of nausea emanated from Caroline's stomach at the smell of elderly meat. *Anna's not coming*, it said to her. *She can't find you. She's given up.*

Anna never gives up, Caroline whispered to the dark pit inside her. It was a familiar pit. She tried not to succumb to fear as it widened and deepened. No, this would not do. Agnes had told her that the witch was in room thirty-one. She'd promised to show her during lunch. Caroline needed to hang on a little longer.

I won't give up, she said grimly into the pit, marching after surprisingly speedy Agnes. Twenty minutes later she leaned across the Formica table and reminded the old woman of her promise.

"Tomorrow," muttered Agnes, picking up the paper plate and licking it. "Or maybe the next day."

Anna isn't coming, heard Caroline.

Whoosh. The contents of the water jug hit Agnes full in the face. Caroline found herself standing with the empty jug. She had no memory of her action. Water flowed out of Agnes's gaping mouth, still with food stuck to her yellow teeth. Water plastered white hair to the skull. Agnes's blue eyes gazed at

139

Caroline out of a younger woman's face. Then she began to shriek.

Nurses converged on Agnes. The few patients in faded gowns sat and stared. In the ensuing confusion, Caroline slipped out of the dining room. Agnes kept groaning very loudly.

"Sorry, Agnes," Caroline whispered. She headed for the staircase she had glimpsed earlier. It had numbers and an arrow. I've got to get to room thirty-one. Tomorrow's no good.

Lunchtime was quiet. Shift changes, guessed Caroline, as she moved down the list of numbered doors. Near thirty-one was a trolley that held a few trays with that familiar unappetizing smell. No one was about, and the door handle yielded to her touch.

Inside, Caroline thought the room was empty. Then she saw her. With one wrist chained to the bedpost, hunched on the floor, rocking, head between her knees, there was Janet. About seventy, her short hair had once been dyed red. Now white roots sprouted as if they had been tugged up like garden weeds.

Caroline knew Janet Swinford from the sickrooms of The Holywell Retreat Center. She recognized that wind-hardened back and hands as wiry as crows' nests. There was even a tinge of Janet's northern accent in her animal moans.

Unlike Holywell's flowers, candles, and incense, the Old Hospital's sterility provided nothing alive. Janet had to have sensed the intruder. She remained crouched; limbs locked. She's a fortress, thought Caroline.

"Janet," Caroline said gently, stepping toward the woman. Unlike Agnes, Janet's nightgown was clean. It was as white as the bedcovers, floor tiles, walls, all a merciless bleached white. The high window added a slab of grey cloud.

"Janet, Janet Swinford," whispered Caroline, again. Someone could come anytime to collect the untouched food.

"Janet, I'm a friend. You remember me. From… from Holywell. I'm Caroline Jones."

The bundle with white and red hair stopped rocking. Her soft moaning grew louder.

"Hush," said Caroline, running to Janet. Putting a wary hand on the bare arm, she whispered, "I can't be found here. Please, please look at me, Janet. What have they given you?"

When the figure began to uncurl, Caroline felt the urge to run back to her own bed. *Anna isn't coming,* came the voice. *You're alone. Even this woman does not want you. You're abandoned.* Caroline bit her lip; she forced her hand to stroke Janet's shoulder.

"I talked to your friend, Agnes," she began. "She, we... want to get out of here. What are they giving you?"

A sudden movement made Caroline gasp. Janet pulled back to the wall and fixed Caroline with bleak brown eyes. She seemed to recognize her from a long way away.

"Go away. I don't want... help." Words forced out of her. "They're not giving me anything. Do you hear? They swapped my meds for a placebo because I wouldn't give him the Key to the Alchemy Scroll. The nurses don't believe me. They're not giving me anything. I can't... I just can't..."

Her eyes, focused on Caroline, turned dark. "Get out of here, you... you traitor." Her voice rose to a scream. "Get out! Get out of here!"

Caroline backed away, horrified. She was halfway down the corridor when the women who brought breakfast arrived. Caroline didn't have to feign weeping.

"Help me, please," she wailed putting both arms out. "I got lost; I spilled a jug of water at lunch. I ran away and got lost. Then I heard shouting. I'm scared... Please, please take me back."

Frowns gave way to muttering. Since the crazy woman did not appear dangerous, they took her back to her ward with the trolley rattling behind. She was deposited in her bed before she could regain her composure.

Agnes snored in the next bed. Caroline shut her eyes. *Anna isn't coming.*

She, of all people, knew what it meant when Janet said that they hadn't given her anything. To stop antidepressant medicine

141

without warning, to take the pills away with no careful stepped reduction in doses, was… unbelievably cruel. Someone was treating Janet like a heroin addict made to go cold turkey.

A long time ago Caroline had tried to quit her medication in similar drastic fashion. After a couple of days, she gave up fighting the psychological pain and insomnia. Her heart skinned raw; she could not stop crying. George, her husband, had been terrified at her sudden deterioration.

That had been her first hospitalization, not like here. In the psychiatric ward of a busy London teaching hospital, there were friendly nurses, compassionate doctors and cakes brought every day, George arrived each evening to watch TV while holding her hand. As soon as she had stabilized, he brought her home. Even so, it took weeks back on the meds before she felt secure.

Janet was being made to suffer. Caroline tried to push away the image of the crouching woman. The dark pit was expanding, and Janet was stuck down there. She'd been kicked into the dark by someone desperate for the key to the Alchemy Scroll. Caroline had no strength to wonder who that might be. *Anna isn't coming*. Anna *had* to come!

CHAPTER 19
JANET HOLDS THE KEY

Caroline woke suddenly. It was very dark. All her senses were unusually alert. The air trembled. Something breathing was close, standing by her bed.

"Let me tell you about witches," came a voice. "And the Alchemy Scroll. You see, Ransome and Le More promised to send it back."

"Janet," said Caroline, sitting up. "Is that you? The Alchemy Scroll. Do you mean that back in the seventeenth century Holywell knew it was taken? We must tell Mary Wandwalker."

"The Key Keeper holds the secret of the substitution. But this Key Keeper is dying. I must initiate another."

"Dying? Surely not," said Caroline. She was horrified. "They love you at Holywell. We must get you home. Are you… are you feeling any better?"

"I'm better at night," came the reply. "In the dark. I've made friends with creatures of the night. I sing the old spells. In the Holywell Infirmary, I stood by the window when you slept. Get up, Caroline. Come on, Agnes is waiting."

"Waiting? For what?"

"To keep watch while I tell you my plan for you and the Alchemy Scroll. Hurry up, Agnes can only manage short periods. She's had too many drugs, and her mind's almost gone."

Too taken aback to protest, Caroline swung out of bed. She was surprised to find hunger pangs crackling in her stomach. Janet sensed her hesitation.

143

"We're going to the right of those red lights for two meters. Then we turn forty-five degrees to get to the door. Take my arm, go on, take it."

"Why talk now?" Caroline muttered into the other woman's ear. Janet smelled clean, too clean. Some pungent hospital soap had evaporated her human smell.

Janet pulled at Caroline to move faster. "Hush, wait till we get downstairs. Between 3 and 5 a.m. no one patrols."

Along the dim corridor and after several turns, Janet continued talking. "I thought you understood. I must pass the Alchemy Scroll key to someone before I die. Agnes is no good. She can't retain anything."

Caroline clutched Janet's arm in response to her bleakness. Janet's hand was an iron grip. She steered her down a flight of stairs gritty with dirt.

"Die?" Caroline squeaked. "What do you mean? You're not going to die."

"Quiet, woman. You'll wake the night guards. They're asleep up there."

The dark was finally broken by a yellow beam. It traced a quick circle on the wall. Fear warred with cold; Caroline hugged her thin gown to her ample chest.

"Agnes with the torch. It means she's found a safe room."

"And," Janet added, feeling the goosebumps on Caroline's arm, "they store blankets down here."

A click produced a blaze across Caroline's eyeballs. Fortunately, her eyes adjusted quickly to find a large basement area with doors leading off.

"Psst, over here! Over here, witch and witch hunter." Agnes cackled. She was enjoying the adventure.

Caroline gulped and followed Janet. The small space turned out to be a storeroom with supplies of toilet paper, buckets, cleaning fluids, and clean laundry, including blankets. There was also a stack of folding chairs. Caroline made herself as comfortable as she could, rubbing her cold feet. Janet handed her a blanket.

144

Agnes grabbed an armful for herself and made a nest on the floor just outside the door. She was obviously used to keeping watch. Caroline was beginning to wonder if there was a whole other community at the Old Hospital that she was just seeing part of. Mostly though, she was preoccupied by Janet and her talk of death.

"Janet, you know I'm here to get you out. I came to find you. We, that is my... my friend, Anna; she'll get us out."

Caroline tried to exorcise her doubts about Anna from her tone. She failed.

Janet turned a ravaged face to Caroline. Misery saturated the tiny room as she sat gripping her hard plastic chair.

"Too late, Caroline. I can't take more of the pain. You know about the pain."

Caroline sighed. She couldn't deny the pain of chronic depression. Janet continued. "It's time to tell you about the Key. I'm going to die here." She stopped.

Caroline suddenly couldn't breathe. This could not be happening. *She* was always the one who was not going to survive her depression. *She* was the one surrounded by kind, compassionate people.

The door creaked open. Agnes peeked into the room like a naughty child.

"Chocolate for Agnes. Agnes a good girl!"

"Yes, yes, later Agnes," said Janet. "Give us a few minutes. You know I get chocolate from the nurse who feels sorry for me. I've saved it for you."

For Agnes, Janet adopted the aura of a soothing professional. Nevertheless, Caroline recognized the strain around her mouth. Time was short. Either Agnes would cease to be a reliable sentry, or Janet would lose control. Or they could be found out by — what was it, the night patrol? A flame flickered along Caroline's wobbly thighs.

Anna isn't coming, came that hateful voice again. *It's no good, Anna isn't coming!*

"Okay, tell me about the Alchemy Scroll," she whispered to Janet. More words tumbled out. "I'm listening on one condition." Her throat was very dry. She looked at the charcoal around Janet's eyes.

"Condition?" Janet gave her a wounded look.

Caroline had the sensation of holding onto a rope with Janet attached. If Caroline let go, the mud of The Old Hospital would close in and smother them.

"Yes, condition," Caroline repeated. "You can tell me about the Alchemy Key. I'll take the knowledge and look after it for you. I'll be the one who bears this... this responsibility, but *only if you stay alive*."

Janet sat back, outraged. Caroline did not care.

"The Key binds us," she insisted. "Until we get out of here. We're leaving — together." Caroline gave a shuddering breath, "or not at all." She looked hard at Janet. "If you don't come with me, the Alchemy Key will die."

Caroline's stare locked onto Janet.

Slowly Janet let her shoulders relax. She took a Kit Kat out of her pocket and opened the door, handing it to Agnes. Caroline heard her say that she had to eat it very, very slowly. Caroline held her breath until Janet sat down. As if looking down a long tunnel, Janet began to talk about the Scroll.

"I love the Alchemy Scroll. We Key Keepers knew that it was not the original that came from the East via Mother Julian. Le More made the copy for Francis Ransome. But this Scroll too has magical properties. From the moment I first saw it, the paper warmed to my touch. I know it came alive as I held it. Did you know there's a serpent on the back? Some say it's a dragon. It winked at me. Its lashes are gold." Janet's voice was touched by the marvel.

"You held the... er... newer Scroll? In St. Julian's College?"

"Yes, in my bare hands. Only the Keyholder is allowed to do that. It's part of the initiation. The former Keyholder does not have to be present. You can do it alone."

146

"Don't say that…" Caroline began, when Janet raised her hand.

Caroline obeyed. Maintaining a connection with this woman was essential. *Oh, the uses of chronic illness*, she thought to herself with some of Mary's wry humor.

"I'll tell you how I became Key Keeper. If you know my beginning, you'll understand."

CHAPTER 20
JANET'S STORY

Janet began with halting words, but soon it rolled out of her like a pent-up wave. Caroline saw she was the kind of gruff countrywoman she'd encountered in her own childhood, working the farms and markets around her rural Cotswolds home. There was something unexpected, though. Born to a family of hill farmers in Cumberland, Janet had a twin brother named Jim. The pair grew up chasing chickens, playing hide and seek round high stone walls, and tumbling down muddy slopes. They were wiry as saplings in the wind of the wild moors.

Both children were destined to inherit their parents' sheep-rearing business. As they became taller, they trained. By the time they were eleven, the twins could castrate rams, bottle-feed newborn lambs, and herd stragglers with a pair of collie dogs. Often their high remote farm floated for days above the clouds. Their world belonged to a landscape in which the family was virtually self-sufficient.

Everything changed one biting autumn with a plague of scabies that ended lamb exports from the Lake District. First, the Swinford family lost their business, then they could not pay the interest on the farm mortgages. Finally, they sold the remaining buildings, including their house, to clear the debt.

Bred to be unsentimental, the twins did not cry until the sheepdogs had to go. Janet hid her face on her brother's shoulder as the collies were loaded into a trailer. His tears came twenty minutes after hers, just like his birth. A week later, the family was living in a two-bedroom council flat in Keswick.

149

After two months, the twins' father would only leave the cramped rooms for the local pub. After three months, reeling home after dark, he started punching their mother. So shortly before the twins' twelfth birthday, they ran away. Hitching rides south down the motorway, they claimed to any curious driver that they were seventeen.

No one believed them. For Janet and Jim were a slight pair in identical grubby jerseys and jeans. Both had bouncing brown curls sticking to their necks. However, the drivers were lonely; they saw many odd types on the road, especially at night. Accustomed to trading stories for a ride, the drivers responded to the pugnacious chin of Jim and defiant eyes of Janet.

Arriving in Manchester, the twins knew that the police would be on the lookout. Although their father was stupefied by cheap beer and supermarket whisky, their mother would have alerted the authorities, so they were careful to choose backstreets and never stole enough to attract attention.

All this time they did not have a plan; or rather, could not agree on a plan. Janet wanted to go to London, attracted by brightly lit stores she'd seen on TV. Jim wanted to find somewhere remote, like Norfolk, he said, and try to get work picking crops. They bickered amiably, taking time to drain their fears. It never crossed their minds that they would not end up together. Then disaster struck.

Janet's life would never recover. Stealing food was better done singly; shopkeepers instinctively watched children who coordinated. Laden with two packets of sandwiches and a couple of cokes, Jim slipped toward the entrance of a run-down Tesco when he made a wrong turn in an overloaded aisle. Colliding with a big man wearing a uniform, Jim left his denim jacket in the store guard's hands. He darted out of the shop and over the road. In his haste, he tripped into the path of a delivery truck.

From the opposite side of the street, Janet saw everything. In her recurrent nightmares, she was forced to watch gigantic wheels gnash the slight torso. A pink mist rose from under the screaming tires. By the time the lorry braked, Jim was dead, and Janet had vanished.

She disappeared a second time. Crushed out of the human world, she fled like an animal. She ran because she could not stop. When she boosted herself into truck cabs strewn with chocolate wrappers and crisp packets, the men looked at her and turned away. None of them tried to talk to her on the route to London.

In London, Janet became a child of the dark. She would slip into night cafes with the coins she had begged on the street. Never a regular, always wandering, sleeping in snatches in parks, she curled up under bushes. When it rained, she would head for the docks and find shelter in an abandoned warehouse or factory. Mostly she haunted train stations whose Victorian shabbiness made it easier to discard her identity.

It did not matter where she went, because everywhere she could see the pink mist of Jim's blood. Every day was punctuated by the snap of his bones.

Ultimately, even she, barely human, got noticed. After six weeks in London, the chill of the changing season began to penetrate, and a woman dropped a pound coin into her dead twin's cap. The woman peered at Janet.

Janet had placed the precious relic between her feet at the entrance to Peckham Rye Station. At all costs, she avoided talking. But this morning she'd made the mistake of sitting on a bench, and the woman sat down too. Janet shifted away. She was just about to slide into the rush hour when the woman left for the Station Café.

Janet knew she should run, yet she was very tired. The woman was back with a hot cup of tea and a bun, placing it between them on the seat. Janet picked up the polystyrene cup. Its warmth felt good. She began to sip; the hot sweetness went immediately to her cold toes and chilled ears. With a shaking hand, she took the paper bag and licked the white icing off the currant bun before cramming it into her mouth.

She ought to run, yet she could not face spilling the tea. There was an arm around her. Janet didn't move; they sat while she drained her cup. The woman didn't ask any questions. She began to talk about a safe place she knew. It was called the Holywell Retreat Centre, far from London, in the country. It had been a refuge for hundreds of years, she said, surrounded by fields and sheep.

Janet shifted at the mention of sheep. Without thinking, she told the woman that her brother Jim might have liked it there. Questions about Jim led to the story of his death and of why they left home. Janet began to wonder if the woman was a social worker, a species she feared almost as much as the police.

"No, I'm a witch," said the woman, smiling. Janet knew she ought to be afraid. Wasn't this what happened in storybooks? In the dark forest, a witch will eat you.

"I'm a good witch," said the woman, putting a comforting hand on Janet's. "We call ourselves the Wiccans of London, and we try to help people, especially girls, in trouble."

She didn't add that "in trouble" had once, prior to legal abortion, been a very specific term requiring herbal remedies. Now the Wiccans worried about young runaways like Janet. A decade or two later, their concern would extend to trafficked and enslaved women.

Janet trudged away with a telephone number and a scribbled address. If she wanted to go to Holywell, she could telephone, and someone would meet her at Paddington Station with a ticket. One of the Holywell counselors would meet the 6 p.m. train. It was up to Janet. She could disappear into London's underworld or keep the appointment.

Janet kept the appointment. At Holywell, she found the old house in mellow stone familiar. The sheep and countryside, I suppose, she thought. The ache of that recognition was no longer unendurable. After a few days, she asked if she could work in the old orchard. A year later, it was a flourishing vegetable plot supplying Holywell with seasonal produce.

Meanwhile, the women registered Janet as a home school foster child. No one enquired too carefully about the kind of education she was getting. In five years, her herbalism combined magic with plant chemistry; in ten years, she could have lectured at a university. In fact, she refused offers as an instructor at several Oxford colleges when they balked at the inclusion of astrology and spells.

One day, Janet met a friendly organic grower at Oxford market, and, after a brief liaison, she gave birth to a stillborn boy. She had planned to call her baby Jim. Shrouded in grief, Janet redoubled her devotion to the magic of the earth. Gaining agreement to extend the vegetable garden into the paddock where the last of the Holywell horses grazed, she found its occupant fascinating and frightening.

Mercurius was an old black stallion. A biter in his youth, he moved close to Janet, who was staking out another quarter of his patch. She did not budge or show fear. Snorting in disgust, he galloped to the far corner to sulk.

After a few days, Mercurius merely stood and glared. Janet built a fence of wooden stakes. Something had to stop that damn horse from nibbling the carrot seedlings. Thereafter, Mercurius would trot over and watch her dig. She would look up into his dark eyes. He knew her. He's a horse, she said to herself. I'm seeing intelligence and understanding, *in a horse*.

She brought oats to Mercurius, who licked her hands. One day she came with the oats soaking up the icy rain. No Mercurius in the field; only a black heap.

She understood immediately. Watching his corpse pelted by Oxfordshire sleet, she felt a curious sensation of tickling on her forehead. Slowly, a black, horse-shaped shadow climbed out of the dead animal and trotted over. The oats fell from her fingers. Mercurius's horse-shade came closer and closer until she could see right through him, and all her senses contained him.

Without a thought, Janet went to join the elder counselors. That morning they were struggling to nominate the next Alchemy Scroll Key Keeper. Janet cut through their dilemma.

"I'll do it. Mercurius told me to. He died last night."

*****

"You see, the Alchemy Scroll isn't like a book," Janet tried to explain to Caroline. "I mean it *is* a book, a very old one, but it's so much more. It's a practice, a magic that is alive and needs feeding. Like a creature. We care for it, and in turn, the Alchemy Scroll sustains us."

"Like Mercurius?" wondered Caroline aloud.

"Yes, Mercurius," said Janet. "The name comes from a sort of trickster in alchemy. Also... the baby. And Jim. They're all part of the Alchemy Scroll. That's why I told you my story."

Caroline wanted to ask if this was the Key. Was the Key Keeper the bearer of stories? Instead, she said, "We have a story, too, I mean me, Anna, and Mary Wandwalker. It's about the Alchemy Scroll at St. Julian's."

"It's all right, I know," said Janet. "The Key Keeper has always known about the Le More copy and the real Scroll going to America. You see, she was one of us."

Caroline nearly fell off her chair. "*She*? You can't mean...?"

"Yup, Roberta Le More passed as a man. Women like her had to in those days. Otherwise, she'd be burnt as witch."

"You're saying she was a witch? The alchemist Robert le More, who did the Scroll copy, was Roberta, a Holywell witch?" Caroline found it hard to take in.

"She was one of us," repeated Janet. "Before she went off with Ransome, she was the Holywell Key Keeper."

Caroline groaned and put her hands on the sides of her head. God, her curls felt greasy.

Where, oh where, was Anna?

154

PART FOUR
CALCINATIO

CHAPTER 21
AN ARSONIST AT THE OLD HOSPITAL

Agnes had smeared chocolate all round her mouth. Janet took out a clean tissue and spat on it. The old woman submitted to being cleaned up. Caroline decided she liked Agnes. Her childlikeness was comforting. Janet gave up trying to get the brown stuff out of the deepest wrinkles. They needed to get back to their wards. Janet's story had taken too long.

"That'll have to do, Agnes. Give yourself a good wash tomorrow. Don't let the nurses get too close before you do."

"When do we go home?" wailed Agnes, looking at Caroline.

"My friend, Anna... she's coming for us," muttered Caroline. She hated her anxiety at the thought of Anna.

It wasn't far off dawn. Soon the gigantic porridge cauldron would bubble; women and men in uniforms would be arriving at the parking lot, locking their cars, and leaving their lives behind. With blank, institutionalized faces, they would become cogs in the underworld of The Old Hospital. *Anna isn't coming.*

"Your Anna isn't coming," said Janet to Caroline. Caroline saw her own lack of hope.

"Trust Anna?" The question came from Agnes.

"Usually, yes," said Caroline, tired and miserable. She began to lead Agnes up the stairs. Janet brought up the rear. "But... she should have been here — before now."

All at once, there was an eerie noise. It began as a humming and escalated quickly into a throbbing alarm. Finally, it grated like bells horribly out of tune.

"Aaarh," shrieked Agnes, clutching her head.

157

"What is it?" whispered Caroline, terrified.

"Don't know," replied Janet. "It's an alarm I've never heard before. People are coming. Get back to your ward, quick. I'm this way."

"No," said Caroline. "No, this is our chance, it could be our only chance. Come on. Back down the stairs. We've got to hide."

Caroline pulled both women back down to the basement. She shut the storeroom door and hushed them. Shouts and cries rumbled above their heads. There was a lot of thumping and grinding, followed by more shouting and creaky wheels.

The horrible jangling continued. Caroline opened the door a crack, but they could not make sense of the unusual level of activity.

"When it's quiet, we'll try to find the way out," said Caroline. "Could it be a mass escape?"

"Not likely," said Janet, wearily. "Too many drugs." She gestured to Agnes who was fast asleep wrapped in blankets. Janet lowered herself to the floor and put her head in her hands. Now that she'd told her story, her energy had vanished.

"I'm going to take a look," said Caroline.

"Trust Anna." It was Agnes. From sound asleep, she'd sat up wide awake. Caroline's jaw dropped.

"I will, Agnes," she said. There was no time to argue. In fact, she felt relieved. Leaving the two women, she crept halfway up the stairs. After sniffing the now silent corridor, she ran back. It was bad news.

"Fire!" she gasped. "There's a fire. I smelled smoke. It's all quiet up there. They've emptied the ward. We could be trapped."

Janet and Agnes rose as one. Even Agnes looked alert. Then her eyes clouded, and she began to whimper.

"I think there's a way out down here," said Janet.

"You *think*?" yelled Caroline, panicking. The smell of smoke crept into their nostrils.

"It's what I've been told," said Janet levelly, "by the woman who gives me chocolate sometimes. She brings bed linen from outside via a basement door, she says."

Where is Anna? thought Caroline desperately. She glanced at Janet. Surely a woman with a death wish wouldn't lie to her. Would she?

Agnes sniffed and mewed; she lunged past Caroline for the door. The other women joined her in the corridor, where they all started coughing.

"Come on," said Janet. "Any door to the outside's gotta be down here."

Caroline took a deep breath, then wished she hadn't.

"Go ahead with Agnes, and take the torch," said Caroline. "I'm right behind you."

Thin acrid smoke was starting to pool by their knees. It grew hotter behind them as they trotted, as fast as Agnes could go, along the corridor that grew dirtier and more like a tunnel. Then they came to a locked door. Janet froze.

"We go back to the stairs," she began. There was a roar and a crash. All the lights went out. Agnes screamed.

"No time!" shouted Caroline. "Get that door open!"

Caroline had been scouring the walls for fire extinguishers. None. There was nothing to use on the meshed glass window in front of them.

"Gimme the torch," said Caroline, grabbing it from Janet. She tried not to cough as the smoke seared her lungs. "Hold onto Agnes."

Caroline held their only source of light. The torch was fading in smoke now as high as their chests. Caroline grasped the cylinder in both hands and ran at the pane of glass.

Thupt. Nothing. Perhaps a tiny crack, but not all the way through. Caroline struck again and again with all the force she could muster. Agnes was wailing. She and Janet huddled in the corner between concrete wall and door, trying to keep their noses above the smoke.

159

After what could not have been more than a minute, Caroline started to cough uncontrollably.

"I'll try," shouted Janet. At Janet's second blow, there was a noise that could only be shattering glass. The torch died. If the breaking glass is the torch not the door, then we're going to die of smoke inhalation, and soon, Caroline thought.

"Caroline, the window glass is gone. But I can't break the mesh. We still can't get to the lock." Janet's voice was punctuated with gasps.

"There's got to be something to cut wire." Caroline swallowed, "I'll... I'll go back to that storeroom." Fingernails dug into her arm.

"Are you nuts?" croaked Janet. "Back there is where the fire's coming from. You'll be dead in minutes."

"Other storerooms... did we pass...?" Caroline wobbled. She was starting to lose control of her arms and legs. She tried giving in to coughing. It seemed to bring her round, a bit.

Whack, Caroline reeled from the slap on her left cheek.

"Wake up. Come on. You don't want to die. Nor does Agnes."

"Nor do you. Do you? You... bitch of a witch!" Caroline was too terrified to care about words. Anger roared. She swung round to where the blow had come through the clouds of smoke.

"This is all your fault. I came here to rescue you. And you didn't even want to escape." Both women were lashing out wildly.

"No... one asked you to come..." barked Janet, trying to slap Caroline and missing.

"You don't want to live," screamed Caroline, seizing a lump of Janet's hair.

"YES, I DO," shouted Janet. Caroline staggered back. So did Janet. Caroline tripped over Agnes who stumbled to her feet.

"Agnes found; Agnes found."

She pressed a small sharp object into Caroline's arm. Despairing, Caroline automatically put out her hand. There must be less than a minute of oxygen.

"Agnes found. Look, look."

"Stop it, Agnes, I can't... oh. What is it? Oh, OH. Get out of the way. Let me at that door."

"What is it?" came a croak.

"Nail scissors, I think. From Agnes's pocket. Yes, yes. Oh, god, which way is the lock? Help me, you, you... stupid effing witch."

With a rattle, the door suddenly opened. Caroline fell forward onto her knees. She staggered up, then pulled Janet and Agnes through. Shutting the door behind them, she leaned against it tasting colder and cleaner air. There was a tiny click and a fluorescent light flickered in what was now unambiguously a tunnel.

"Must be on a separate circuit," muttered Janet. She didn't look at Caroline.

"Go, go," rasped Caroline. With the scissors in one hand and the sleeve of Agnes's robe in the other, Caroline followed Janet's unsteady steps. The next and last door was an anticlimax. Only bolts on the inside secured it. Recently greased, the bars slid easily, even in their shaking hands.

Pushing the metal door open, they found themselves outside. It was morning. With the brick walls of The Old Hospital behind them, they climbed steps leading to a courtyard. Caroline looked back to see black smoke pouring out of the windows where glass had melted. Grinding came from the conflagration devouring The Old Hospital.

The women gazed blearily at the deserted yard. It must be used for delivery trucks. Caroline knew they ought to get moving. They had to hide. The problem was that she could not move at all. Agnes sucked her thumb while Janet stared at the treetops visible over another flaming wing of the hospital.

Screeching brakes interrupted Caroline's daze. An androgynous figure in black leapt from the van marked "Grocery Supplies."

"Caroline, you've got her. Over here, get in quick."

161

"Anna," said Caroline faintly. "You're here. Where did you get the van?"

"No time. Just get in. Are we taking the other one?"

"Yes," said Janet, looking warily at Anna.

"Quick, before they see us," hissed Anna. She bent to push Agnes's rump into the back of the van.

"No, no," wailed Agnes, helplessly.

"Hush, Agnes," said Janet, taking a seat beside her. "These are… friends."

"Cab door's unlocked," said Anna, running around to the driver's side. Nevertheless, Caroline got into the back with Agnes and Janet before slamming the doors. The van growled into reluctant life, swerving wildly as sirens screamed from behind the burning building.

CHAPTER 22
THE FIRE BETWEEN THEM

Anna woke Caroline at 6 p.m., setting a paper cup of tea on the table next to the bed. The dark outside seeped into the motel room. Lamplight from the pink shade radiated a rosy glow that Anna associated with porn movies. She did not say this to Caroline.

"Wake up, Caroline. I made tea."

"Um. Ah. Go away."

"Janet says you've had too many drugs to go on sleeping. Drink this while I get us a sandwich from the nearest gas station."

Anna sat on the bed, jiggling Caroline's hand until the older woman heaved herself up on her elbow. Caroline flinched as she picked up the hot tea and set it back down. Across the room was a long mirror. Someone with grey skin looked back at her.

"All right," she grunted. "Okay, Anna."

"Are you awake? Get up so you won't fall back to sleep before I'm back."

Anna kept her expression in the shadows. Her jeans were creased, and the designer tops she usually wore had been replaced by an old T- shirt of Caroline's with the faded logo: "Reedbourne Infants Sports Jamboree 1998." In a former life, Caroline taught small children.

"Where did you find that old thing?"

Anna shrugged and reached for her jacket. A smell wafted over to Caroline that she did not expect. Anna usually wore expensive perfumes. Caroline never enquired about their origin. Mary worried that Anna shoplifted. This smell was no perfume.

163

It can't be. Yes, really, that's paraffin. The truth blazed into Caroline. She threw back the covers, scrambling into a sitting position.

"Anna, it was you. You, you started the fire?"

At the door, Anna's hand froze.

"We'll talk later."

There was a plastic card nailed to the door half concealed by Anna who would not turn around. Fire Safety Regs, realized Caroline. The irony ignited her.

"Get back here!" she ordered.

Anna did not turn around. She leaned with her forehead on the door. Caroline was used to Anna being evasive. Not usually with her, though.

As Caroline swung her feet to the floor, Anna at last turned to face her. Anna's hands dropped to her sides. Two red patterned twenty-pound notes fluttered onto the pink carpet. Caroline shivered at the reminder of blood.

"You set the fire," she said quietly. Each word was distinct. "Don't deny it. Don't lie. We could have been killed. People could have *died*. How do you know they didn't?" Caroline choked. Then she coughed. Her saliva tasted of smoke.

Anna had huge black eyes.

"No one died. Online I found…"

"Online," spluttered Caroline. She wobbled and put her hand. Her palm met wallpaper cold to the touch. Caroline clenched her fist. Her fingernails were brown from smoke. Her wrists throbbed from scorch marks.

"Online," she yelled again. "Do I look like I'm online? Does Janet or Agnes? We were *there*. People breathed that smoke…" Caroline's tirade was interrupted again by coughing.

Anna dashed to the bathroom and reappeared with a glass of water. Caroline tossed the contents into her mouth, then held out the empty glass. Twice more Caroline forced liquid down her throat before she took the glass in both hands and sipped, then placed it next to the tea, which had acquired a whitish scum. Not for one second had Caroline's fury burned down.

"You can't trust online," she forced out. "We've talked about this."

"Caroline, beloved..." wheedled Anna, looking at Caroline's set jaw. "Calm down. It's not good for you to get so upset. Come here." She made as if to pull her lover into an embrace. Caroline wasn't having it.

"Fuck off, Anna."

Anna hissed. Caroline *never* swore to anyone. She wasn't finished.

"Tell me that you can be certain that no one died. *Because of the internet.* Like there are no lies there? No... jiggery pokery."

In the seconds of silence stretching between them, Caroline stared at Anna's flushed cheeks. So rare that Anna betrayed consciousness of having done wrong. Was this all she was going to get?

Anna knew that Caroline was referring to her own cyber-trickery. For years she had falsified data for a criminal gang. For the Agency, she was prepared to do the same.

Previously, Caroline had been blithe about Anna as an online Robin Hood, while Mary hoped against hope to rein her in. The search for the Alchemy Scroll had propelled the Agency to action before the three of them could hammer out parameters. Now they were divided in the rosy lamplight. Caroline's anger must be fueled by fear.

Anna shook herself like a dog in from the rain.

"I couldn't get into the building," she said, frustrated. She kicked the bed frame with one of her sharp-toed boots. "First, it took too long to find that... that prison hospital. I was so worried about you; about how you were coping..."

She shot a sly look at Caroline. She'd expected challenges from Mary. Miss Wandwalker, vigilant leader of the Agency, promised challenges. But Caroline? The woman who slept nightly in her arms and moaned in pleasure when they made love? She who cried down the phone if they parted for more than a day. Where was that Caroline now?

"You know how much I love you." Anna's trump card slowed Caroline. Her breathing became more regular. "I couldn't bear to leave you in that place a second longer." Anna switched her body into submissive mode. Caroline sighed.

"You can't do this, Anna. You can't make love an excuse. Not for a fire. Not with all those people."

Anna bit down her irritation. She made herself tell the story in her normal voice.

"Caroline, get real. Listen to me. I hacked into where they ordered food. The balance sheets included numbers of meals served each day. So, I could count patients and staff as they left the building. As soon as I realized you weren't coming out the front, I went to the only other exit. There you were, all three, making the numbers right."

Caroline stared past Anna. "Not me," she said in a strangled tone. "Not even me and Janet, whose picture you studied. Me, Janet, and Agnes. Just numbers. A slip of a digit online."

Her scorn scorched. "You can't tell me you knew, you *knew* us, us three women had not come out. People, not numbers, Anna. Agnes would have died because people like her always die. No one cares for the Agneses."

"You did," muttered Anna.

"Not me, Janet."

"You're saying I don't care. About people?" Anna tried to sound disbelieving.

Caroline swallowed. That was not it, exactly.

"Anna, I suppose you care. Well…in principle. But you're a survivor. You call what you do cybercraft, and you are a cyberwitch. The online world is more real to you than anything else. Even me." Caroline was shocked at her bitterness. "People are what you manipulate; to survive."

"I care," whispered Anna.

Caroline did not believe her.

"No, you *don't*," Caroline's voice cracked as she forced out the words. "My hair stinks of smoke, even though I shampooed it twice. We were dying in that fire. And you stayed *outside*. You

166

set that fire to smoke us out like animals. Animals," Caroline ended with a shout. Anna stood frozen.

Bang! Bang! Caroline and Anna jumped. The door was being hammered.

"Let us in," came a muffled voice, Janet, probably. Yes, there she was, with Agnes behind her.

The older woman was clean yet confused. Her big grin fell off when she saw Anna and Caroline. Janet waded in.

"Stone the crows, as my Grandma used to say. You two can be heard from the parking lot. What's going on?"

She sounded far too cheerful for Caroline. I'm in shock, Caroline realized.

"Stone... crows?" Anna sounded strained.

Caroline lifted her exhausted head. "Nothing. It's all nothing."

The energy in the room ebbed away. Janet sat beside her and took her hand.

"Poor Caroline. You should give her some of those tranquilizers, Anna. They've done wonders for me and Agnes."

Caroline raised her head and saw that Agnes was smiling. She could not look at Anna. Caroline heard a zip savagely ripped. Another glass appeared in front of her. It held something sticky and red. Then Anna's olive hand appeared with two pills and tossed them in. They fizzed into bubbles.

"What?" said Caroline, bleakly. She took the glass and stared at it.

"Just drink." Anna said at her most haughty.

Caroline glanced at the three other women: Anna enigmatic, Janet frankly curious, Agnes puzzled. Caroline considered the probably illegally obtained drugs in the cocktail. Could she trust Anna like she always did, or did until now? There was a long pause.

"Anna gave it to me and Agnes hours ago. We're fine," said Janet. Her tone reminded Caroline of a bell that rang unexpectedly high.

"Agnes like. Agnes like." An unsteady hand approached Caroline. Agnes wanted it.

Caroline clasped both hands around the glass and drained it quickly. There was a pleasant sugary taste, a fizz in the mouth with a mineral undertone.

She handed the glass back to Anna, who placed it in the sink without comment. Her face had taken on the veiled look that Caroline remembered from when they first met. She had waited too long to reassure Anna about her trust. Even so, she remained too angry to lie.

"We're going out to dinner," said Janet brightly.

Agnes clapped her hands, "Yes, yes, yes."

Caroline groaned. Anna ignored the suggestion. "I'm getting us sandwiches from the gas station we passed."

"Nope, we're going to The Olive and Dove. I booked a table for 7 p.m." Janet was revoltingly pleased with herself. Caroline looked hard at her. Hard to tell in the rosy light, but Janet's pupils could be dilated.

"Janet, are you feeling all right?" Caroline was starting to get a pleasant buzz somewhere in the region of her ears. "Anna, did you put coke in this…this cocktail?"

Long ago Anna had slipped her cocaine when her depression was at its worst. Caroline had run around the garden for two hours unable to stop. There'd been tears, followed by talking into the night, and promises. How much was Anna prepared to toss away?

"No, I didn't." Anna was stung. "It's not coke." She stopped. Caroline and Janet had identical raised eyebrows. Agnes giggled.

"Grass," said Janet, with assurance. "Found it powdered mixed with sugar shoved down the side of the seat in that van. Good idea to make it into a tea. In the circumstances," she added to Caroline. "And I mean it about going out to dinner. Anna has a wad of cash, and we need somewhere we can pretend to be normal, even if it is just because there are other people. We've

168

got to stick together," she added meaningfully to Caroline, "to make a plan."

Caroline flashed back to Holywell, where the counselors gathered after a meal, conversing, making plans. With her stomach melting, Caroline had no answers. She recalled that someone connected with the Alchemy Scroll was looking for Janet. Food might stop their insides from shuddering. Let Janet try her crazy notion.

"What about Agnes?"

"She's coming, of course. Now, Anna, what about that trash bag of clothes you said you kept put in the van?"

Minutes before 7 p.m., a colorful crew startled the sober patrons of The Olive and Dove. Agnes wore a sliver elasticated skirt, a sky-blue jumper, and bright pink lipstick rather too liberally applied. Janet patted her khaki trousers lightly stained with engine oil and a man's brown jacket with a green wool scarf. Both exclaimed loudly at the succulent odors, log fires and the horse brasses polished to winking gold on every wall.

Touched by the simple joy in Agnes, Caroline was warmed by the glow coming from Janet. Janet has shifted balance, she thought, either from drugs or the fire. She looked like her story, a countrywoman-become-herbal-witch. Surely, she could sense the land calling her home.

Caroline had shrugged into her own navy raincoat. She supposed that Anna bringing it meant something. It wasn't enough. By contrast, Anna was superbly attired in scarlet satin culottes and a black silk top. She had brushed her hair until sparks flew.

After the star-roofed countryside, the Olive and Dove proved to be a thatched building bursting with light. Expensive cars lined the hedges on each side. The old brick and beam front remained a traditional pub, while the restaurant glittered in the glass atrium at the back. At the spectacle of faux coziness, hot food, and warm company, Caroline blinked.

169

CHAPTER 23
A GOOD MEAL AROUND THE FIRE

The oddly attired women were shown to a table next to a fire, whose hearth had been built of brick into what had once been the back of the old cottage. With silver birch logs, the peaks of flames burned red and gold. Caroline could hear the crunch of splintering wood under the chink of glasses and rising hum of voices.

"Not here," she said. "Not by the fire."

Janet silently rose and touched Anna's hand. Agnes gave a squeak and scuttled further into the glass interior, where there were a few empty tables. She had promised to be very quiet. They joined her at one of the two free tables furthest from the flames. Janet tilted her head up to the glass membrane that separated them from the country night.

"We'll sit here, thank you," Caroline heard herself say to the waiter.

"Of course, Madam. I'll bring the menus and be back to take your order for drinks."

Caroline recklessly ordered a bottle of wine. In for a penny, in for a pound. She could see the answering gleam in Janet as they touched glasses. She was not looking at Anna. Still subdued, they agreed on roast chicken, exchanging remarks as if passing a baton. They ate slowly and passionately, hardly exchanging words.

"Sweet, sweet," whispered Agnes.

171

"Yes, Agnes, I know. I promised her dessert," said Janet to Caroline and Anna. "Sticky toffee pudding for all of us please, and don't hold back on the ice cream."

It took the sweet butteriness of the dessert to remind Caroline of how much she loved comfort food. Too much, of course. Hence the failing dieting that was her usual fraught relationship with eating. At least the clean jeans that Anna had brought for her were looser after The Old Hospital. However, when the pudding had been served, Caroline found she could not begin.

She stared at the oozing brown sludge over butter sponge. A dollop of ice cream was melting into a yellowish pool; she watched it, fascinated. A volcano of cake poked through the hot lava of caramel. Caroline giggled; she looked around guiltily. *Must be the marijuana,* she thought. She put out a finger and twirled sugar strands, then dunked it in the puddle of ice cream. The sweetness flicked a switch inside her. Caroline met Anna's eyes for the first time in hours. She looked away.

"It's good, isn't it?" Janet said to Caroline. "The pudding, I mean. They used to make it on my birthday at Holywell, always with homemade ice cream."

"Yes, it's good." Caroline even managed a smile.

"Agnes like. Agnes more." Not yet finished, Agnes held out her bowl as the waiter blinked and nodded. Janet scraped the last of her softening ice cream. Caroline sat transfixed by the beauty of the yellow cream in the blue bowl. She felt tears gathering. Her throat was thick, and not from smoke.

"Caroline like," she said croakily. Janet stared at her, then chuckled. Agnes swallowed the last of her ice cream, apart from the blob on her nose. Even Anna relaxed.

"Here, Agnes, let me wipe that," Caroline said applying her napkin to Agnes's face.

"We've escaped, Caroline," said Janet. "Haven't we?"

"Yes, I think we have," agreed Caroline. "You were right about coming out to dinner, even though it's crazy."

172

"Definitely crazy. Shall we have coffee? And there are chocolates."

Anna's phone buzzed. She took it out, then said to Caroline quietly: "It's Mary. A text. And another."

Reading it, Anna tensed. "She wants us to meet her in LA. Soon, when the airport reopens after the snow. We have to go to her because they won't let her leave." Anna shot a wary glance at Caroline, then answered the question on her lover's face.

"There's been a murder at the Museum. The Alchemy Scroll is gone, and she wants us to track down the killer."

PART FIVE
SEPARATIO

CHAPTER 24
MISS WANDWALKER ON THE TRAIL

The day after the terrible discovery of D.P.'s body, Mary woke to the radio station announcing a lull in the blizzard. With more snow forecast for later, the freeways would remain closed, the Mayor's office said.

Mary switched on the TV to see a skinny woman with a bare neck turning blue. Her honey hair looked brittle in the freezing wind. While flashing perfect teeth, she explained that snowplows would arrive today from ski resorts in the mountainous regions of the state. Apparently, the once-in-a-century storm, as they insisted on calling it, was localized to LA County. Elsewhere, the ski season was done.

Mary pulled back dusty curtains to confirm that nothing was falling from the steel sky. After tapping at her laptop, she took the elevator down to the deserted hotel lounge and ate some stale cereal. Then she headed for the streets, pleasantly surprised to find the sidewalks cleared of snow.

Mournful shop workers shoveled the snow, enabling about half the businesses to stay open. Supermarkets were the stores attracting lines of customers. Mary managed to dodge around figures in double coats and ski hats, as she made for the address she'd found online.

For Mary had decided to track down Professor Cookie Mac. He had connected his obsession with the Alchemy Scroll with something called The European History Foundation and its Alchemy Symposium. A quick search online and Mary discovered that this organization shared the address of a bookstore on

177

Fifteenth Avenue. Cheered to find an open coffeehouse across the street, Mary took the opportunity to sip a cup of restorative coffee.

Probably the EHF had the offices upstairs; but why not be located on a university campus? Mary had a hunch about their sponsorship of Cookie Mac's Symposium. The fact that Cookie Mac desperately wanted the Alchemy Scroll had begun to give her ideas.

Meanwhile, she inhaled the sacred odors of fresh-roasted Brazilian. Waiting for a lull, she then nipped to order a second cappuccino, trusting that her quarry was not equally fast. No one dared to ask for sprinkled chocolate at Java Giotto's. It had a century of old-world purity to uphold.

While scanning for the missing professor, Mary checked her priorities. Her case was the missing Alchemy Scroll. Yet, the murder of D.P. changed everything, didn't it? Money worries also could not be ignored. The Agency's credit card was liable to expire any day. Mary reflected gloomily that her Agency would be up in smoke if they did not get paid for something, and soon.

Free facts, thought Mary, how can I find information requiring neither expensive purchases nor travel? This morning on Google she had exhausted her online talents. That was Anna's realm. Old methods, thought Mary, to check out the EHF. Lurking in the folds of her handbag, a dusty address book contained relics of affairs and intrigues. Here were the sticky secrets in the academic world, in the incurable gossip of scholars.

Mary searched through past lovers for suitable scholars. The third cappuccino provided the energy to make the call. After an enjoyable twenty minutes chatting to a sleepy history don from Oxford's wealthiest College, Mary had a better idea of Professor Cuchulain Macdonald. Just as she thought, truly incendiary material.

"What? You're sure you are describing Professor Cookie Mac Macdonald?" she prompted.

"That's horrible, unbelievable," she said. "Yes, the twenty-first century has gone mad. I can see that The European History

Agenda would make it poison to a real university. Any more info would be great. Can you get your grad students to dig on social media?"

Mary hung up with, "I'm relying on you, Jerry."

Or rather on the call of your stomach, Mary said to herself, having recklessly bribed the academic bon viveur with a meal at a London restaurant of his choice (she'd have to rethink that one for expenses).

Mary Wandwalker was shocked at what she'd heard. The European History Foundation included known white supremacists, some never tenured, some quietly retired from their academic posts. She grimaced. The Alchemy Scroll attracted attention, and some of it was not good.

Perhaps Jerry could get something more. Over a decade ago, they'd spent a delightful weekend in Florence while he gave a keynote. Uncomplicated sex and sophisticated culture had been her way of staving off loneliness. It never worked, but Mary refused to think about that now. She had a murder and a lost Alchemy Scroll to find.

That's right, she said to herself. The murder and the Scroll are connected. I will not abandon D.P. It may be ridiculous, considering the police have the resources. Nevertheless, I... Well, there's Sam to consider. He's vulnerable: so young, distraught, and a foreigner, at a crime scene in LA. There's racism here. I can't walk away from Sam. We must find his brother's murderer. Anna could do her cybermagic on the EHF website. Their homepage tantalized with multiple levels of access in return for donations.

Mary was also worried about Caroline. A laconic text from Anna stirred up more questions than answers. Anna merely said that she'd gotten Caroline and Janet Swinford out of The Old Hospital. They were hiding in some motel. Mary frowned at the wording.

CRASH: then breaking glass. Mary dropped her phone. Peering through the ice on the café window, she saw the backs of teenagers scooting down the street. Boys — all wore

179

baseball caps. Her eyes swung over to the hole in the Academy Bookstore's window. Cracks radiated from it. She did a double take. While she'd been talking to Jerry, someone had spray painted the door.

Mary grabbed her bag and made for the street, remembering at the last moment to go back for her phone. Exiting the coffee shop, she glimpsed a man running after the youths. Something about him seemed familiar. He wore similar clothes to the fleeing boys down to the ubiquitous baseball cap.

From the Bookstore, there appeared two white men in near identical dark suits and red ties. Naturally, they were on their phones. Mary could hear sirens getting closer... until they mingled with other vehicles crunching over refrozen snow.

She wasn't the only spectator from the café. A motley crowd of young people who looked to her like students held up devices to take images. Many seemed confused by the graffiti. Older folks like Mary stared in disgust at the blood-red swastika.

Before Mary could decide what to do, a squad car drew up and two cops got out. One, an older man, tightened his mouth at the damage. Confirming the absence of suspects, he nodded at his female companion, a young woman with beautifully dreadlocked hair tied back. They made their way to the young men waiting for them expressionlessly. At that moment Mary noticed snowflakes drifting down.

The small crowd thinned. Mary kept her eyes on the police. She felt, rather than saw, the silver backs of laptops snap open in the café behind her.

The female cop pointed at the damage and asked her questions. Pale youth one as Mary thought — they really were very alike — appeared to be making a complaint. He gestured down the street in the direction of the running boys. The cops turned to each other briefly before getting back in their squad car and driving off. Mary did not think there was much chance of catching anyone.

"Miss Wandwalker."

Mary jumped and turned around. For a millisecond she was flooded with fear. Then she recognized the young man.

"Sam... Sam Murphy. You startled me."

"Yeah, sorry. Were you looking for me?"

"Yes, no ... That is, I'm looking for that man from... erm, the Museum. Where've you been? The police want to question you."

"Yeah, I bet they want to question *me*," said Sam, bitterly. "Why are *you* out here now, Miss Wandwalker? It's starting to snow again."

He went on defensively. "*I'm* looking for my brother's killer!"

The snow was intensifying again, gentle in its deadly beauty.

Mary took a step toward him. "It was you, just now, wasn't it? You were running after those boys. I thought the man looked familiar."

"Yeah, I was in the bookstore when the brick came through the window. Sounded like a gunshot. When nothing else happened, I ran out, saw them making a getaway."

"You didn't catch them." Mary sympathized.

"Actually, I did. Two of 'em. They told me something real important. But we can't talk here."

"I've got a hotel room."

"No good, they're bound to be watching you."

"They? Who?" Mary leaned forward.

"The cops. Whoever wants to pin my brother's death on me." His eyes slid away from Mary's. She realized with a shock that he did not trust her either.

"Come with me. A friend has lent me his apartment while he's away. It was supposed to be a break from D.P.'s nagging." His voice trailed off as he guided Mary down a side street. "It's always like this with cops," he continued angrily.

Mary opened her mouth to protest, then remembered Captain Lascelles. What did she know about being young, black, and male in America?

"D.P. told me what you said. About the Alchemy Scroll not being his culture. He thought it was funny. I don't. He studied for *years*. Now he's dead."

"I'm really sorry, Sam…" Mary was mortified. Her mistake lived on. "I suppose I deserve it," she said. "I really didn't mean… I knew D.P. was a master's graduate."

"People like you never *do* mean it. You think we all live in sink estates and our parents don't care. Our parents are fucking professors."

He swung his arms and starting walking again. Mary dropped behind.

"Keep up," he called. "You're not so special. We've got to talk."

Mary put her head down and strode as fast as she dared. When they were side by side, Sam continued. "Yeah, so I messed up with drugs in high school. That was years ago. I came here with D.P. These days I'm clean and taking classes at UCLA.

Sam was a volatile mix of grief and resentment, Mary realized. As for her, she could forget pride.

"Look Sam, I understand that I hurt D.P.'s feelings. If he could laugh about it later, I'm… I'm glad. Please let's start again," she said. "I want to help find D.P.'s killer; I really do."

Sam glanced down. Mary had a flash of seeing herself through him: an old woman with tired eyes, determined jaw, and a weird lavender coat. She was also the last person to see his older brother alive.

He indicated a side street. "Five minutes, down here."

His long strides were hard to match. She could hear him on his phone:

"Mum," he said. "Yeah, it's me, Mum. I'm with that woman I met in the Museum. The one D.P. sent you that last text about. Yeah, I need to talk to her. Then I'll come to your hotel. I love you too."

CHAPTER 25
THE EUROPEAN
HISTORY FOUNDATION

Sam steered Mary Wandwalker to a tiny apartment that smelled like the gym. A collection of jeans and sweatshirts and socks lay tangled on the floor. On a Scotch taped poster, a jazz musician that Mary could not place sweated into his trombone. Sam nodded her to the sofa bed piled with multicolor cushions. He pulled a book from his backpack.

"Look at this. I got it from the Academy Bookstore. It's published by 'The European History Foundation.' They're racists, fascists. This book proves it."

He thumped down a garish paperback next to Mary. She picked up the offending item and scrutinized its Contents page. Titled: *How Political Correctness Stole Our Heritage*, it had chapters on various history curricula, ranging from state-funded high schools to midrange universities.

Turning to the back cover she found a blurb that turned her stomach. The gist was overt: African American, "women's," Latino, and indigenous histories were insidiously depriving White America of its glorious European origins.

"Prejudiced," said Mary carefully. "And incorrect." She did not want to fuel an already smoldering Sam.

He grabbed the book back. "Look here," he said, turning pages to some badly reproduced color illustrations. "This is what got D.P. killed; this alchemy shit."

Mary examined the text around what claimed to be alchemical images. As a former archivist, she could tell these

183

used modern pigments. The words told her why Sam was so upset.

"Alchemy," she read aloud, "once a pure Aryan science, has been rewritten to propagate the lie... Oh, that's enough. This is sick." She felt sick and dropped the book to the floor. Noting the chapter's author, she regretted all that coffee. It was bile in her throat.

"Cookie Mac wrote this... this racist and false account of alchemy. Another indication that D.P. was killed over the Alchemy Scroll," said Mary, slowly, trying not to rush to judgment.

"Yeah. My brother got attacked over another racist book from the old days." Sam kicked the book half under the bed.

Mary took a deep breath. Wrong to characterize alchemy so, he wasn't reading the EHF book accurately, and no wonder. It was a clever perversion of the complex and multicultural alchemy she had researched during the night flight from London.

"No, Sam. This..." she picked up the book and opened it at the alchemy images again, "this... trash is not what alchemy is. Believe me, this is not what D.P. lived and died for. He loved *real* history. You know that, and I saw it. He loved the Alchemy Scroll even if he never had the chance for a proper look."

Mary tried to connect with Sam's burning eyes. "You're right though, that the EHF is spreading racism and lies. I checked with an old friend, and you have found evidence to confirm it."

Sam stood up, his whole body radiating angry heat. He snatched the book from Mary and threw it at the door.

"I said *lies*," said Mary. She held out a hand, willing him to focus. "Look at me, Sam."

He growled at the book splayed on the floor. Then he threw himself on the opposite end of the sofa to Mary and put his head into his hands. Mary noticed his shoulders shaking. She did not dare touch him. Perhaps he could listen?

"Sam, you loved your brother. I only met him the once, and I could see he was... remarkable. Think about who he really was, what he devoted his life to. You can't believe what's written here. The EHF book is a travesty. Don't buy into their narrative, their hatred. Do you want them to win? D.P. didn't. He knew alchemy came from all over the world and is for everyone. Not what these people say it is."

Frustrated and confused, Sam rubbed his eyes. Then he rose and started pacing, even though the room permitted only six strides. His fists jammed into his jacket pockets. Anguish gripped his whole body. Mary could see his youth. What would be the right words?

"D.P. went to college; I went to jail," he said suddenly. "And I'm the one that's alive."

"Do you want to get your brother's killers, or to destroy them?"

Suddenly, it was if Anna was in the room.

"Destroy them." The response was automatic. Then Sam realized what he'd said.

"Don't talk, Sam. Let me think for a moment."

Sam sat down again, watchful, and unconvinced. Mary reviewed her recent encounters. The dysfunctional Captain Lascelles thought Sam a likely candidate for theft of the Alchemy Scroll and, she remembered, with a small shock, for his brother's death.

Mary was certain Sam was innocent. And yet, she realized that she had no evidence to exonerate him, so why was she so sure? Because he felt like D.P., she realized. And D.P. needed more from them.

"D.P. got killed by the thief who took the Alchemy Scroll, which is very valuable. Did you know that the Scroll itself was originally Muslim. It was sent to Mother Julian of Norwich — an English medieval nun — by a great Islamic scholar. They corresponded out of mutual reverence for each other's learning."

Sam took out his phone and began tapping. Mary remembered something.

"In fact, Sam, I've just remembered that Alchemy originated in Egypt. The word comes from, 'Land of Black Earth.' So, if you go back far enough, alchemy is African."

"Ah hum..." Sam remained absorbed for a further five minutes while Mary watched him. Finally, he shoved his phone in his pocket, leaned back, and said, "So you mean fight fire with fire. Their alchemy is bad, but D.P. was onto the good stuff?"

Mary relaxed some of the tension in her jaw.

"That's it, Sam. D.P. died protecting precious African learning that enriched both Islam and Christianity."

Mary's last sight of D.P.'s warm smile had been on the frozen steps of the museum, just before he'd helped her into a cab. It was her turn to be fired up. Her stomach groaned. Sleuthing required sustenance.

"Erm, um, what about a hot meal? Some restaurants ought to be open. Right now, the snow's not too bad."

CHAPTER 26
MARY AND SAM

Mary and Sam agreed that tracking the Alchemy Scroll would assist in capturing the killer of D.P. A project without being a plan of action, she realized. With Mary's passport confiscated for the duration, she was stuck in snowy LA. So, what to do next?

What were Caroline and Anna doing, she wondered? Those two gave her range: Anna backed up Mary's intuitions with her occult online skills; Caroline was their soul. Together, the three could plot, feel, and imagine into enigmas. Before meeting them, Mary never relied upon other people, only files of data, so why did she feel so cut off now?

Mary was still racking her brains for a way to chase after Cookie Mac when Sam steered her to a Jamaican restaurant in East LA. On his advice, they ordered D.P.'s favorite meal, a rich pepper stew with chicken, chilies, and garlic, with a crisp green salad.

"We've gotta find that white Prof," Sam said, waving away the waiter. Mary nodded in agreement. She was rather amused at the waiter's astonishment at Sam's similar accent to her own. Sam went on. "Macdonald, yeah, I saw the way he was looking at me. Yesterday I followed him out of the museum. He got the only cab I've seen since the snow started. So of course, I lost him."

"He's evaded the Los Angeles Police too," said Mary, tiredly.

"Shall I order coffee?" Sam remembered to say.

187

"Yes, please," said Mary, her jet lag beginning to close in again.

"How d'you get the LAPD to tell you things?"

Mary blinked.

"Like who they're looking for?" Sam explained.

"I phoned earlier from Java Giotto's. It took a bit of arguing about the Alchemy Scroll and my having rights to follow its trail. I may have mentioned the words "official consultant." I was thinking of St. Julian's, of course."

Mary decided to tell Sam the full history of St Julian's Alchemy Scroll and her commission to get it back. Trying to make him understand about Anna and Caroline took them through D.P.'s special dish, a stew that required slow chewing and several jugs of water.

"So, what about Macdonald?"

Mary noted Sam speaking more calmly.

"Miss Wandwalker?" Sam's patience was for an old woman, Mary realized. She sat up straight.

"Sorry, I was just thinking... Yes, the police told me Cookie Mac's disappeared, off the grid."

Sam frowned. He's so vulnerable, Mary thought.

"Sam, are you going to be okay? About the police, I mean."

The young man laughed. "LAPD is no match for my Ma. She's hotfooting it over there with a lawyer first thing tomorrow. I should stay out of their way until he could read them the riot act for chasing a murder victim's brother simply 'cos he's Black."

Mary winced. "Glad to hear it," she muttered. Heat flushed her cheeks as she took out her phone. She found two voice messages. The first made her exclaim. The other found her plopping back onto the chair in frustration.

"Miss Wandwalker, are you okay?"

"I don't believe it." She turned back to Sam. "Message from Sergeant Rivera. At this very moment, Cookie Mac's on a plane to London. Apparently, they let a few planes take off during today's break in the snow. He got a flight to Las Vegas connecting to Heathrow."

188

"Does that mean…?"

Mary raked both hands through her hair. "To cap it all, Anna, my associate, will arrive in the morning. They've got a reduced service into LAX. Snow expected to die down overnight."

Sam took a big breath. "The prof dude's gone to the UK. Why?"

"The question is what with?" returned Mary, acerbically. "Has he taken the Alchemy Scroll to England? I thought he wanted it *here*. He's the star of the symposium funded by the EHF, remember? At least he is if he has the Alchemy Scroll. He made that clear at the Museum."

Sam nodded while Mary continued to dredge her memory. "The Symposium's bicoastal: a tryout on the West Coast, then the East. A big corporation is backing it, or so we've heard."

"So, why's he gone to England?" repeated Sam.

Mary's phone rang. It was Rivera again, and she had further news.

"Yes, Sergeant, I got your earlier message about Cookie Mac. I thought you were supposed to be stopping *all* the suspects leave Los Angeles. You took my passport…"

The voice from the phone changed tone. Mary felt her senses shift into gear.

"Does this mean you are no longer looking for Sam Murphy? I believe his mother is bringing a lawyer…"

"Ah, well, if I do see Sam…" Mary winked at the young man, who grinned.

"You want me to do *what*? Surely the police have resources…"

Mary waited while the young woman repeated her difficult request.

"You're sure he took the Alchemy Scroll, Cookie Mac? Yes, yes, I realize that it does not necessarily make him a murderer. But still…"

"Oh, I see. Lascelles has collapsed and with snow paralyzing much of the city…

"My Agency will keep in touch. Thank you, Sergeant."

Mary switched off her phone. Although Sam's eyes popped with questions, she wasn't sure how much to tell him. Her plan assembled itself at lightning speed.

"So damn infuriating, Sam. Anna will arrive tomorrow morning. while Cookie Mac passes through UK border checks at Heathrow. At least the police delivered my passport to the hotel. You see, I must go back. Someone over there could be in danger."

"From Cookie Mac? If he took the Scroll, and you was saying he did..."

Mary licked her lips. "The police found more CCTV," she said, carefully. "Cookie Mac exiting a cab in the right time frame for D.P.'s death. They have him running an hour later the next street to the Museum. He's clutching a long thin package."

"Running in the snow?" repeated Sam.

"Yes, he falls over yet gets up, runs again. Apparently, he was desperate to get away."

"I'm going after him." Sam grabbed his rucksack from the floor and began to root through.

"No, Sam, not you. *I'm* going after him. Or rather my detective Agency will. You remember me telling you about Caroline and Anna? Rivera says Lascelles is in hospital. She's been taken off the case because of the weather emergency. No chance of permission for her to go to the UK on this evidence anyway. She wants to know if I can track Cookie Mac in the UK, not the least because of something he was heard saying at LAX."

"Which is?"

Mary was silent. Cookie Mac had paid over the odds for his flight. Even so, he had to virtually force himself onto the plane. A stressed flight attendant put his rant on Twitter. Sergeant Rivera forwarded it, and so Mary showed Sam the clip.

"*I gotta find a witch in England,*" Cookie Mac shouted. "*She has secrets, alchemy secrets. My research will make millions if I get to her.*"

Sam opened his mouth, then shut it again. Mary tried to contact Anna. No reply. Cookie Mac had to be on his way to Janet, the Key Keeper of the Alchemy Scroll. With Janet in peril, so would be Caroline and Anna. Mary did not want to go into details with Sam. She probably trusted him, but should she let him get more involved? He was so young.

Sam's stare became an appeal.

"Look, Miss Wandwalker, D.P.'s my brother. I'm going after that man whatever you say."

The hurt in Sam's voice burned into Mary. He'd assumed he was part of her team.

"Sam, it's not that I don't value your help. My business, the Agency, is so new. I don't know how to look after someone like you."

Shocked by her own words, Mary spoke quickly.

"My... our Agency has debts. This is our first big case. It's make or break for us."

"Yeah, but *your* brother isn't dead."

Mary bit her lips. He deserved more.

"Sam," she said with unwonted gentleness. "I never had a brother or a sister. My parents died a long time ago. Later, I had a baby." Her voice dried.

"I never tell anyone. My associates in the Agency are Caroline, my dead son's wife, and Anna, his... his girlfriend. We're an investigating team, almost a family."

Mary wanted Sam to understand. "I understand how much you want to be involved," she said. "For D.P.... well, I care about him too. You want justice for your brother. So do I. My Agency was brought in to get the Alchemy Scroll back to its rightful home in Oxford."

She could not believe what she was about to say.

"Murder and theft, it's one case. Best we work together for both our families, Sam."

The young man nodded. "Okay,"

191

Time to stick her neck out, Mary thought. "Since your mother has squared the police, I'll get you with us on the plane to London. But only if it is okay with your parents. Phone them."

Sam banged the table. Then his grin turned into a chuckle. "Hey, Miss Wandwalker."

"Yes?" Mary was putting on her coat and pulling her hat out of a deep pocket.

"Shouldn't we find out if Cookie Mac has the Alchemy Scroll with him before we get on that plane?"

CHAPTER 27
FLYING APART

Mary Wandwalker and Sam Murphy met Anna at Los Angeles Airport. The young woman swanned out of the arrivals gate wearing a peach suit with silver accessories. Hair swept up in a French pleat and lips scarlet, Anna only lacked dark glasses to convince bystanders she was a movie star, any movie star. Perfect, just perfect, thought Mary, on Anna's unbeatable style.

She probably slept all the way, concluded Mary. Anna could sleep anywhere she could curl up like a wildcat. Mary sought in vain for rest on planes, and she was facing another long transatlantic crossing. As Anna approached her tense associate with her most enigmatic expression. Mary became more uneasy. What had she forgotten about Anna this time? Oh yes, her tendency to surprise.

"You will go back to find Cookie Mac. I have your tickets. I'll stay. I have work to do here."

"Hello, Anna," said Mary. "Nice to see you, too. How is Caroline? *Where* is Caroline?"

Anna sniffed. "Who's your man?"

Sam in green fatigues under his rucksack shifted from foot to foot as if the cold floor was red hot. From the instant Mary pointed out Anna, he had been unable to concentrate. Anna smiled; she was used to it.

"I'm Sam Murphy," he muttered.

"Sam's helping us," said Mary. "About Caroline...?"

"She's fine. Will meet your plane at Heathrow and take you to Holywell. We know that's where Cookie Mac is going. He

193

insists on meeting Janet. She forwarded her emails from him after she made us take her home."

"Yes, I got those before you landed. Dorothy too wants our help with Cookie Mac's visit. Do any work on the plane? Anna, pay attention. Did you find the whereabouts of the Alchemy Scroll? We don't know for sure that Cookie Mac took it to England."

"Clues," said Anna unhelpfully. "Clues to follow up. Likely he left the Alchemy Scroll over here, which is why I'm staying."

Anna was not prepared to tell Mary Wandwalker about successfully hacking into LAX surveillance cameras once the plane reached American airspace. Identifying Cookie Mac was no problem since she could compare his furtive figure with multiple images from his website.

Anna was especially proud of spotting the murder suspect placing a cylindrical parcel in a LAX locker. Only then did she acquire a headache, made worse by ordering too much whisky. What to do with this dangerous and potentially lucrative information?

Given her encounter with Leni in the police cell, and the blackmail of Godric St. John, Anna felt lost. Caroline would say to tell Mary. But Caroline wasn't talking to Anna. As people scurried toward the Gates, and Sam hopped as if between fires, Mary Wandwalker stared as if able to read Anna's mind. The young woman saw doubt in Mary's grey eyes darken like a storm cloud.

Just who was she working for? Anna wondered. Right now, she did not know. I'll find out if the package Cookie Mac left is the real Alchemy Scroll. Then I'll decide about telling Mary, Anna promised herself. To escape from those penetrating eyes, she addressed Mary loudly.

"I'm staying to break the firewall around the European History Foundation. You wouldn't understand. I see you printed out the plane ticket. Now I must get another one for the boy. It's no problem."

Anna took out her special laptop and set it on a metal seat near the Terminal desks. After about a minute of furious tapping, she skipped to the nearest printer point and typed in a code.

Anna's not telling me everything, thought Mary. Should I be worried?

"There." Anna was back with a paper with a plane ticket code on it. "This gets you two seats together on the plane back. You need to go to the departures desk to redeem them. I'll..." She paused.

"Yes, Anna, you'll what? What aren't you telling me... um us?"

For the first time Sam looked at Anna with something more than wonder.

"Go now," said Anna, firmly. "Forty-five minutes until your flight. Not much time. Good, you have no suitcases, since you missed the bag drop."

Mary glared at her.

"Okay, now I'll tell you," said Anna, taking Mary by the arm and drawing her toward the departure escalator. Sam followed.

Anna was giving Mary her patient-you-don't-understand-cybermagic look.

"I've located The Alchemy School here in California," she said with satisfaction, ignoring Mary's combination of cough and groan.

She continued. "The Symposium begins in five days," she said. "Cookie Mac is keynote speaker and has sent a box of books on ahead. These may hold the Alchemy Scroll. I'll get to it."

Well, she was *almost* confiding in Mary. There was only about ninety miles between the locker at LAX and The Alchemy School in the hills above Santa Emilia.

"It won't take all three of us to follow the Prof..." began Sam, forgetting his resolution not to get between the dangerous young woman and the scary old one. Mary scowled at his unhelpfulness. Meanwhile, Anna simply folded her arms. What was Anna up to? Mary drew in her last card.

195

"Anna, what about Caroline? I know you rescued her and Janet, from the fire. Another woman too. With Caroline's poor health, she must be traumatized. Anyone would be, depression or not."

Asking about Caroline did not go as Mary expected. The air around Anna bruised. She moved her hands across her face. Something wasn't right.

"How *is* Caroline? Mary insisted. "You haven't said. I've been very worried. Being stuck in The Old Hospital is quite an ordeal." Anna flashed her eyes angrily; she turned away.

"Anna? What haven't you told me?"

"Who's Caroline?"

"*Shut up, Sam,*" snapped both women. They glared at each other. Mary was reminded of Western gunfighters, fingers hovering nervously over their holsters.

"Ahm… I'll just be over here." The women ignored Sam. "Don't hang about, Miss Wandwalker," he called over his backpack hump.

Mary's frown raked Anna's face. She found something she wasn't expecting — a bleakness.

"Caroline is fine. She's at Holywell. She likes it there. I can't return to England just now. As well as Cookie Mac's box, I must… I must…"

"Have to *what?*" It came out sharper than Mary intended. Anna seemed to be about to open up. Then she gave the tiniest shake of the head.

"Mary don't forget the other suspects. On the site of the Alchemy School were the registrations for the Symposium."

Anna warmed up. Mary wasn't getting it. "Delegates from Oxford, from St. Julian's College. That Dame Eleanor, Godric St. John and Ravi Patel have all registered in the last forty-eight hours. And that's not all. I got into the payments; they were all paid for by Mer-Corp." At that name, she got Mary's attention.

"That name again; Mer-Corp holds the mortgages at St. Julian's. They want Cookie Mac to verify the Alchemy Scroll.

I'd forgotten he has two reasons for going to the UK, Janet, and the College. Something's going on."

"Did you read the reports I uploaded to you two days ago?" Anna was on sure ground that Mary hadn't. They came to over three hundred pages. "As well as being a huge pharmaceutical business, Mer-Corp's the biggest annual donor to that Los Angeles museum where you found the Alchemy Scroll."

"Where the murder took place." Mary's mind was buzzing. "Anyone from the museum going to the Symposium?" Anna took out her phone and scrolled down.

"Dr. Melissa Oldcastle, Director, from The Los Angeles Museum of Early Manuscripts."

"I met her. You're right, this is important," said Mary, playing for time. "But I still don't see…"

"Mer-Corp," said Anna with brooding patience. "It's turning up in too many places. I *have* to have more time to break the firewall. Particularly," she said significantly, indicating Sam waving at them, "particularly to find any links to your European History fascists. At the same time, I can search Cookie Mac's box at The Alchemy School. No, Mary." Anna put up a hand. "Don't ask me about Caroline. She'll tell you herself."

Mary resigned herself to running to make the flight. She wasn't fooled. Anna wasn't telling her everything, this was evident. However, Anna had a point that their suspect pool could not be limited to Cookie Mac. Mary gave her young colleague her best "this-isn't-over" look, then picked up the handle of her roller bag. Sam was beckoning frantically. Mary made up her mind.

"All right, Anna. Since our suspects will be heading to California, it makes sense for you to stay until Caroline and I can join you. Where exactly is this Alchemy School?"

"Ninety miles north of LA, in the hills above Santa Emilia. They have spaces available for the Symposium, so I'll book us in. Does that mean him too?" She jerked her thumb at the disappearing back of Sam.

"Him too. I must run. I'll be in touch from the UK. Be very careful, Anna. Do *not* let Americans like Homeland Security catch you doing cyber-spells. *Ever*. I mean that."

Mary felt a tug on her arm. Sam had darted back. "Gotta go," he said, pulling her toward the departure gate escalator. Mary started to trot with him.

"Oh, one more thing," called Anna.

"No time. Email me," yelled Mary. "All right, Sam, I'm coming." Mary looked back over her shoulder for Anna. She was nowhere to be seen.

CHAPTER 28
BETRAYAL

After Mary and Sam ran for the Departures Gate, Anna did not go far. Jetlag never bothered her. Her raging headache was from another assault on her body. She went in search of sugar from the most immediate source: candy. Cakes, cookies, and chocolates were her way of blocking out memories. Afterward, she would ruthlessly starve herself, so that her body remained a fine-tuned instrument of her will.

Caroline knew. Caroline's problem with food was obvious. It was a war she lost every time she tried to diet, unlike Anna. Once Caroline found Anna eating bar after bar of chocolate alone in their bedroom, silver foil and paper scattered like leaves. The look of ferocity she received made her back out at once.

Eating to dull pain in public was like stripping naked. In fact, removing her clothes would have bothered Anna not at all. She went straight into the nearest Starbucks for a caramel latte and began chugging it down. Given what she was about to do, she was glad that she'd left it for when it was too late to tell Mary about Cookie Mac's passage through LAX.

Let Mary and Caroline get entangled with him in the UK. The fuss over his connection to Janet Swinford would give Anna cover. It would keep Mary busy. Although she and Caroline remained estranged, it was Mary's suspicious nature that Anna feared. Caroline was her lover, after all.

Or was she? After the painful outcome of Caroline's sojourn in The Old Hospital, could Anna depend on her? Could she

199

count on Caroline's affection to outweigh well... her outrage at Anna's methods?

Anna swirled around the last inch of sugary drink with her finger, blending the caramel, coffee, and milk into a silky sludge. She was surprised how much the rift with Caroline hurt. Scrunching her paper napkin into her fist, she thrust her chin up to swallow the last sugar hit. The buzz in her blood did not solve her problems.

"Addiction," Mary had unkindly put it when the cake supply had mysteriously turned into a handful of crumbs and a lone raisin. In response, Anna snarled that she'd been too young for hard drugs when first trafficked into prostitution.

Control of child prostitutes rarely involved drugging them because they too easily died, she explained in short hard words. Anna was fully trained by the time her abused body could tolerate such extreme measures, or so her keepers thought.

Perhaps she'd order another caramel drink to sweeten what she was about to do. For she was about to betray the Agency, betray Mary and Caroline.

If they could only make it work, Mary used to say. If the Agency could become a container for something neither Anna nor Mary had known before: a family. Now, without Caroline depending on her, Anna was alone. It did not taste good. There were voices inside: I am risking everything; *I could lose everything*. Too bad, she said with some of the bravado of the old days.

Opening Cookie Mac's locker was second nature to someone with Anna's past. She whipped out the wrapped cylinder and glided from the terminal, elegant and unnoticed. Only one security guard followed her, taking photographs on his phone. He thought she was some celebrity in disguise.

Outside, Anna barely noticed that it had stopped snowing and that the temperature was rising rapidly to normal. She sat in the taxi like foreign royalty. Unlike Mary, she did not listen to the driver's exclamations about climate change and the rumor of a wildfire in the mountains. In the hotel, the young woman rested the cylinder on the huge bed. Unwrapping the brown paper, she found that the tube was made of leather and had a lock.

Anna set to work with her picklocks — another item from the old days. Fortunately, she could disguise them from security screens by folding them, so they became the spines of her elaborate handbag. Lifting the cylinder lid, she pulled out a white bath towel with something hard inside.

Anna hesitated. The Alchemy Scroll had been stolen from the museum here in Los Angeles shortly after Mary and that young man's brother had found it. That the brother was dead, probably because of the theft, Anna knew.

"So much blood," Mary had said. Although Anna had seen death, she was not indifferent to it. For a moment, Sam's strained face haunted her. She tasted salt; it brought her to Leni's tears and the trafficked girl's terror in the prison cell.

Anna unwrapped the towel slowly, coming to a cardboard tube smelling of incense. She placed it carefully on the bed. There was something about wearing gloves if the Alchemy Scroll was not being used to heal. She slipped on leather mittens she'd purchased in the airport gift shop, (a replica of those used for wrangling horses), and ever so gently eased out the velum. Without taking a breath, she began to unroll it.

Yes, here were astonishing colors and animals wilder than any cinematic dragons. Layers clung to each other, suggesting they were anointed with oils in some distant past. The smell of spices grew more intense.

It was dizzying, that a riot of color: flying creatures with silver and gold wings in an azure sky. Mountains were speckled with bearlike animals, some dancing. Over them were great birds wheeling around a crescent moon.

She turned to the strange writing. Definitely spells, she decided. Unrolling further, a red man and a pearl woman embraced in a glittering pool with a star above their crowned heads. Here a distinctive perfume, more like a modern fragrance, began to rise from the book.

Anna bent closer to the vellum. Her loose hair fell onto the surface page forming a black cloud around the figures. Suddenly, she jumped back, grabbing her long hair to shake it free of the odors. Not working. Rushing to the musty bathroom, she gagged at the mold in the shower, then tipped her toiletries bag onto the floor to retrieve her emergency supply of shampoo. Over the sink, she washed her hair and scrubbed her neck with grim efficiency.

Returning to the bed, now a shrine to the Scroll, Anna stood a step away. She had never been alone with something this old, this precious. Remembering tales of miraculous powers and seeing the golden serpent breathing within the vellum, Anna was moved by its magic.

"Don't harm me," she whispered. "I will treat you well."

The Alchemy Scroll is alive, she felt. It quivered with magic reinforced by the devotion of generations of Holywell Key Keepers, like Janet. Or not like Janet, she remembered. Janet's Alchemy Scroll was the seventeenth-century copy. Nevertheless, this Scroll had hundreds of years at St Julian's. The Alchemy Scroll is a ghost of those who treasured it, thought Anna. She thought she heard whispers from muttered prayers. Anna knew fear.

"The witches of Oxfordshire shall keep the Key," she whispered.

PART SIX
FERMENTATIO

CHAPTER 29
ANNA WITH THE SCROLL

The next day Anna decided to take a train north to the coastal city of Santa Emilia. It was the nearest she could get to The Alchemy School without hiring a car. Although she could drive, she did not like American freeways. Plus, traveling by train gave her time before making decisions that were irrevocable. Everyone wanted the Alchemy Scroll. There was Godric St. John's blackmail over Leni, Mer-Corp, good for a hefty sum, reckoned Anna. Cookie Mac had friends with deep pockets; and yes, Mary Wandwalker and St. Julian's.

While Anna cared nothing for that heap of stones, she knew the depth of Mary and Caroline's commitment to their Agency. Failure to recover the Alchemy Scroll meant the Agency might not survive. No Agency — here Anna struggled to understand — no agency meant no family. The three of them would go their own ways.

Together with Caroline's fury over the fire at The Old Hospital, Anna saw Mary's stormy grey eyes. Why would Mary reject a huge sum extorted from Mer-Corp in favor of handing the Alchemy Scroll back to the impoverished college? How, how *strange* Mary was. Unless, unless...

Anna kept moving, as if she could escape what she'd done. Striding into the pillared elegance of Los Angeles Central Station, even here Caroline's accusations haunted her.

"*I started the fire to get you out*," Anna howled internally for the fortieth time. Caroline's stern face never wavered. Would she and Caroline ever be lovers again?

205

Anna clenched her teeth and climbed the train's steps. Behind her, the guard heaved up the suitcase containing the Scroll, before getting back on board. She snatched the handle and dragged it down the mainly empty carriage. Whistles blew. With sulky abandon, Anna shoved her luggage under a seat by a window and sat down opposite it.

Impersonating a regular passenger, Anna removed a container of tea from the small brown bag she had been given at the station kiosk. Her hand was not quite steady as she sipped the hot liquid. It tasted plastic. Staring into the clear evening light as Los Angeles slipped away, she made herself return to the imaginary conversation. How would it go if all was well between the three women of the Agency?

"My cyber hacking is contemporary alchemy."

Anna's research online had resulted in this epiphany. Hacking dissolves one machine into another. Networks are soluble. Each one has a different voice or tone, like living beings in cyberspace. Hackers *talk* to them, ask them to do more than usual stuff.

"Helps you steal things," Mary would say with her divided soul. Her criticism would not be as disapproving as she wanted it to be.

"It's cyberlove," Anna wanted Caroline to say, with glee. But Caroline wasn't talking to her since the fire. Her reproaches kept seeping through.

"How could you take such risks with other people's lives. How *could* you, Anna? How could *you*?"

Anna stared at the suburbs retreating into the setting sun. A shopping mall with a near-empty parking lot was lit up, trying to woo customers off their internet habits. Little chance of that, even with the ice melting on the streets. Anna reopened the brown bag to remove a ubiquitous American sandwich, a wodge of salty turkey, one slimy leaf, and a yellow square remotely related to cheese.

As Mary would see it, she thought as she unwrapped the plastic. With a grimace, she took a bite that necessitated opening

206

her jaws as wide as a snake swallowing a rabbit. If her digestion did not revolt in the hours ahead, she would be bouncing off servers up and down the California coast.

Which website first? Mary wanted her to get into the European History Foundation. Although part of that shady crew, Cookie Mac deserved his own deep trawl, as would the other suspects. Anna stretched her scarlet shoes to rest on the dusty suitcase.

"Do you use the Dark Web, Anna?"

The voice was Caroline's two months ago. She'd been watching Euro-TV, a show about agents chasing cybercrime across the continent. At Caroline's question, Mary paused in the doorway with the tea tray. She'd stiffened. That meant Anna could not use the tricks of a lover to deflect the inquiry.

"Never," she said, not turning around. "No Dark Web." She glued her eyes to the keyboard where her fingers danced. Mary put the tea tray down and coughed. The room subtly shifted.

"Anna?" That was Mary.

"Mary?" That was Caroline.

How could Anna explain? She did not want to admit, would *not* admit, to certain things.

"Cyberhackers don't need the Dark Web." Too long a pause.

"We're asking you," said Mary, pointedly.

Anna stopped typing. She wore a plait down her back over a magenta blouse. Clearing her throat, she snaked her hand behind to the red ribbon. Pulling it off, she shook her hair until it flickered with sparks. She began typing again.

"I don't use the Dark Web now," she said expressionlessly. "It's very dangerous. Stuff can...can get out."

"Quite," said Mary. "Would you like some tea, Anna?"

"Not just now."

"Just Caroline and I then."

CHAPTER 30
OVER WATER, BACK TO EARTH

Of all forms of travel, Mary hated overnight flying the most. It was all right for those who could afford the obese luxury of first class. What with beds, unlimited alcohol, exotic food, the latest movies, blankets, hot towels, and the equivalent of country house staff, you could forget the endless hours and nasty smell in the toilets. Very few of her lovers had such forgiving expense accounts.

By contrast, she and Sam were crammed into a row of tiny seats at the back of the economy cabin. There Sam fidgeted while trying to fit his long legs into about six inches of space. Thank you, Anna. Mary winced as they were served cold reconstituted mashed potatoes with grey-looking meat, orange gravy, and a slice of tomato. With this came a chocolate biscuit packaged to look like a dessert.

In mute appeal, Sam pointed to the pay-for-drinks menu. His lost puppy expression was too much for Mary. Sighing, she promptly doubled their orders: Sam for American beer, herself for several tiny bottles of fiery red wine.

She could never sleep on planes. At least Sam's consumption of beer helped him stop kicking Mary's freezing ankles. Sam found a film about zombies on the tiny monitor, while Mary stabbed appropriate areas of her screen and found an old British soap opera.

Halfway through the third episode, a massive thump on her left side caused her elbow to crash into the table, spilling the last drops of wine. It was sleeping Sam toppling over. Mary extricated herself and propped Sam up. Then he began a full-throated snoring.

Mary shut her eyes. It was going to be a long night. She slid down in her seat and returned to the charmingly dysfunctional family. Their problems got solved every twenty-five minutes, just in time for the Ad break. Perhaps she could pick up tips.

After nine hours of dodging Sam's elbows and shifting shoulders, Mary thrilled to Heathrow's baggy clouds. Even though the white sunshine drilled into her skull as they tramped the endless corridors of Terminal Three, she could silently cheer that their passports worked at the E-Gates.

Steering Sam through the "Nothing to Declare" cave that was Customs, they almost fell through the last doors into the Arrivals atrium. A towering wall of glass dazzled. The elevators were glass too, rising and falling as if through water. On the marble floor were weary taxi drivers holding out placards, like fishing nets.

Mary could barely keep her eyes open as she scanned for coffee.

"Over here, Sam," she grunted.

Arriving at the Costa Coffee shop, she and Sam saw a short round woman in jeans and a none-too-clean rust-brown sweater.

"Caroline, thank God," said Mary.

"Coffee," grunted Sam, ignoring Caroline and lurching for the counter.

To Caroline's surprise and pleasure, Mary grabbed the younger woman in a hug. "I've been so worried about you. Anna wouldn't tell me what The Old Hospital was like. There was a fire?"

A shadow crossed Caroline's features. Then she smiled a real smile at Mary, who noticed the strain around her eyes. Caroline grabbed Mary's roller bag.

"You must be exhausted. That's your double cappuccino on that table over here, next to my coat."

Mary made for the sweet vista. Caroline sat opposite with plain black coffee. Mary recognized the thrift store coat.

Caroline insisted on buying clothes for next to nothing "until my weight stabilizes." She was always trying to diet, and it never seemed to work. Mary suspected the side effects of whatever antidepressant she was trying.

Caroline began brightly. "Is that young man Sam? I am so sorry, Mary. About the murder and all you've been through."

Mary tried to smile. No, coffee first. She scalded her tongue on the first sip. A male voice broke in.

"Um, Miss Wandwalker, have you got any pounds? They won't take my American money." Sam looked disgusted.

Mary choked and put down the cup.

"Ah, Caroline, do you have any cash for Sam? I'm down to a few pennies."

"Of course." Caroline went rooting around in her new handbag. Given to her by Anna, the stylish bag (hopefully a knockoff) was grubby from the trunk of the car.

"Here's a fiver," she said cheerfully, holding out a folded piece of green paper.

Sam took the money, "Er, Thank you," he said. He stared at the crowd of morose travelers desperate for stimulants. Sam hunched his shoulders and prepared to do battle.

Meanwhile, Caroline was sipping her coffee with a dissatisfied expression and studying Mary.

"Have some of this milk," said Mary. "It'll help when you want to go for the biscuit tin later." Caroline gave a rueful grin and held out her cup.

"I'll get you another coffee."

"Yes, you will." Mary took another swallow and began to feel slightly human. "First, tell me about Janet. Is she feeling better? Back at Holywell? Has Anna been in touch about Cookie Mac?"

Caroline looked remote.

"I mean recently, in the last couple of hours?" continued Mary. "What's he doing here bothering Janet?"

Caroline picked up her cup and ran her finger around the inside rim. Her green eyes glinted at Mary.

211

"Janet's okay. After a couple of nights in a motel, she insisted on going back to Holywell. Anna had left for the airport. I took Janet home. We'll see her later."

Mary's head swam. Oh yes, jetlag: like being hit over the head with a brick. Yet, Mary recognized that Caroline was being evasive. She had not replied to the question about Anna, had she?

"Caroline, I thought *Anna* was the one for games..."

Mary's grip on her empty cup was covered by Caroline's cool fingers.

"Sorry, sorry, Mary. I've never flown to the States, so I don't know what it's like. No. Janet's gone back to Holywell because Professor Cuchulain Macdonald claims to be her long-lost cousin. She wants to meet him with maximum moral support. That's us."

Mary's jaw dropped.

"Long-lost *cousin*? she queried. What's he after?"

"The Alchemy Scroll Key, probably," Caroline began. "Now that he's got the Scroll, we think. That's Janet's assumption. However, she's sensitive about family, so agreed to meet him."

"This coffee tastes different," The table jolted as Sam jerked a chair so violently that it wobbled everything.

"Welcome home, Sam," said Caroline, twinkling at him. Mary held out her cup in mute appeal.

It would be a two hours' drive to Holywell, Caroline reckoned. She glanced at the two arrivals. Sam Murphy stared around the Terminal, as if unsure what country he was in. Mary Wandwalker had her head on the table. That meant she was fast asleep.

PART SEVEN
AUGMENTIO

CHAPTER 31
REUNION AT HOLYWELL

The next day at Holywell, Dorothy frowned at Mary in the pre-dawn kitchen. Sitting at the Formica table, Mary screwed up her eyes under the merciless overhead neon. She put her head in her hands. Dorothy banged a huge kettle on the stove to get Mary's attention.

"We had a gathering last night."

Mary opened one eye, saw reproach, and shut it again.

Dorothy raised her voice. "We met to decide if your Sam Murphy could be here at Holywell. Caroline vouched for you and said you vouched for Sam. However, Miss Wandwalker, you should have warned us. You should have asked permission"

Mary began to understand. "Sam? Ah, I'm sorry, Dorothy. Okay, he can go to his family's house in London."

That was a problem. Mary hastened to explain. "You see, I promised his mother I'd keep an eye on him. Until they can bring D.P. home for the funeral, his parents are stuck in Los Angeles."

Mary paused. The implications of bringing Sam to Holywell began to burn in her cheeks.

"Dammit, I didn't think about how the trafficked girls would react to a young man"

"No, *you* didn't think," said Dorothy, uncompromising. "Fortunately, Caroline did. She talked to us about Sam's grief. Then we gathered the young women. At first, they were shocked and scared. Caroline told Sam's story. She'd pointed out to us

215

witches that we want our women to acclimatize to young men of Sam's age. They will be fellow students at St. Julian's"

Mary got to her feet and swayed, grabbing the table for support. *She* had retraumatized trafficking victims. "I'll take him away this morning," she managed to articulate. "I'm so sorry. I'm not as good at this enquiry business as I thought." She choked.

In response, Dorothy began to relax. She waved Mary back to her chair.

"No, Miss Wandwalker, Sam can stay for a few days. On a trial basis, you understand. Janet backed up Caroline by saying that Sam was part of an investigation that included her kidnapping. Naomi came in having grilled Sam to within an inch of his life. She's made him understand more about human trafficking than he ever wanted to." Dorothy almost smiled.

"Plus, Linda and John did a few scrying spells. They said Sam's aura was gentle questing, but what really turned it…" Dorothy turned around to light the gas under the kettle,"

"Yes? What really turned it?" Mary found her knuckles on her lips.

"What really turned it was Leni. Out on bail, she reminded us that the charges against her are inflated by prejudice. Sam too has suffered from prejudice, as well as from the death of his brother. You see, Caroline shared from your emails. So, Leni said that since your Agency is helping her, she would give back a bit of trust. To Sam." Dorothy grimaced.

"You have no idea, Miss Wandwalker, how important those words are to Holywell. If the trafficked women can learn trust, to distinguish between those out to exploit them and those they can relate to, then our therapy is succeeding."

May blinked. "I'm so glad."

"Trial basis," repeated Dorothy, firmly. "We need to talk about Leni. What exactly happened with Anna in the police cell?"

"Not sure yet," murmured Mary. Her heart still beat too fast from this nerve-wracking conversation. "I will check with Anna."

"She's innocent of those charges. There's even talk of upping them to attempted murder. Godric St. John is up to something.

"Very probably," muttered Mary. Her throat was parched.

"What are you going to do about it?" Dorothy demanded.

The big kettle on the stove began to gurgle. It was 5:30 a.m.; Mary had been awake for an hour; guilt is exhausting.

"I expect you'll want coffee," said Dorothy, resigned.

"Not right now, my stomach feels peculiar," said Mary, still trying to recall details of Leni's arrest. Anna told her remarkably little about her visit to Leni's cell, she realized.

"I'm making tea," said Dorothy. "I've not been sleeping. With the girls restless, I wake early."

She switched off the gas, then addressed Mary's dazed expression. "Leni's assault charge is bad enough. It also puts at risk our plan for the trafficked women to become St. Julian students," she said, leaning back against the cupboards.

"Yeah, I see that. Tea's fine. Anna visited Leni ... last week?"

"That's right. I don't know what Anna said to her. She was very tight-lipped. However, I do know Leni was calmer afterward. Pass me the tea bags from the shelf above your head." Mary rose automatically.

"I haven't had a chance to get a proper report from Anna," she said, subsiding into the chair at the kitchen table. "Not about her visit to Oxford police station. Except I know she went to see Godric St. John too. He insisted on it. They must have discussed Leni."

"*He* laid the charges against her," said Dorothy frowning. "Assault, attempted theft, and more. She's so thin; a victim, not a criminal. It's a nightmare."

Dorothy bashed tea bags as if she could see St. John's face at the bottom of the huge teapot.

217

"So sorry," said Mary again, accepting a mug of tea. She gulped down a couple of mouthfuls. Miraculously, her head began to clear.

"Yes, okay, Dorothy. We should have reported back to you before now," she said. Her eyes focused properly for the first time since the flight. She felt bad. *I should have been more careful about the trafficked women*, she said to herself. *I could kick myself for bringing Sam to Holywell. Yet, I know Dorothy wants practical solutions not breast-beating.*

"I will get on to Anna and make a proper plan," Mary announced, putting her empty mug in the kitchen sink. "Don't worry, I'll find out about Anna's meeting at St. Julian's."

"Today, please," said Dorothy. Her steel met Mary's dignity, and she relaxed. Mary began to mentally organize the next few hours. *Nothing on her phone, Anna is being even more difficult than usual.* Mary's delicate stomach developed a knot.

"Look, Dorothy, do understand the complexities. It's not just Leni; it never was. Whatever's going on at St. Julian's and Godric St. John is related to the Scroll *and* to the kidnapping of Janet."

Mary's tired brain dragged up items gleaned from yesterday's car journey with Caroline and Sam.

"You know Janet could not identify her captors. Not only was she drugged, but Caroline says she has no idea who forged the transfer to The Old Hospital."

Dorothy sat down again, her expression troubled. Mary continued.

"At least Janet's back here at Holywell. She's told you what happened. Caroline Jones risked her life to find her. There was a fire, you know."

Dorothy sighed and refilled her mug from the giant teapot. She pointed the spout at Mary who shook her head, then wished she hadn't.

"Janet's never been chatty, but this was different," Dorothy admitted. "She's told us about escaping the hospital through dense smoke. What a terrifying ordeal. She'll need time to recover."

Dorothy's smile was wan. "Of course, we're very grateful to the Depth Enquiry Agency for rescuing Janet. Although starting a fire to do so, seems well... extreme."

Mary looked away. She too felt horror at what Caroline had relayed in the car. Now she wished Janet had been discreet about Anna's methods. Dorothy did not need to continue. She and Mary understood each other very well.

"Yes, um, Anna," muttered Mary.

"Quite," returned Dorothy.

*****

A couple of hours later Caroline, Mary and Sam went to find Janet Swinford in her vegetable garden. Sam followed Mary with a lost puppy look. To him, Holywell was strange to the point of uncanny, she realized. Mary's ears hurt from loud exclamations by witches and trafficked teenagers over breakfast. As for Sam, after a few scowls in his direction, the young women ignored him, chattering in several languages. They ran around to seize boxes of cereal or dip spoons into the bucket of porridge on the stove.

Unlike the teenagers in denims and bright sweatshirts, the witches were sartorially diverse. Chinese Linda had a brilliant scarlet silk jacket over jeans, with a jade and gold dragon over her back. Cherry, adding raisins to her bowl, had a spattered striped apron in navy and white that almost grazed her shoes. Mary was greeted shyly by Naomi, who wore a charcoal robe with blue embroidery. Stitches matched the sky-blue ribbon that threaded through the silver plait down her back.

Janet, on the other hand, wasn't in the kitchen at all. After Caroline enquired of Dorothy, wearing a pinstriped wool blazer (visiting Leni's solicitor, she said), Janet was agreed by the witches to be outside.

219

"Already?" one of the Congolese women wondered. That's probably Sarah, thought Mary.

"Janet likes her own company," muttered Linda as she spread homemade jam on buttered toast.

"And being in her garden," agreed Naomi. "She pretty much lives outside during summer."

"It's not summer," said Mary, tart.

Linda grinned. "Janet's catching up. Most of her friends are things she grows, you know."

Caroline skipped breakfast. Mary made a mental note to ask about the inevitable diet. Sam shoved in soggy cornflakes and pulled a face at the milky tea. His eyes never left his spoon in the four minutes he gave to breakfast. Was it the witches, or the trafficked women, that most spooked him? wondered Mary.

Driving from the airport, Caroline tried to prepare him for Holywell. She'd described the counseling work, emphasizing the benign character of its witchcraft. Sam's jaw dropped at the word "witch."

Mary reflected that Sam's image of the "craft" was likely to owe more to Disney's malicious hags than to Caroline's wise women as Keepers of the Key to the Alchemy Scroll. No wonder Sam shifted nervously from foot to foot while waiting for Mary to finish breakfast. He darted out of the door as Caroline approached. Mary put her mug down and followed.

They walked into a still morning with few clouds. Early sun softened the remains of frost. Mary looked up to trees misting green against hills dotted with sheep. Caroline led past the ancient well to the extensive vegetable beds. Tiny dandelions and thistles poked above the glistening soil as they approached Janet stomping about in Wellingtons and a muddy raincoat, pulling fiercely at the weeds. Mary got straight to the point.

"Please stop a minute, Janet. I know we only met last night but I must ask. After all you've been, though, why let Professor Macdonald come here to see you?"

Mary meant to pierce the wool in her own head by the crisp interrogation. It was not well received by Janet. The rescued

220

witch muttered curses at the bindweed tearing her raw fingers. She turned her back on Mary and resumed weeding.

Caroline shook her head at her friend. She'd noticed that Janet's hair had been trimmed and dyed to match the bits of color she'd seen in The Old Hospital. Taking a deep lungful of the scent of turned earth, Caroline touched Janet on the arm.

"Your hair looks nice. Do come and sit with us, Janet. For a moment."

Janet sniffed and gave a grudging nod. After one last pull on a dandelion root, she followed Caroline to a nearby bench. It formed a pentagon around a huge oak tree. Caroline beckoned Mary. She hesitated over Sam several meters away staring back at the house.

"Um, Sam, why don't you go back to the kitchen and help with the dishes. They don't have a dishwasher."

Sam looked beseechingly at Mary. She tilted her head. He sighed and headed back in a reluctant lope.

"How is Agnes doing?" Caroline said confidentially to Janet.

Agnes? Then Mary recalled the old woman rescued along with Caroline and Janet. A friend, Caroline had said, with no further details.

"Still in the Geriatric Ward," said Janet to Caroline. "If they can't find any relatives, and the doctors agree, I'll ask if she can live here. She'd like the garden."

Mary could wait no longer. "The police are still investigating your... your abduction?"

"Yeah." Janet gripped her knees. It was obvious she wanted to be left alone.

"Do you feel safe now?" Caroline again, hand on Janet's arm. Mary sat on Janet's other side.

Janet sniffed. "*He* sent me letters, that Macdonald. Well, photocopies anyway. Found them waiting for me when I came back. Family letters. I must see him. Here is safest."

"Cookie Mac had your family letters?" Caroline knew Mary wanted to be sure of details.

"Humph. Says we have Scottish connections. It could be. I remember family talk." Janet spoke gruffly, realigning her body to include both Caroline and Mary.

"The letters he sent are real old. Early eighteenth century, he said. They are from a mother in England to her son in the Connecticut colony. The name is Hepzibah Janet Macdonald."

"And that was enough to convince you?" Mary tried to keep her tone neutral. She failed.

"No," said Janet shortly. There was a pause.

"Dorothy says he'll be here at 10 a.m. today," said Caroline conversationally. "You know he's a murder suspect for that poor boy in Los Angeles. We think Cookie Mac stole the St. Julian's Scroll. *Your* Scroll."

"The Alchemy Scroll," muttered Janet. Then slowly, "The healing Scroll. Yes. I'd like to see the real one." Mary sensed Janet quiver with energy.

"We believe he has it," she said, encouragingly. "We want to get it back. St. Julian's commissioned our Agency to do that, as well as find you. You know St. Julian's is in a financial crisis?"

Ignoring the reference to the College, Janet dug one callused hand into her army fatigues, drawing out a handful of sepia photographs of family groups. Some were of individual children with corrugated sheds and farm animals in the background.

"Family, his family," she said. "Not eighteenth century, of course. These are about one hundred years old." She knelt on damp grass, laying out the images.

"This one." She pointed to a small fair-haired boy grasping an adult sized pitchfork as tall as he was. "You see...?" Janet gazed at Caroline with intensity. There was something she did not want to put into words. Mary began to wish she had not accompanied Caroline into the garden.

"Oh, oh, yes, I see." Caroline touched the sepia image with her fingertips, then took Janet's hand. "It's Jim, isn't it? This boy in the old photograph looks like your brother Jim. This must be an early twentieth century Macdonald."

222

Mary knew this story from Caroline's emails. Jim was Janet's brother who died. She saw him die on the streets of London. Mary stood up. She spoke quietly.

"Would you like to see Cookie Mac alone, Miss Swinford?"

Janet began to collect the photographs as Mary went on. "We'd like to talk to him too, but this is your meeting. Perhaps we can question him after you've talked."

Still kneeling with indifference to damp, Janet surveyed her garden.

"Caroline can be with me," she said. She concentrated on a crow balancing delicately on a beech branch.

"Fair enough," said Mary, gamely. "I need to contact Anna, anyway.

CHAPTER 32
PIZZA AFTER THE STORM

Days later, all involved agreed that Cookie Mac's visit traumatized everyone at Holywell. Even though only Janet and Caroline experienced him firsthand, his tantrums seeped through stone walls. His rage and hysteria flamed so much anxiety that the young women were dispatched to their bedrooms, where they huddled together. Mary smelled cigarette smoke.

As the shouting got worse, Mary and Dorothy exchanged horrified glances and moved to intervene. Fortunately, at that moment Cookie Mac flounced out. Snarling at Dorothy, he flung open the front door and continued yelling until he slammed the door on his hire car. Mary saw the unfortunate vehicle leap into the air at every bump on the muddy track that led away from Holywell.

Wide-eyed, Mary and Dorothy found Janet weeping in Caroline's arms. The younger woman nodded reassuringly, so Mary pulled Dorothy away.

"Marvelous woman, your Caroline," muttered Dorothy, before ducking into the kitchen to reassure the other witches. Surprised, Mary found herself nodding.

Dorothy decided to declare a pizza night, a treat for the trafficked women. She was set on a return to the normal rituals of Holywell. A pile of insulated boxes arrived in a van from Oxford. After the emotional storms of the morning, the atmosphere of relief felt almost festive.

After casting a calming spell, Dorothy chatted with Mary over dinner as if a murder suspect and Scroll stealer had not

225

stormed off the premises with threats and curses. Although the witches preferred vegetarian soup, tonight they would dig into the girls' favorite dishes. They are family, Dorothy said, not inmates.

Mary and Dorothy observed from one end of the long dining table. The young women clustered at the other, where most of the pizza boxes were piled up. Sam sat next to Leni, back from jail pending her trial. On his other side was Sojourner. Mary could just catch a few words. He shared some unusual ingredients of American pizza. On "pulled pork," the young women giggled.

"Are the girls feeling better after today's... erm, disruption?" said Mary under her breath to Dorothy. Naomi answered.

"The *women* aren't fazed by racists like Cookie Mac," she said, with determination. "They've had treatment like that for as long as they can remember."

"And I," said Caroline, with a brave smile, "don't mind being called a 'dumpy little nothing.'" Mary winced. Getting angry would help no one. Nevertheless, she was about to give a forthright summation of Cookie Mac when Janet spoke, spare and sad.

"That man is no family of mine."

The women around Janet grew still. Like a stone in a pond, the ripples spread until even the teenagers shot understanding glances. Janet rose, moving a couple of empty boxes to the sideboard. She picked up two plates of Holywell's apples stored from last October.

The last word had been spoken on Cookie Mac. Mary and Caroline exchanged nods. Slipping away from the table, they made for the room they shared upstairs.

"I'll bring you up some tea," called Linda as they closed the door.

"Are you really all right?" said Mary tentatively. Caroline gave a hollow chuckle.

They sat opposite each other on the two single beds. Each had a colorful patchwork quilt of many fabrics, from jersey to silk. Caroline told Mary they'd been made by the young women as part of their art therapy.

"That man," Caroline began. "He thought he could bully Janet. That didn't work. I couldn't have stood up to him like she did."

"Yes, you could have," said Mary firmly. "Tell me more. You didn't have a chance to go into details earlier. Cookie Mac's a suspect, remember, for murder and theft. Anything he let drop could be a clue."

Caroline sat up to rack her memory. "He said the Museum Director showed him the Alchemy Scroll a week before the murder. That night he went back to check it was genuine if you can believe that."

Caroline looked as skeptical as Mary.

"I don't think that's why he was creeping around at night. More likely planning to steal the Alchemy Scroll for himself. I wonder how he got in," muttered Mary.

"He didn't say. But he mentioned a Museum trustee being a fraternity brother. What's that?"

"Ah," said Mary sagely. "An American university thing. I'll explain later. Go on about the night of the murder. It was good of Janet to question him on it."

"She said the Key Keeper would not allow murdering hands on the Alchemy Scroll. Okay, Cookie Mac admitted going up to the attics near the time D.P. was killed. All he found was the empty chest, he said. He left, planning to return the next day and confront Director Oldcastle about the theft. That's when you met him."

"Lying bastard. He left D.P. lying there. Did he even check to see if he was dead?"

"He said he did not see any body. It was dark."

"No, it wasn't. Not only would he take a torch, but he's so obsessed with the Scroll and his rights that he'd switch on the lights. He left D.P. in a pool of blood."

Mary gave a shuddering breath. The vision of D.P. in his own blood fired her insides. Caroline extended her hand. Mary brushed it away, angry again. Sighing, Caroline lay back in the bed and continued describing Cookie Mac's charm offensive.

"Red-eyed from jetlag, he burst upon Holywell barely noticing the watchfulness of its inhabitants. Smelling of those cheap rental cars, he anticipated triumph. Thus, he greeted Janet." Caroline had memorized every word:

"My long-lost cousin, a delight to find you at this... this commune. What an exquisite coincidence that we are both engaged in care of the Alchemy Scroll? My dear Miss Swinford, I, Professor of Alchemy, am the expert summoned to confirm St. Julian's Hall's loan. You, my newfound relation, have an intimate knowledge of its secrets. Key keeper and Alchemy scholar, together at last. I know you will help me in my research."

Mary felt sick. "How did Janet react?"

"Told him she would never reveal its secrets. I thought he'd leave when she was so firm, but it turns out he had a second reason for his visit. At first, Janet was pleased he asked about her family. Unfortunately, those photographs he sent are all he has. Unlike Janet, Cookie Mac has no stories from earlier generations. His parents are dead, and he is estranged from the rest. Later we could guess why."

"So, what made him seek her out now? Did he always know the Alchemy Scroll connection to the Key Keeper?"

"Worse than that." Caroline tensed. Mary saw that she did not want to say it, but she would. "Cookie Mac let slip that tracing family was an idea from The European History Foundation. He'd been ignoring me, so I asked if the EHF wanted to trace early American alchemists, like Francis Andrew Ransome. It was obvious from how he reacted that they cared about... something else."

Mary was puzzled. Then she looked disgusted. "I get it. They're white supremacists. I bet they wanted to know if he had nonwhite relatives. He wanted to check Janet's records. After all, the colonists did intermarry with Native Americans."

"*He* wanted to know," said Caroline as if she had bitten into a Holywell apple and found a worm.

228

"Well, it's possible. If the Macdonalds went over in the eighteenth century."

Caroline broke in. "They could have had slaves."

Mary sat back; she'd been naïve. She remembered the fire in D.P.'s eyes.

"I see. You're right. They could have had slaves. Well, given what we know of him, that would explain... how he left Holywell."

There was a tap on the door. Caroline jumped up to receive a tray with a teapot, mugs, milk, a bowl of sugar and a plate of homemade shortbread. The sweet scent was bewitching. Caroline made a face, then smiled at the young woman, who did not return the favor. Caroline placed the tray on the dressing table while Mary shut the door.

"That was Leni, out on bail, not Linda."

"Oh, Leni," said Mary. "The one who assaulted Godric St. John."

"So, *he* says," said Caroline darkly. "You saw how slight she is. She couldn't kick a mouse."

Perhaps I'm more cynical, Mary thought. "The provocation could have been extreme."

"You mean like today?" Caroline rejoined. "Cookie Mac throws open the door yelling that Janet is raising demons, along with a bunch of whores and a dumpy little nothing. They all heard him, you know. The girls from upstairs and witches in the kitchen preparing lunch."

"At least it got his invitation rescinded," said Mary practically.

"Dorothy was marvelous, wasn't she? Telling him that he was the one possessed by a demon of his own making. To go back where he came from and take his devil with him. I wonder if she meant that literally. That his racism is a demon."

"Who knows?" said Mary, not concerned with the witch's deconstruction of bigotry. "At least Sam cheered up hearing her telling him to get out. He was more comfortable with the women tonight and they with him. Now tell me about Janet's papers."

"Yes, that was really fascinating," agreed Caroline. "Who knew that the Key Keepers have an archive? She has letters from the fifteenth century, Janet said. She hasn't read them all. A few are in Latin."

"She showed Cookie Mac a letter?" ruminated Mary. "Why shouldn't she show it to us? If the letters go back that far, there might be something about Francis Andrew Ransome, our aristocratic purloiner of other people's manuscripts."

"Brilliant idea, Mary. And you are right because Janet told me that Roberta Le More was from Holywell. Amazing that a woman could pass as a man in those times."

"There are historical precedents," said Mary.

"But how will going through old papers help us find the Alchemy Scroll and the killer today?"

"Ah," said Mary, the former Archivist. "You'd be surprised at the potency of old papers. I'm going to use anything we find — even if it's nothing — to interrogate Cookie Mac and his academic rival, Godric St. John."

Caroline poured the tea. "Do be careful. We've seen Cookie Mac's temper, and we don't know what Godric St. John was up to with… with Anna."

Mary grinned.

"It's time to be proactive with both gentlemen. I'm going to shake the trees and see what truths falls out. Tomorrow, Cookie Mac meets Dame Eleanor about the Alchemy Scroll. Now that it's apparent that St. Julian's doesn't have it, she wants me present. At the same time, Caroline, could you…"

"…Ask Janet to let me see the Key Keeper letters? Of course. And do you know, Mary, I think it will really help us. I've got a feeling."

"I guess that's a start," said Mary Wandwalker. She hid her doubts. At least Caroline had not pushed about Anna. She had a strange sensation about that young woman, as if Anna was alone in the wilderness.

CHAPTER 33
A PHONE CALL TO ST. JULIAN'S

Before sleeping, Mary phoned the harassed St. Julian's Principal. Even though Mer-Corp knew that the Alchemy Scroll was missing, thanks to Cookie Mac, Dame Eleanor remained frantic about publicity. She was inclined to blame the Depth Enquiry Agency.

Mary pointed out that so far neither the Twitterverse nor the newspapers had connected the murder of a trainee in a Los Angeles Museum to a rarely seen manuscript in Oxford. Director Oldcastle and Cookie Mac knew it was not in their interests to spread the story.

"For now," said Dame Eleanor. "And what do I do with Professor Macdonald tomorrow? He is, after all, the Mer-Corp auditor. I expected better of you, Miss Wandwalker. Mr. Jeffreys was so certain your Agency could handle delicate tasks."

Mary's hands clenched. She'd been through fire, what with a murder, and white supremacists. And what about Caroline, who had gone undercover to rescue the Scroll's Key Keeper? Where were the College's thanks for that? Then there was Anna's secret meeting with Godric St. John. No, she would not dwell upon Anna tonight.

Miss Wandwalker took a deep breath — recalling a wit in the Archives who once referred to her as Pod, standing for Princess of Darkness.

231

"Dame Eleanor," she began. "When I met Professor Macdonald in Los Angeles, it was at the scene of a crime. An innocent young man lay dead; his blood..."

A rush of salt stopped her tongue. She swallowed and continued. "Macdonald is a murder suspect. The Los Angeles police asked me to report on his movements in the UK, and I will. You told me yourself you had a call from a detective in Los Angeles."

She needed to focus. "You hired us to find the Scroll. Here's what you do: *before* Professor Macdonald arrives tomorrow. Tell Mer-Corp that St. Julian's rejects an auditor who is under investigation for a capital crime. *You* insist that they appoint someone else and submit a resume for your approval. That will buy the College, and us, time."

There was a heavy silence on the line.

"They might go for it," came the grudging response. "Mer-Corp knows how vital this loan extension is to us. Unfortunately, the state of the College's mortgages is an open secret."

Mary thought fast. "Then inform Mer-Corp that you have appointed me as your representative. I'll negotiate for St. Julian's."

After all, it wasn't only St. Julian's that had everything to lose. Restoring the right Scroll to its rightful place would enable the Agency to keep going. Mary held the phone tight.

"Very well, Miss Wandwalker, have it your way." Dame Eleanor sounded tired. "When Professor Macdonald arrives tomorrow, I will refuse access to our seventeenth-century Alchemy Scroll. If he cannot see our copy, then he cannot declare it bogus. Your point about him being a murder suspect is a good one."

"I will be present," Mary said at her most unchallengeable.

"You and Godric St. John," agreed the harassed Dame. "Godric knows him, I gather. Academic rivalry, I believe. After our no doubt delightful encounter, I'll tell Mer-Corp that Cookie Mac is too tainted to be their auditor. And that you've been appointed to vet his replacement. That should enable

232

your *Agency*," sarcasm dripped into Mary's ear, "to get the real Alchemy Scroll back in time."

Mary heard a pause of desperation.

"St. Julian's is relying on you, Miss Wandwalker."

Oh, for the days when it was possible to bang down the receiver to end a call. Mary prepared for bed while unclenching her jaw.

That night she dreamed of Mr. Jeffreys. Inscrutable as ever, she could not tell if he was sneering or regretful about her enforced retirement. He wasn't in his spacious quarters near St. Paul's Cathedral in London. No, he was in St. Julian's Quad, the age he was now. Blood ran from his forehead. His fine suit soaked from being thrown into the fountain all those years ago.

CHAPTER 34
TROUBLE AT ST. JULIAN'S

Waking before dawn, Mary listened to Caroline's soft snores. She never woke this early; something had to be wrong. It was hours too soon to head for the St. Julian's meeting; yet, the anxiety burning her stomach would not die down.

I'm going now, she decided, throwing back the bedclothes. Holywell was a house of sleepers as Mary crept out. Clambering into the silver car, she drove the back roads into the city, headlights picking out overgrown thorn bushes and tiny nocturnal creatures. Gears ground too noisily, as if the car was trying to tell her something she refused to hear. She had to be early. She was not early enough.

Turning onto Oxford High Street at sunrise, Mary slammed on the brakes. She was trapped in a chain of cars, trucks, and buses, all hardly moving. Low sun blazed behind the fog, making the city's spires and towers spectral. Mary could not tell if the murk was pollution or the typical refrigerated atmosphere of Oxford.

Inches at a time she finally got sight of Queen's Lane. She blinked, not at first understanding what she saw. That street was blocked off by the police. A No Entry sign topped barriers, and... was that really crime scene tape?

Mary groaned as she saw that the entrance to St. Julian's was barred. Three police cars crammed the gate, stuck at odd angles. It was as if they had tried to get through simultaneously.

Now came the sirens, the loudest from an ambulance approaching from the other end of Queen's Lane. It materialized

235

out of the gloom, parking just before the College. And Mary could do nothing, stuck in the endless procession of vehicles.

Drawn agonizingly slowly up the High Street, Mary had time to see paramedics race into the Porter's Lodge. Two of them carried a stretcher. Then, in a sudden blast of horns behind her car, she was swept onward to Carfax Tower.

It took another thirty-five minutes for Mary to locate a parking space. She ran back to St. Julian's so fast that one of her heels caught in a gutter. She almost fell before stopping to put her shoe back on.

"You can't go in there, Ma'am: the College is closed." The uniformed policeman was huge with the sun blazing behind. He loomed, blocking St. Julian's entrance.

"What's happened? You must let me in, officer. I have an appointment — with the Principal." Mary thought about saying: "Let me pass, I'm a licensed detective."

Unfortunately, that wasn't true, and she wasn't Anna. This police officer was about twenty. He stuck out a badly shaven chin and stared straight through her. It was another "older woman invisibility" moment. Mary recognized it in an agony of frustration.

Shouts came from inside the College. Mary stepped aside to listen.

"Get me the American Ambassador," came a male voice familiar from the day before as well as from Los Angeles. With the rage came a new note: fear. "Call the President; the *American* President, you Mexican trollop."

A woman backed into Mary's sight line, leaning for support against the stone of the Porter's Lodge. It was Dame Eleanor. Something in blue, a scarf, was sticking out of her cream pantsuit pocket. What looked like blood was dripping from the turquoise silk onto the flagstones. Drops of scarlet stained Dame Eleanor's beautifully cut trousers.

"Dame Eleanor," she yelled. "Over here! It's me, Mary Wandwalker."

The woman swiveled. Mary stepped back. Dame Eleanor's usually olive skin was chalky, her eyes chips of coal, sightless. Perhaps it was the blood smeared on her hands. She looked down at them, puzzled, then up at Mary.

"This is your fault, Mary Wandwalker" she croaked. "You should have told me." Her defeat was frightening.

"Why? What's happened?" shouted Mary over the shoulder of the young policeman as he tried to edge her back into Queen's Lane. "Can you get them to let me in?"

Before she could get out any more words, two policemen rounded the corner with a struggling Cookie Mac. He was able to grip his briefcase because his wrists were cuffed in front.

Mary gasped. Blood covered the front of his white shirt; his velvet jacket had a rip down the right sleeve. As soon as he glimpsed Mary, the yelling began.

"Wandwalker, you did this to me! You set that witch on me to steal my Scroll. I'll get you; I'll get you all. You'll pay. None of you will ever get the Scroll. Never," his voice rose hysterically.

Mary saw a smear of spittle on his unshaven chin. The two policemen said something sotto voce. Ignoring Mary, they hustled Cookie Mac through the barrier and into one of their parked vehicles.

"Wait, wait," called Mary, running after them. "Let me talk to him. You must tell me what's going on. I can help. I want to make a statement."

She stamped her foot in frustration at being ignored. The car pulled away. Cookie Mac twisted to glare out of the back window.

"Really, Miss Wandwalker? So glad you are keen to help us."

Mary jumped at the woman's voice from behind. Clad in a hijab as well as police uniform, the lines around her eyes said sleep deprivation, not age. Her dark jacket had a stain on the shoulder that she could have told Mary was the result of burping

237

her baby. Mary later decided that Moira Coombs would intercept a bullet before she would confide such a personal detail.

"The Chief Inspector's asked me to take statements. We'll need one from you."

Mary caught the emphasis on you. "Tell me what's happened, Sergeant" she demanded, facing authority with her own. "And why does everyone think it is my fault?"

"That, Miss Wandwalker, we want to know," said the Sergeant calmly, leading Mary across the quad.

Dame Eleanor had vanished, presumably to do something about the blood. Mary decided that the office she was being escorted to belonged to the College nurse from the posters about STDs and safe sex. How soon could she shake answers from Dame Eleanor? I want Caroline, she thought, maybe even Anna.

Moira Coombs sat her across a desk with nothing on it. She gave no indication of taking notes; instead, she fiddled with a phone to record their conversation.

"I'm not talking until you tell me what's going on." Mary folded her arms. Coombs exchanged glances with the Constable standing in a corner. After a measured stare at Mary, she spoke briskly.

"Professor Godric St. John suffered a brutal attack early this morning. He's still alive, but only just. The ambulance took him to the John Whitcliffe." Coombs's expression drilled into Mary.

"It wasn't me," Mary said automatically. "Oh," she realized as events slotted into place: "Cookie Mac did it."

"Evidence suggests just that," said Coombs, sitting back. "For now."

She furrowed her brow at Mary, who realized she too was under suspicion. "The American Professor Macdonald was discovered kneeling beside the victim. Not only was he covered in blood, he became hysterical. We can't interview him in his current state. *We* want to know why everyone seems to blame you, Miss Wandwalker."

238

Mary thought furiously. The idea of Cookie Mac hitting, nay nearly killing, Godric St. John made no sense to her. Cookie Mac already has the Alchemy Scroll. If he did not bring it to Oxford, then he secreted it somewhere in the States. All Cookie Mac is after is the Scroll Key, and that lives with and in Janet.

"Godric St. John is a *modern* chemist," she said to herself. "The Key Keeper's secrets are nothing to him."

"Who? What? Miss Wandwalker? Please answer my question. Why are the American and Dame Eleanor blaming you?"

Moira Coombs had a trace of a Scottish accent. Her persistence chilled Mary. Prevaricating would be no good.

"Sergeant Coombs, I really don't know why Cookie Mac yelled at me."

Mary shook her head, then stopped. There was something Cookie Mac had yelled as he was taken away. That's right. He'd accused Mary of *setting a witch to steal the Alchemy Scroll* from him. Could that... could that possibly be Anna?

It might explain why she was still in the States and not answering her phone. Mary coughed and put her hand up to hide her face from the inquisitive Sergeant. It was true. She knew in her bones. Anna had the real Alchemy Scroll. The Agency was done for.

"Really, Miss Wandwalker? I find it hard to believe that you do not know why people blame you." Sergeant Coombs was stern, her gaze unwavering.

Mary's thoughts speeded up. "Dame Eleanor too," she said. "No idea why she says it is my fault. She can't blame me for the attack on Godric St. John as well."

The woman pounced. "As well as what?"

Mary coughed. "Client confidentiality."

"You're a lawyer?"

"No, a detective, private. Er... we're not licensed... yet."

"Then you're *not* a detective."

Mary bristled. "Nevertheless." (She liked that word) "Nevertheless, I will keep Dame Eleanor's, that is, the St.

239

Julian's, business, confidential. I can assure you that it has nothing to do with assaulting a Professor of Chemistry. Why I am being blamed for that crime, I cannot say. And really, it's I *can't*, not I won't."

She ended by defiantly meeting Coombs's neutral stare. She had nothing to hide about this morning's violence — probably.

Coombs jerked her head at the other policeman. He melted from the room. The Sergeant remained seated, ostensibly playing with her phone. Mary had no doubt she was dispatching instructions to dig up the dirt on a Mary Wandwalker, who claimed to be some sort of detective. Find her known associates. Mary winced. Caroline was no problem; while she hoped that Anna's cybercraft was convoluted enough to conceal her past.

This was not the day for the police to discover that Anna had received a conditional pardon for crimes committed while imprisoned by a trafficking gang. It was conditional on her remaining in the custody of Mary Wandwalker, and ten years of a clean record. *Not just unconvicted. She must be clear of any taint of crime*, Mr. Jeffreys insisted.

How ironic, Mary thought, that Anna's association with me could get her pardon revoked. With a sensation of her world crumbling, Mary reviewed her participation in the Alchemy Scroll affair. Was the irony wearing thin?

CHAPTER 35
ST. JULIAN'S IN TURMOIL

Summoned by a text from Sergeant Coombs, Dame Eleanor strode into the office with the young constable whose mustache was wet with perspiration. She glared at the Sergeant, then took a seat farthest away from Mary. The room contracted.

"I resent being dragged in here when my College is in chaos."

"This won't take but a moment, Dame Eleanor," said Coombs smoothly. "We're interviewing everyone who came to the College this morning. Think of this as saving your valuable time."

Dame Eleanor took out an unusual gold and peach lipstick, applying it with a none too steady hand.

Mary felt fed up being organized by others.

"Dame Eleanor, you said this was all my fault. What did you mean? I was nowhere near the College when the violence occurred. You made our appointment yourself, for hours later."

"You know what you did — what your so-called Depth Enquiry Agency did." Dame Eleanor would not look at her.

"No, I don't." Mary spoke sharply. "Please look at me." She'd had enough of unspecific accusations. "Either tell the police what you know or leave us out of whatever mess you've got the College into."

"*I've* got the college into..." Dame Eleanor's voice rose. With rage or shock, Mary could not tell. "Our Porter told me he'd never forget the arrival of Cookie Mac. The man came into the quad yelling something about witches, whores, and the evil

241

Alchemy School." She shot a glance at Moira Combs's raised eyebrows, then paused for breath.

"Yes, Miss Wandwalker, I know about the Alchemy Symposium in California. Months ago, they asked for photographs of our Alchemy Scroll, which I refused, of course. This morning I checked their website. The symposium was canceled two days ago. I opened my email and found a horrifying message from The Alchemy School's President."

Dame Eleanor's choked; a glass of water appeared in front of her. She knocked it back like hard liquor, then continued in a quieter register while checking her phone.

"The President is... a Dr. Jez R. R. Wiseman." She turned to Mary, seething. "Did I know that The European History Foundation is a front for white supremacists? That Cookie Mac had been funded by them for years, and was the — unnamed — author of much bogus and racist material on their blog?" She visibly struggled for calm. Mary began to feel sympathy.

"Dr. Wiseman, the President, is shocked. He blames *me*. No way would his Alchemy School collaborate with the EHF or host Cookie Mac. They'd received unequivocal proof from an unknown hacker of the EHF website."

Anna, it had to be. Thank God for Anna, Mary whispered to herself. At last, she'd breached those firewalls, or whatever one does to them. It was worth her staying in America. Dame Eleanor spoke again, this time to Mary.

"I know, I just know, your Agency sent The Alchemy School the evidence. I remembered that Mr. Jeffreys said you had a brilliant web investigator. Like magic, he said. And you'd warned me about the EHF."

Mary decided it was time for a few well-chosen words. After all, the police were present.

"Dame Eleanor, you can't possibly believe... None of what you say makes it my, our, doing that Cookie Mac..."

After a strangled grunt and another look of resentment at Mary, the Dame tried to pull herself together.

"You pushed Cookie Mac over the edge," she accused. Then her steam ran out. Her heart was no longer in it.

"Dammit," Dame Eleanor moaned. "I suppose I'm wrong to make it all the fault of your Agency. Dr. Wiseman enclosed a copy of the email sent to cancel the speaking contract. It was calculated to enrage Cookie Mac with all that stuff about the pernicious and fraudulent nature of his writing for the European History Foundation. Miss Wandwalker, couldn't you at least have warned me?" The Dame's self-pity had taken over.

Mary could see the chain of events. It hadn't ended well for Godric St. John, nor for St. Julian's.

"I didn't know," she said, feeling compromised. "Anna did not tell me about the EHF website. She should have consulted me. I don't know why she didn't."

Dame Eleanor sniffed. "You too have a subordinate out of control. I suppose that's what happens with an inexperienced Agency. I shouldn't have listened to Mr. Jeffreys."

"Wait a minute," began Mary crossly… but Coombs held up her hand.

There was a knock on the door.

"Come in," yelled Mary and Dame Eleanor together. It was Ravi Patel, horror etched upon his face. His jaw sagged at seeing Mary. Probably came from the airport, she thought.

"Who are you?" rapped Coombs,

"I'm… I'm…" stammered the young man.

"Ravi Patel," said Mary.

"Professor St. John's research student," said Dame Eleanor, without interest. Moira Coombs sat up.

"Ravi, I see you've just got back from the States. Me too," said Mary quickly.

"I… yeah, from Heathrow on the bus. The news… is it true Dame Eleanor that Professor St. John is dead?"

"Not dead, sir." Coombs said with an edge. "A text from the hospital says they are prepping the victim for surgery."

Ravi gripped the table. There was no chair for him to sink into.

243

"And another thing," said Coombs, staring at the phone as if she found it hard to believe what she saw. "Professor St. John managed a few words before the anesthetic took effect. The nurse told the officer he said: "Must see Mary Wandwalker.""

PART EIGHT
CIBATIO

CHAPTER 36
READING AND GARDENING

Caroline wished she'd paid more attention to Mary's stories about the Archive. Or better still, had asked more questions of the self-taught expert. Sitting on the bed at Holywell, she groaned. Try as she might, the aged papers spread out on Mary's bed appeared to record bird tracks rather than words. And these were the letters in English.

There must be some secret to old handwriting. She could not ask Janet because of her pained expression when Caroline approached her previously about the Key Keeper's letters. Was it unwillingness to leave her beloved vegetable garden, or was Janet avoiding some secret in the ancient documents? Now curled on the bed, Caroline reviewed their earlier conversation.

*****

Janet had thrust the fork into the ground and stood up. She contemplated the petitioner with those faraway eyes.

"The Letters? Why do ye want... No, don't tell me." Janet gazed sternly at her rows of shining earth speckled with shoots. "I need to garden today. After yesterday. That man, that... false alchemist, Macdonald."

She stabbed the earth with her big fork as if she could make Cookie Mac's blood sprout from it. Then, surprisingly, she drew out a bunch of keys from her jeans pocket.

"The oldest is the key to the chest with the letters. It's in my room."

247

While Caroline searched for words of thanks and reassurance, she realized that the two of them were no longer alone. Olga and Leni had crept up the gravel path with Sam sloping behind. Janet surveyed the young women without expression.

"Sorry Janet, it was me," said Olga, looking at the wet earth Janet had dug.

"It was me," said Leni, staring past Janet's head. A yard away, Sam nodded. He put his hands in his pockets.

"What was?" said Janet.

Caroline was surprised by the gentleness and the sadness in her eyes.

"I, we, wanted money, so I rang the phone number we were texted. I knew it was wrong when they said they wanted Holywell secrets." That was Olga. Her gaze was traveling slowly up Janet's body.

"I wanted that job at St. Julian's. So, I copied the medical chart on you that Dorothy has," said Leni, focused on Janet's left ear.

"I see," said Janet. "Thank you for telling me."

"We… are… sorry."

Janet picked up her fork, and the two girls jumped. Janet put it down again. She addressed them firmly.

"You're brave girls. At Holywell, no one will hurt you if you admit a mistake."

Leni and Olga relaxed. Leni turned to Sam and smiled. This time he nodded enthusiastically. She ran into his hug. Olga started to slip away as Janet called out:

"How about a bit of practical alchemy in the garden?"

There was a sudden eruption of gravel, and all three youngsters vanished. Caroline giggled. Janet put her head back and gave a belly laugh which made Caroline laugh even louder.

"Would you like some help?" Caroline said, tentatively. "I can come back after I've looked through the letters."

Janet spoke to a blackbird pecking a few meters away.

"I want to get those lazy bitches out here," she said without malice. "Do 'em good. They need some proper dirt under their fingernails." She flashed a shy smile at the younger woman. "So thanks, Caroline, but today I want it to appear I need an extra crew. That'll get the other witches on board."

She returned to skewering the damp soil, then crouched to tug up handfuls of young grass.

Caroline almost skipped as she navigated the circular beds of aromatic herbs. She too felt the rebound from that horrible confinement in The Old Hospital. The boost to her mood would not last, she knew. But why not enjoy it? Looking up, she marveled at the pearl strands of mist hugging the chalk hills. She recalled that Holywell was rooted to the center in the valley, at the confluence of two ancient streams.

Passing the remains of the medieval well, originally also a shrine, Caroline stopped and touched the stones edged with deep green moss. The water smelled of buttermilk. It had magical healing properties in the olden days, the witches said. Today there were too many contaminants from farmers' pesticides.

Caroline saw that the sundial near the well was the twin of one she had seen in St. Julian's main Quad. Mary said it was seventeenth century. So, the sundial was from the same era as Francis Andrew Ransome's theft of the Alchemy Scroll. She idly wondered if there was a connection.

Janet's room was snug in the attic. As she climbed the final oak spiral stairs, a ping announced the arrival of a text from Mary. Something had happened at St. Julian's. They weren't telling her what, but she would find out and get back to Caroline. Could Caroline check the letters for Francis Ransome and then get in touch with Anna?

Anna, the name stabbed into Caroline's heart. She hesitated, then opened Janet's door, inhaling the scent of lavender polish. *Anna*, sighed Caroline again, sitting on Janet's bed. Anna, who had failed to answer three phone messages over the previous day. Perhaps the Key Keeper's letters would speak louder than her lover's silence?

CHAPTER 37
LETTERS ACROSS THE ATLANTIC

Back in the bedroom she shared with Mary, Caroline's bright mood dimmed at the thought of Anna's silence and their estrangement. A dark pit waited to swallow Caroline at such moments. What had a therapist once advised? Ah yes, distill the dread, stop it from seeping into her being. Yes, here it was, the thought she'd avoided so far. Torn apart by the case, the family of the Agency was disintegrating.

Caroline shut her eyes and opened them again. What would Mary do if she was here, and Caroline told her of her fears. She'd say get on with it, Caroline guessed. Nothing else to do.

Two hours later, Caroline stood up to ease an aching back. She was holding a letter that referred to the original theft of the St. Julian's Alchemy Scroll. If only she could decipher it. The signature began with an R. Could it be Roland, or Roger, or maybe Robert? Perhaps, Robert Le More.

Robert Le More. Caroline scrolled through the case notes that Mary had insisted they keep, adding to them every day. Unlike Mary, Caroline kept hers on her phone. Yes, here was Robert Le More. He was the alchemist who'd copied the Alchemy Scroll.

Brought by Francis Andrew Ransome to St. Julian's on several occasions, the college failed to realize that his beautiful copies were *for them,* not for Ransome's voyage to the American colony. Not for centuries would the college know that switching manuscripts had allowed Ransome to steal the original Alchemy Scroll to take to New England.

251

But the Key Keeper knew something. What was it that Janet confided in that terrible place, The Old Hospital? It blazed back, like that time she tried gin: Robert was Roberta. She was a woman, a *witch*, or alchemist from Holywell.

"I bet she was a Key Keeper," said Caroline aloud. "She must have planned to go with Ransome. They wanted the Alchemy Scroll to help treat the sick in America." She screwed up her face. "That's right, he did work as a physician, Mary said."

Part of the address said "Conetticut," which had to be an early spelling for the colony. Caroline could not find the address on Le More's letter. Had the woman traveled to America with Francis Andrew Ransome?

Oh, why wasn't Mary back to help her. The old paper felt like sunburnt leaves, thick yet fragile. Caroline texted Mary again. Nothing. Suddenly, she saw faint writing below the signature. Was it another name? She took out the magnifying glass she had begged from Dorothy.

Yes, another name; but the first part was familiar. It was Roberta, Roberta Africanus. Caroline had already Googled Robert Le More to find only the brief mention sent by Anna. Now she tried "Roberta Africanus" on her phone. The results made her hands tremble. What did it mean? Mary must see this, and soon. If Mary would not be returning to Holywell, then Caroline needed a ride to Oxford.

CHAPTER 38
IN THE DOLDRUMS

Dorothy agreed to give Caroline a ride to Oxford. Good timing, she said, since she was about to leave with Leni for what should have been a simple check-in at the Police Station. Given the recent violence at St. Julian's College, her bail condition had become a summons for an interview. The police would not say why they demanded Leni's presence for an unspecified length of time. However, Dorothy could guess after twice listening to Mary's terse phone message. It had been recorded after Godric St. John had been whisked off to hospital.

With her forensic eye for detail, Mary outlined what had to be considered the second attack on Godric St. John. Both are bound up with the missing Alchemy Scroll, she explained. As perpetrator of the first assault, not even the arrest of Cookie Mac could save Leni from suspicion.

Dorothy played Mary's long message for Caroline while Leni grumbled and whined about going into Oxford. With Mary's phone switched off, Caroline was glad to learn that Mary now planned to visit Godric St. John at the hospital. At his request, she said, and Caroline heard Mary's astonishment and fatigue. Switching off the speaker phone, Dorothy informed Caroline that she did not share Mary's pessimism about Leni's position.

"I shouldn't say it, but surely this horrible attack means that Godric will drop his ridiculous charges against Leni."

253

From the kitchen, she beckoned the young woman, who was whispering in a corner with Sam. Caroline caught swear words about the police.

"Come with us, Sam," said Caroline. "You can help cheer Mary up, or, if you prefer, take a look around Oxford."

Sam brightened, exchanging glances with Leni. "Sure, Caroline. Let me get my coat," and he ran off.

Dorothy nodded absently, her mind on Leni's troubles. "What happened at St. Julian's this morning is far more serious than that thing with a mop bucket," Dorothy said. "And Leni's *here*. She's been with us all this time. Naturally, the police called earlier. They had to confirm her appointment for this afternoon."

"They'll want to question her," suggested Caroline. She knew the shadows under Dorothy's eyes matched her own.

Dorothy shot her a glance. "If we go now, I'll have time to swing by our solicitor's," she said, resignedly. "Really, this is too much, accusations against a girl like Leni!"

Caroline thought of Anna's remarkable history. She prudently said nothing. Once she'd overheard the trafficked women whispering about hitchhiking to Oxford at night to let off steam. Leni's alibi may not be as perfect as Dorothy imagined. Caroline decided to keep quiet. Nothing must complicate the enquiry into Cookie Mac.

On the drive to Oxford, Leni curled up in the back of the car. Gazing at grey fields, she gnawed at her lower lip, seemingly oblivious to the pink lipstick she chewed on. Close to the city, Caroline saw the overnight fog remained wrapped around Oxford's towers. After Dorothy left her off at the John Whitcliffe Hospital, Caroline watched the car disappear down the brick-lined street. At least Dorothy and Leni would have the Holywell solicitor for their next joust with the police.

Minutes later Caroline found Mary slumped in the visitors' canteen. It was the dead time of the afternoon. Having twice been refused access to Godric St. John, Mary lacked the energy to leave.

With the smell of blood on her sky-blue jumper, she could not yet face the labyrinth of corridors, all painted the same blend of yellow and cream. Mary had had enough of the muffled tannoy and running figures in sage polyester. She dreaded passing the rows of trolleys with drips going into grey arms that she'd glimpsed near the ER. The canteen was both quieter and emptier. At least it was until Caroline burst in.

"Mary, thank goodness you're still here! *Why* are you still here? What's the news of Professor St. John? Have they charged Cookie Mac?"

Very slowly, Mary rose to her feet and embraced Caroline. She held her close for a moment.

"I...I... that is, he..." Mary wobbled, grabbed the table, and sat down quickly. "Just a bit lightheaded," she said.

"Oh Mary." Caroline drew up a chair and hugged the older woman again. She noticed four dirty paper coffee cups. She recalled that Mary hated coffee in disposable cups.

"I failed, Caroline. We failed. This case... we can't do it."

The words were jerked out. Shocked, Caroline could not believe what she heard. Mary never gives up, was her immediate response. What once fired the formidable Archivist now inspires the Agency. "There's no limit to what we three can achieve, *together*," Mary once said. Yet, Caroline knew despair; she could taste it in the harshly lit canteen.

"You haven't eaten have you, Mary? Not since breakfast."

"Not hungry," Mary mumbled, her head down.

"Eat these; the witches made sandwiches. I don't want them. It's vegan cheese, I'm afraid."

Mary sat up reluctantly. She opened the Tupperware box that Caroline had fished out of a Sainsbury's shopping bag that seemed to go everywhere with her.

"I've been meaning to talk to you about your ridiculous diets," she said, snappily. "I'll eat a sandwich if you eat the other one."

Standoff. Two determined expressions. A very fat man in a stained apron was shutting down the deep fat fryer at the other end of the long room. In a corner, a small woman with hair an unlikely orange was changing the till roll. Everyone else had disappeared after a greasy lunch.

Flinty grey eyes met luminous green. Caroline stared at the sandwiches. Was that the homemade bread emitting sweet and yeasty scent? Her mouth watered, and she picked up the sandwich. Now she could smell the salt and sour milk aroma of cheese. Caroline smiled at the sandwich, not at Mary. She took a bite.

Mary began to eat. I'm overstressed, overcaffeinated and being ridiculous, she thought ruefully. Their Agency case was nowhere. Police on two continents thought her capable of murder. She had yet to devise a way of making Cookie Mac give up the Scroll he'd taken in Los Angeles.

No, it's even worse, she thought wearily. My brain is going. Anna stole the Alchemy Scroll from Cookie Mac. That was one of the things he'd yelled at me, and there's no reason for him to lie about it. Why Anna took the Scroll is anyone's guess. The Agency is finished before it ever had a chance. None of this could she bear to say to the woman sitting in front of her.

Instead, between bites of the sandwich, Mary uttered grim sentences. With every word, she imagined throwing the Business Plan for the Agency in the fire. It was the one pinned up in her office at home.

"Godric St. John's in a coma." Mary cleared her throat. "His injuries are just like, like... D.P.'s. In Los Angeles, the killer picked up an axe from the Ransome trunk. This time it was a hammer from a toolbox left on an adjacent staircase. The Police have charged Cookie Mac with attempted murder. He denies it."

Mary gulped. This was the hard bit. "Caroline, you won't like this. Cookie Mac alleged that Anna stole the real Alchemy Scroll from him. No, don't look like that. He is not lying. Our police got his phone and showed me the footage so I could identify Anna. She broke into his locker at Los Angeles airport.

"Don't look at me like that, Caroline," Mary said resting her forehead on one hand. "LAX Security emailed Cookie Mac when they found pictures of someone getting into his locker without a key. Some guy followed lots of women in the airport and then got nabbed for photographing without permission." Mary paused while Caroline got a tissue out and blew her nose. She nodded at Mary to continue.

"That's why Cookie Mac went crazy this morning and stormed into St. Julian's. He assumed Anna'd been sent by the College to snatch the Scroll. If only that were true."

Mary sighed. "So angry was he that he admitted taking the Alchemy Scroll from the Museum in LA. He demanded that Dame Eleanor and Godric make Anna give the Scroll back — to him. The police told Dame Eleanor, and she spilled the beans."

Mary paused. This is so much harder than I thought, she reflected.

"Caroline, I've been texting and calling Anna for hours. She's gone. I'm so sorry."

Mary turned away. It hurt to look at Caroline. "We must accept it. Anna's gone, and the real Alchemy Scroll is gone with her."

PART NINE
PROJECTIO

CHAPTER 39
ROBERTA AFRICANUS

Lights dimmed in the hospital canteen. It was a subtle hint. The catering staff would prefer the two women to leave during their afternoon break, Mary realized. However, Caroline did not move.

"Anna's not gone," said Caroline, her voice quiet yet firm. "No, Mary, she's not been in touch. I just know she's not gone."

"Oh, Caroline, you're…" Too trusting, in love, naïve, Mary was too tired for the right words.

"I've got news for you too," Caroline was shifting nervously on her seat. "An email from Dorothy arrived as I finished that sandwich."

Nervous, not distraught, noted Mary. She leant on her elbows amongst the crumbs to listen.

"It's Sam," said Caroline. "Sam and Leni. They're both at Oxford police station being questioned about Godric St. John. Picked up buying train tickets to London. Leni must have given Dorothy the slip.

"Whaaaat! *Sam*… and Leni…?"

"Don't panic, Mary. They haven't done anything. Or so they say. Just hitchhiked into Oxford last night. The girls do that from time to time. It's unfortunate there was an attack…"

"On someone in a position to send Leni to prison. No doubt their night out leaves Leni without an alibi for early morning."

"Well yes, apart from Sam. Fortunately, Dorothy says the Holywell lawyer is excellent. He's at the Police Station now and is confident he can get them home to Holywell tonight."

Mary groaned and clutched her head. "If this is what depression feels like..."

"You haven't got it," said Caroline as if protecting unwanted territory. "You're exhausted, not depressed. It's quite different, and you know it. Pull yourself together, Mary."

Suddenly furious, Mary blazed at Caroline who forestalled her.

"I know. You never say that to me. But then, you're not me."

Too honest not to agree. Mary scowled. "I'm responsible for Sam. How could he..." she muttered. I feel rather silly, she thought, privately.

"How could Sam make friends with a girl of his own age?" Caroline tried not to smile. "Sam's inexperienced but still a young man. It is I and Anna who really need you, Mary."

Mary sat for a moment. She stared at her aging hands as if seeing them with new eyes. "You really think Anna...is... coming back?"

"Yes. Don't you feel it too?"

Mary's expression went enigmatic. "You're right about lots of things, Caroline. I hope that you are right about this. It is too late to get to see Godric St. John today. Let's have a few words with Sam and Leni. By the way, what about those letters at Holywell?"

It was a companionable walk to where Mary had parked the car. They drove out of Oxford as rush hour traffic began the dawdle to the suburbs. Caroline described how she'd tried to decipher the Holywell letters. Mary longed to say, "Cut to the chase," but she could see that Caroline wanted to tell the story in her own way.

"Some of the packets are very old," she said. "Some papers aren't letters at all. Maybe torn entries from ledgers, with lists of stuff. Those were thick as cardboard, whereas the actual letters were tightly packed and almost transparent. As for the writing, it was so hard to make out. Many letters are in Latin, and one might be French, or a sort of French. You know, Mary, the Key

Keeper's records go back to the founding of St Julian's Hall. I saw language like the Chaucer I did in school."

Mary gave up being accommodating. "Get to the point, please Caroline. It's been a long day." It was all she could do not to sound cranky.

"Okay." Caroline speeded up. "Well, listen to this. It's amazing. There was a separate folder of letters from the American colony. That's what the label said. The dates spanned over a hundred years, starting with one of the first signatures I could make out: Roberta Africanus. She and her daughter were living with the Holy People. I guess that's the Native Americans. Hers was a such strange name that I Googled it with the date in the letter." Caroline paused.

They were out of the streets now, nosing onto a dark country lane. Their headlights glinted off hedges that were spiky with the lack of true foliage. Above the Oxfordshire countryside, a sickle moon grinned.

"And?" Mary's voice was strained. Despite her tiredness, she was driving carefully. Caroline was a nervous driver. Mary had decided not to risk her on Oxford streets or on hazards lurking on the dark roads.

"A slave!" The voice beside her in the dusk went hoarse. "Roberta was one of the first runaway slaves to be as living as a free woman with Native Americans. I found her in Wikipedia on early American slavery. She's thought to have escaped from the household of... guess who? Governor Francis Andrew Ransome after he died in... what was it?"

There was a rustle as Caroline took out a notebook from the handbag at her feet and angled it to the radiance from the instrument panel, "Yes, here it is, 1673. I managed to photocopy all those letters to show you. You'll be able to read more than I."

Mary almost stopped the car at the news. Instead, she braked for the turnoff to the track to Holywell. "I had no idea there were slaves that early in New England."

She did not mention the racism of Cookie Mac. What might this mean for St. Julian's distinguished thief, the future Governor Ransome? Caroline was continuing.

"Me neither, about slavery that early. So, I looked that up too. Seems that a few Africans were taken to the colonies right away. In fact, some scholars suggest that even the sixteenth-century landings were caught up in the transatlantic slave trade."

Both women were silent, chewing on this news. Approaching Holywell, the lighted house shone like a beacon. "Slaves here too," said Caroline softly, thinking of the trafficked young women.

"What? Oh, yes," agreed Mary. "Let's get inside. It's about time for dinner. Afterward, I want a close look at the photocopies."

*****

Poring over the letters after an unusually silent meal (Dorothy, grey, withdrawn; the young women subdued over Leni and the revelation of their night excursions), Mary and Caroline were disturbed by a burst of voices from below. Mary stood up, then realized the ruckus was celebratory. Male boots drummed up the stairs, and Sam burst into the room, followed by Leni. The young woman looked relaxed and happy — a first in the experience of Mary or Caroline.

"Mary, I found you. That Holywell lawyer was awesome." Sam grabbed Mary in a hug. Then he sat down hastily to hide his embarrassment. Leni joined him on the other bed.

"I'm very glad, Sam, but really…"

"Yeah, he wouldn't let them separate us. He got us out real quick when it became clear they had nothing on Leni for today or last night. Whenever that mean old guy got whacked."

"That's true? Nothing to connect Leni or you to the recent attack?" Mary wanted to be sure.

"Nothin', nothing. Yeah, we hitched to Oxford last night, Miss Wandwalker." Sam took a breath. "Leni *wanted* to go

264

and confront that lying professor, but I talked her out of it. We arranged to meet today and run away to London..."

"*Not* a good idea," intervened Mary. She could not help the smile.

"Well...anyway, we didn't. The cops stopped us."

"It wasn't Sam's fault," said Leni with more animation than before. "He kept telling me to trust you both. Anna too..."

Mary and Caroline blinked at the mention of Anna. Their eyes met; Leni continued. "I didn't listen until Sam told me about his brother, D.P., and St. Julian's Alchemy Scroll getting stolen in Los Angeles."

The room dimmed for Mary. She could still see D.P.'s smile through the snow like a friendly flag. It had warmed her on the doorstep of the museum. Sam, too, looked gruff. He swallowed, and Leni squeezed his hand. In the silence, Sam's eyes fell on the letters spread out on the opposite bed. Caroline handed one to him.

"Roberta Africanus? She's a legend, a made-up story, my teachers said. Does that say she's a slave living with Indians? But Mrs. Jones, that's not right. Not if she's *the* Roberta Africanus."

"What do you mean?" Caroline was a bit put out.

"'Roberta Africanus...' that name's been haunting me," said Mary, slowly. "Not just because we know she's Robert Le More."

"Le More, he's the guy who... is that right? He faked the Alchemy Scroll back in the... whenever it was stolen by that Governor?" Leni was asking Sam.

"Not a guy," said Mary, twinkling. "A woman."

"No way!" Sam's jaw had dropped.

"It has to be," jumped in Caroline, green eyes glowing. "Because the letters say that Roberta Africanus goes to Connecticut with Francis Andrew Ransome. So does Robert Le More or rather Le More comes out as a woman in the New World. Anna said that nothing more is heard of Robert Le More in the history of alchemy."

"Making it more likely that she traveled with Ransome." That was Mary putting together the pieces.

"Le More," means African." Leni's voice was clear, even bold.

"African, babe? ... how..." Sam's affection for Leni spilled over his curiosity, thought Mary. Leni put her hands together.

"If Le More was originally, the Moor, you know, with two 'o's and no 'e's. Sarah told me that some Africans are called Moors. One of the witches was going on about Shakespeare and race. She was saying... oh, I didn't really listen. It was different races having a history in England.

"There were Africans in England and in Ancient Rome," said Caroline. "The school I used to teach at had history posters all 'round the walls. Also, there is a story that the ancient Carthaginians reached America. They were in North Africa."

"We're getting off the point," said Mary. "Sam, you were saying... something about *the* Roberta Africanus not being a slave."

"Yeah, not a slave," said Sam. "You see, D.P. always said I'd never find peace until I could see history for myself, I'd just be letting it happen to me."

"You mean the racism," said Caroline.

"Yeah, Mrs. Jones. You know, D.P. was so...so *right.*" Sam turned to Mary. She felt her eyes prick.

"Is so right. He's still here." Mary's words tumbled out. *That's what Caroline would say.* Caroline gave her half a smile.

"Yeah." Sam stopped. "I always thought my parents liked him best. He could do exams, you see. None of that really matters, does it?"

Mary was ill-equipped for this. Caroline wasn't. "Of course, your parents love you just as much. They'll be so proud of you, you'll see. So please, Sam, are we sure *our* Roberta wasn't ever a slave in America?"

In the pregnant pause that followed, Mary's chest tightened. Roberta Le More, brilliant artist and alchemist, could not have been enslaved in the seventeenth-century colony, could she?

266

Mary found herself wanting to drive up to Governor Ransome's house to protest. She could not explain why this was so important. She just knew it was.

After scrolling his phone for a couple of minutes, Sam beamed. "Wikipedia is wrong about Roberta Africanus. Yes, she's listed with Africans who married Native Americans in the colony. I found it on a website D.P. sent me. I guess the others could have been slaves before they escaped. Not Roberta, though. I got sent an anonymous text. It has a link to marriage records in the Connecticut colony that have come online this week. Governor Ransome married twice, the second time to..."

"Roberta Le More," Caroline clapped her hands.

Mary briefly closed her eyes, then began to summarize

"I think we know who sent that text, Sam. Thank you for sharing. We're as certain as we can be that Roberta Africanus is the Robert Le More who visited St. Julian's College with Francis Andrew Ransome. A few women did 'pass' as men in the period — it would help in becoming an artist with alchemy training."

"Don't forget we know she was from Holywell too," added Caroline. "That's why we have her letters. She kept in touch."

"She may have had correspondents all over Europe," said Mary, thoughtfully. "After all, Alchemists were powerful people."

"Like witches," said Leni eagerly.

"Exactly," said Mary. "Women alchemists might even *be called* witches. They had a lot in common. That could be why Roberta decided to disguise herself as a man."

"They were healers, those witches were," insisted Leni. "Back then and like now, here at Holywell. Linda's been telling me the old stories."

Mary became brisk. It had been an exceedingly long day. "Right, we know that Francis Andrew Ransome was a physician-alchemist because of what he practiced in America," she said. "He wanted the Alchemy Scroll for medicinal purposes. Roberta Le More went with him willingly. Perhaps they were already lovers. She took the name Africanus later when she lived with Native Americans."

"And had at least one child," broke in Caroline.

"And Leni said, 'cos she's seen letters too," broke in Sam. "Go on, tell 'em, Babe." All eyes were on Leni. Mary could see the sulky lines she usually hid behind. The girl reminded her of Anna. She knew Caroline was thinking that too.

Leni visibly tried to relax. "What did you find?" said Caroline gently.

"Well, Linda showed us a couple of them letters. It was when that gardener-witch, Janet, was gone. I thought..." Leni faltered. She was unused to people hanging on her every word. "I just knew," she said with more confidence, "that she'd never been a slave. She was strong; she made choices."

"She spoke of being loved!" Caroline exclaimed. She was holding one of the photocopies into the light.

"Yeah," said Leni, cautiously. She glanced briefly at Sam. He nodded, smiling.

The four of them passed around the letters. Even Mary found it hard to decipher the faded ink of Roberta Le More, the African artist and alchemist who went to live in New England.

After a while, Caroline told Leni and Sam to get some sleep. Both she and Mary were privately speculating whether the pair would retire to one bed or two. Mary cocked an eyebrow at the closing door; Caroline smiled. Since it was none of their business; they did not speak of it as they prepared for the night.

*****

Ping. Caroline, a notoriously poor sleeper, woke when the text arrived at 2 a.m. Mary had her head under the covers; she was lightly snoring. When Caroline saw the glowing letters in the dark, she shook Mary awake. Excitement made her ruthless. She switched on a lamp. Mary flung, an arm over her eyes.

"Aaargh. Go away, Caroline. I'm asleep."

"Mary, you've got to look at this. Come on."

"Morning. In the morning."

"No, now. It's from Anna."

Mary forced her eyes open. "Anna? What's the time? 2:07 a.m. Drat the girl. Give me that phone."

The text was simple. In reply to Caroline's question about the Holywell letters, Anna had sent: 'Roberta Africanus married Ransome then Indian Chief.'

"Wow... Do you see?" mused Caroline.

"Anna's back," said Mary, throwing the phone onto Caroline's bed. "Now, for heaven's sake, get some sleep."

CHAPTER 40
MERCURIUS

Morning brought no further word from Anna. Mary didn't like it. They still did not know where Anna was, let alone her plans for the Scroll she'd purloined. Above all, Mary needed the Alchemy Scroll to fulfill the Agency's contract. Yes, she cared about solving the murder and attack on Godric St. John, but those crimes secured police resources. No point in being starry-eyed about Caroline and Anna, Mary told herself. Only she possessed the dogged determination to restore the Alchemy Scroll to St. Julian's.

Right now, the Oxford police were being "unhelpful," Mary said to herself as a message arrived from Sergeant Coombs during breakfast. Left on Dorothy's office voicemail, it ordered that no one staying at Holywell was to leave the area. They were to make themselves available for further questioning as required. Mary chafed at the breadth of the restrictions.

She tried to get Coombs on the phone to ask if Cookie Mac was talking. The constable on duty said the Sergeant was busy. With Mary's prodding, she eventually condescended to pass along the query. Fortunately, Dorothy had a source at St. Julian's amongst the administrative staff.

The police are crawling all over the College, she said, conducting searches for bloodstained clothing. No, they were not asking about the Alchemy Scroll. Word on Godric St. John was cautiously optimistic, even though he had not regained consciousness.

271

"I need to be told as soon as he wakes up," said Mary to Dorothy. "I'm not spending more hours in that canteen waiting for him to come round. Can you get your contacts to pass on any news?"

"Of course," said Dorothy. "They're primed. They're on Leni's side too. That St. John can be a right bastard to the staff."

I bet, said Mary to herself. She beckoned Caroline outside.

"We've got to plan. We've got to organize, and we've got to work this out," she announced as they took a stroll around the lawn. Frost turned to wet, making the grass a brilliant green spotted with patches of clover. Some of the tiny leaves could be daisies.

"You're feeling better, aren't you," said Caroline. "But we can't make a plan until we know more; until we talk to Anna."

"The occasional text is no good." Mary coughed. It had come to her in the middle of the night: "We're going to have to go and get the Scroll from Anna ourselves. Physically go to where she is. First, we need an idea of where she's heading. Is it this Alchemy School? That College where the Symposium was to be held?"

"Mary, the police said we weren't to leave."

"That's what they said in Los Angeles too. I think we can convince them that fetching the Scroll is the key to the case around Godric St. John *and* Cookie Mac."

Caroline looked doubtful.

"Oh, do keep up, Caroline. Godric St. John is not dead. D.P. Murphy is. That sergeant in Los Angeles can persuade the Oxford police to let us, me at least, to return to the States. They've got a murder to solve."

"Sorry." A pause.

Mary put her hand on Caroline's arm. "No, I'm sorry for snapping. It's just… this is our first case. We've bitten off more than we can chew. If we weren't desperate for money, we'd have waited six months, got proper training…"

272

Caroline looked understanding. Mary continued. "Let's go and sit on the bench over there. You're not too cold? I just needed to get out of the house with all those… emotions."

"Okay, no emotions," said Caroline, smiling. They stared at a small robin with a bright orange chest hopping about. Caroline found a few biscuit crumbs in her pocket. "No drama, Mary, be calm. We'll go over what we know. So where did this all begin?"

"With our hiring," said Mary, almost mesmerized by the robin's delicate dance for more sprinkles. "Dame Eleanor hired us to find out if St. Julian's Alchemy Scroll was in the Ransome bequest at the Museum. If so, we, that is, I, was to negotiate its return."

"Don't forget Janet's kidnapping," said Caroline. "We've rather lost sight of that."

"I could never forget what you went through," said Mary, with warmth. "And you're right. Someone went to a lot of trouble for the key to the Scroll's secrets. Why? We've two main candidates for the kidnapping: Godric St. John and Cookie Mac. One's a chemist; the other a historian. Only one of them is based here in Oxford."

"Since they're both ambitious for more than academic kudos," said Caroline, shrewdly, "could it be about money? The Alchemy Scroll is priceless, after all."

"Priceless, yes. But it's not only money, I'm sure of it. There are easier ways of getting hold of valuable manuscripts. What is it about this one? They both want it. They're not in it together, for sure."

"Ohm, wait a minute." Caroline struggled to articulate something. Janet's experience in The Old Hospital was important, there was something...

"The healing," she almost shouted. It fell into place.

"Mer-Corp," exclaimed Mary. "A Pharmaceutical megacorporation that holds St. Julian's mortgages." They looked at each other.

"Time to get the iPad," said Mary.

273

"Got it in my bag with my phone," said Caroline, reaching for the inevitable Sainsbury's carrier.

A couple of minutes later, Caroline put her hand on Mary's arm.

"Let me try my phone. Yes, here on *The Guardian*'s Investigative Reporting site: 'Mer-Corp funds educational foundations that provide grants and scholarships to advance chemistry and the Life Sciences. Sources state that Mer-Corp began operations in the UK in 2010. It's rumored to be involved financially with the investments of at least one Oxford College…'"

"Yes, we know about St. Julian's," said Mary.

"There's a link here to an article on the origins of Mer-Corp. Oh, it's a PDF. I'll need to download and magnify the print."

Mary stood up, causing the friendly robin to soar up the bare branch of an overhanging apple tree. Stamping her feet to revive her frigid toes, Mary didn't notice the robin's indignation. Nor did she see Janet Swinford popping up over a hedge. The recovering witch returned to digging. She rose again to frown at Leni and Olga. These apprentices were too ready to put down their forks and start tweeting.

"Mary, look at this."

Obediently, Mary pored over Caroline's phone, gripping her right arm. She read aloud:

"Mer-Corp began as 'Mercurius Medicines' founded in 1703 in Boston by… here it is, John Andrew Ransome, so named to honor his alchemist grandfather, Francis Andrew Ransome, Governor of Connecticut, and famous physician. Oh, Caroline, it's connecting at last. Mercurius is the transformative principle in alchemy."

Caroline sat back thinking furiously.

"But John Andrew probably never knew about the Alchemy Scroll. It was in the Governor's personal possessions, locked away since his death. The grandson founding the company does not prove Mer-Corp is behind everything."

"No, that's true. However, we can at least say that Mer-Corp is linked to the Alchemy Scroll indirectly. Who knows what family legends got handed down? Mer-Corp develops new medicines. Don't they sponsor research into alchemy for new compounds? Why didn't Dame Eleanor tell us to look more closely at Mer-Corp?"

"You think she knows about Mer-Corp and the Ransome family?"

"She must. When hiring me, us, she said that the College needed the real Alchemy Scroll because the company owning the mortgages insisted on an expert valuation. Mer-Corp is that company. Cookie Mac is the expert Mer-Corp chose. The problem for the College is being stuck with Robert Le More's facsimile."

"Janet's horse had the name Mercurius," said Caroline, forlornly. "Anna says Mercurius is mercury, the poisonous beginning, the *prima materia* of alchemy. Mercurius is alive, a sort of devil, a trickster. Eventually, he can be a divine spirit or take a female form, such as the Virgin Mary. Mercurius leads to the Water of Life that cures everything."

"Oh," said Mary, staring at Caroline. "Cures… everything." They paused.

"*Prima materia* can also be a state of depression," Caroline added. This she had researched for herself. "They say alchemy is about transformation, including psychological mending."

She smiled ruefully at Mary. "Mercurius is the perfect name for a company selling pharmaceuticals." Something caught her attention on the phone. "Oh, look, Mary. The Ransome family sold half the company to Macdonald Bank of Los Angeles in 1809. They changed the name of the merged company to Mer-Corp Macdonald; the Macdonald dropped in 1871. It says: 'Mer-Corp to this day specializes in chemical research for new household products and medicines. It has a nonprofit arm through which it funds educational charities.' What do you think that means?"

Mary sat back on the bench. Her ungloved hands throbbed from the frigid air. Was that a drop of rain? She glanced at Caroline.

"All those years at the Archive, I never audited financial records," she began. "Even so, Mer-Corp sounds like what Mr. Jeffreys calls a financial predator. They take control of institutions by making loans to them that are hard to repay. St. Julian's would be an easy target. Getting a whiff of the Alchemy Scroll could have been an unexpected bonus."

"Well, don't forget those stories of healing poor scholars," said Caroline seriously. "Everyone knows the legend. Mer-Corp could have picked on St. Julian's for that reason too. Perhaps there's some magical power in the Alchemy Scroll, after all."

"Something that activates the placebo effect."

"You're such a skeptic, Mary. Although it reminds me of how Janet changed when we thought we'd die in the fire. She found she wanted to live. She had to save her friend, Agnes. In an odd way, the fire resuscitated her. I never thought of it like that before."

"That is not quite what's meant by the placebo effect. But I agree there may be more to the Alchemy Scroll. Remember all those prohibitions about touching the Scroll; the need for gloves? Come to think of it, Cookie Mac appeared distinctly unwell. Perhaps he touched the Scroll with his bare hands."

"Anna," Caroline typed feverishly.

"Caroline, Anna's a sort of witch, even if she calls it cybercraft. I'm sure she knows how to treat the Alchemy Scroll." Caroline raised her large green eyes to Mary.

"I'm going to phone her."

"All right. Do it from the car. It's the middle of the night in America, or wherever Anna is. You and I are going to pay Dame Eleanor a visit. She blamed *me* for the attack on Godric St. John, and that the Alchemy Scroll is not yet returned. Her turn to answer questions about St. Julian's and Mer-Corp. I want to know about the funding for Godric St. John's professorship. Meet me at the car."

Minutes later, Caroline thrust her phone into her old jacket's pocket and wished she had eaten breakfast, as Mary had advised. Her hunger growled with anxiety for Anna; although it was absurd to think of Anna as helpless. Nevertheless, the formidable young woman ranged alone in a case that now stretched from California to the Oxford College they were making for. Was Mer-Corp behind these crimes? Time for answers from St. Julian's.

CHAPTER 41
COAGULATION

The sound of a woman yelling stopped Mary and Caroline from leaving Holywell as soon as they had planned. Janet waved madly once her shouts had penetrated. It was Caroline she wanted.

"Go on," said Mary. "Be quick. I'll wait at the car."

Caroline nipped across the damp lawn, gave a comradely pat to the well and sundial, then trotted past the circular herb beds to the vegetable garden, where Janet stood grinning.

"Look at those gals," she said in a stage whisper. "Gardeners? I don't think so!"

At the other end of the vegetable patch, a weeping willow was smoking. Puffs came in two directions from trailing tendrils. It was as if a green-domed house had wonky chimneys. Caroline had to smile, although she was anxious to be off to Oxford.

"Is that what you wanted to show me, Janet? We're just on our way…"

"No, not that." Janet stabbed the earth with her spade a couple of times. Caroline recognized her difficulty. A depressed person often finds it hard to converse or to initiate ideas. She made herself be patient.

"It's those gals. Well, really, it's Agnes. I wanted to ask you…" began Janet with effort. "Oh hell," and she whacked the ground so hard that sparrows fled the hedge nearby.

"It's all right, Janet," said Caroline gently. "You're having a bad day. It happens. You've got an idea about Agnes. Go on, you can tell me."

279

Janet stuck out her chin and addressed a beech tree in Caroline's sight line. "Those gals do not have enough to do. I've heard about their night... activities. So, I'm thinking, what if we got Agnes to live here permanently? They could help me look after her."

"That's wonderful. A great idea. What can I do?"

*****

"She wants me to help her pitch it to Dorothy," explained Caroline in the car. For once she was driving. Mary insisted she build up her confidence. Caroline agreed only after trying to get Anna on a live call, but a mechanical voice said her message box was full.

"A small nursing facility for dementia patients," mused Mary. "They could get funding for that. I have a feeling Holywell's feeling the pinch." She sighed thinking of the financial crisis dogging the Agency. Caroline knew the way Mary's mind worked. Then she jumped as Mary's phone rang loudly.

"Keep your eyes on the road," ordered Mary. Caroline only just made the turn onto the Oxford highway. "Hm... interesting!"

"Mareee," prompted Caroline.

"Yes, all right. One of the texts is from Anna. It's the least exciting. Just says 'ETA Alchemy School tomorrow.'"

"So, we can go...?" began Caroline.

"Absolutely. The Alchemy School is in our future too. I meant it when I said we should go to California for the Scroll, and for Anna. I will need to talk with Dame Eleanor about our expenses."

Mary thought for a moment. "You know, Caroline, I wish Anna'd tell us why she's going to The Alchemy School when our two main suspects are here. Don't forget, I need to square it with the police to release the three of us to fly back to the States. That means Sam too. I don't like leaving him here alone."

"He's not alone. I saw him coming out of Leni's room this morning. And do you know what he said?"

"Cannot guess. Now Caroline, pay attention. This other text says Godric St. John is awake and asking for me. Take the ring road until the exit for the John Whitcliffe. We'll see him first."

"He said, 'It's not what you think.'"

"Who, Godric?"

"No, Sam, of course. So, I asked him. What is it then? He was so sweet. He said he's sleeping on Leni's floor because of her nightmares. 'She needs a friend, not a hookup,' he said."

"Good for him. I like that boy. Did you hear what I said about going to the hospital?"

"Yes, but what about St. Julian's and Dame Eleanor?"

"Later. That's the third text. She's asking us to come at 3 this afternoon. For an international video call, she says."

"Oh, that gives us lots of time."

"Not as much as she thinks. We're going early to have that private conversation about educational funding."

Caroline shook her fading curls and moved the car too suddenly into the fast lane of the highway, forcing a supermarket truck to brake sharply. Mary gripped her seat. A couple of grey spires popped up from behind bony trees on the horizon. Today is more Springlike, mused Mary. With the morning mist dissolved into sunshine, Oxford, here we come.

They found Godric St. John asleep. Under a clean white sheet, tubes stuck out of both arms. The intensive care ward was stuffy and smelled of disinfectant. With his head encased in bandages, there was something odd about the way it rested — on a sort of padded ring. A nurse addressed them in a Polish accent, or so Mary assumed by his name tag.

"He's been asking for you. The doctors finally agreed we could call. Be careful because he mustn't move his head for another twenty-four hours. We don't want any pressure on his brain from the wound. That's the reason for the surgical ring."

Caroline had mistaken the young man for a doctor. Mary knew he wore nurse colors. He had a beatific smile on his unshaven face that made one forget the dark circles around his eyes. Yellow cropped hair stuck out at an angle from under his green-blue cap.

"Miss Wandwalker, the doctor says you and your friend can stay until he wakes. The police explained how important it is if he can remember the attack. They are sending someone soon." The nurse nodded briefly, then left them both on the grubby orange chairs near the bed.

Caroline looked nervously at the monitors. She grabbed Mary's hand. Surprised and not displeased, Mary gave it a squeeze, then patted Caroline's arm.

A gargling sound came from the region of Godric St. John's mouth. There was a minute quiver of hairs on his hunting dog chin. To Mary, his head appeared fragile, as if made of glass.

"Professor St. John," she whispered, dragging her chair closer. "Are you awake? It's me, Mary Wandwalker. You asked to see me."

Caroline hardly dared breathe. The corpselike figure on the bed made a rattling sound. Mary checked the ward; no one in earshot.

"Waaarh…"

"What? What do you want, Professor?"

"Perhaps he means water," said Caroline, pointing at a plastic tumbler with a straw on the bedside table.

"Oh, yes." Mary rose hastily, dropping her heavy handbag on the floor with a thump. Both women looked around guiltily. Machines continued humming. The nurse flashed them a reassuring smile from a desk near the door.

Holding a straw to Godric's chapped lips, Mary saw the lines of pain deepen as he swallowed. Even moving his jaw and throat muscles must hurt. When she heard a tiny gurgle, she pulled back the cup.

"Professor, we'll come back when you're feeling better."

"No," came a voice stronger than expected.

The coherent word was shocking, more so than the wince. Mary sat down and waited. More words came, frustratingly slowly at first, then with more conviction as if each was a tiny flame.

"I'm... sorry about... your friend. And... that girl."

"Friend?" said Caroline puzzled. "He must mean Anna. What did he do to Anna?"

Godric St. John unfolded his story. Without using the term blackmail, he explained his bargain with Anna: the Scroll for dropping charges against Leni.

Truth be told, the girl had not really hurt him. He'd pretended it was worse to frighten her because he never wanted the college to have anything to do with trafficked women. Later he'd realized that the incident could be used further to his advantage. He'd set up the meeting with Anna that confirmed his sense of her having... special skills. Anna would steal the real Alchemy Scroll and bring it to him.

"Was it for the money?" asked Caroline, shocked.

"Was it for the prestige?" added Mary, not shocked.

"Antibiotics," whispered the sick man, and then had to swallow a cough. After a minute's rest, he could go on. "We think, that is Mer-Corp thinks, that the real Alchemy Scroll must be soaked in a very ancient, very powerful antibiotic. That's why they funded my Chair and Ravi's scholarship. He did most of the historical digging, even though he is really a research chemist like me."

Ravi Patel had uncovered references in other alchemy texts that pointed to specially treated herbs combined in unspecified ways. These were the medicines used by physician- alchemists like Francis Andrew Ransome. Unfortunately, the tradition of secrecy meant that the identity of the herbs and secrets of their combination were impossible to ascertain.

Instead of names, the herbs had pseudonyms such as "snakeheart tree," or metaphors like "root of living gold." Eventually, Ravi learned that the St. Julian's Scroll had the only complete sample in its vellum copy. With paper versions, the concoctions decayed. They'd tested the seventeenth-century version to be sure.

Sources hinted that only the Key Keeper knew how to make the antibiotic active. A real Water of Life, Ravi enthused. He'd said it again when he visited Godric a few hours ago, unless the older man had dreamed it.

"Antibiotic resistance is huge, an international crisis," said Mary, understanding.

"That's what Mer-Corp said." The voice was cracking. "A new viable antibiotic..." he whispered on weakening gulps, "billions, billions of dollars. I *had* to find the real Alchemy Scroll... give Mer-Corp. Had no choice. They would not let it stay at St. Julian's. A rival business could..." He stopped, voice dried to sand.

Mary and Caroline leant forward on their chairs. They did not hear a man approaching.

"Professor St. John, what about the attack that brought you here? What can you remember?"

The police constable made Mary and Caroline jump. Godric was silent, then began to gasp. Ticking from the monitor nearest his head turned into a loud whine. At once, the young nurse materialized.

"You go, all of you, now," he ordered. They went.

*****

Arriving at St. Julian's, Mary and Caroline met a wall of sound. Every city center tower and spire have bells that go mad at noon, Mary recalled. It was as if they were dodging chimes as well as hungry bodies. Of course, the students were aiming for the dining hall and lunch. The two women watched androgynous characters in jeans and woolly hats chain their bikes to the racks by the Porter's Lodge.

Mary signaled to Caroline to attach herself to the group. They would slip inside unnoticed. No need to alert the Porters, and via them, Dame Eleanor, to the early arrival of Miss Wandwalker and her colleague from the Enquiry Agency.

Mary saw how much Caroline relished the sensation of being invisible and purposeful. Once they reached Dame Eleanor's private office, Caroline grinned at the way Mary waved dismissal to the confused male secretary.

"Here, you can't just... Miss, um...Wandwalker? No, stop."

"Dame Eleanor's expecting us."

Waiting a microsecond after a couple of loud raps, Mary launched herself inside, followed by Caroline. The Principal rose from her desk frowning at the sudden intrusion.

"Miss Wandwalker. You're far too early. Please return at the correct time."

"We're early because we have urgent questions for you. It's about Mer-Corp."

Mary took the big chair opposite Dame Eleanor. Caroline dragged another from the corner and sat down looking expectant. The secretary remained standing with his mouth open.

"Mer-Corp?" Dame Eleanor ran her fingers through her expensive hair. "It's all right, Jonathan, I'll handle this."

Today her jacket and skirt were dark mustard trimmed with black lace. Caroline glimpsed nails painted to match. She tried not to stare. The Principal lifted a cigarette from her desk drawer, lit it, and took a long drag. She stared at Mary with a haunted expression. Mary's grey eyes didn't waver. Caroline coughed. The Dame looked at her impatiently, then pulled a steel ashtray from her desk drawer and stubbed out the cigarette.

"I guess there are no more secrets now," she said wearily. "I'll tell you about Mer-Corp."

285

PART TEN
DISTILLATIO

CHAPTER 42
MER-CORP

Dame Eleanor rested her eyes on the dead cigarette. Slowly, she recounted her story of a poor Latino family who had an ambitious daughter. The nerd of her high school, Eleanor Martinez refused to be daunted. Never mind the obstacles, she would succeed no matter what. Never mind she lived in a culture where so much was stacked against the poor.

"My parents spent everything they could get their hands on to get me to college, and I worked cleaning rich people's houses. By the time of my doctoral program, my… my student debt got out of control. I'd maxed out my credit cards. The only jobs were minimum wage; especially for people like me."

Dame Eleanor's American accent had shifted. Even to Mary's inexperienced ears she sounded less educated and poorer.

"My folks were undocumented back then." Dame Eleanor glanced at Caroline. "Illegal immigrants, so stuck in the worst jobs, some not even minimum wage. They came over the border as a teenage couple. I was born in the US, so I'm legal; but then the US government started cracking down on migrant families, even in California. When I was starting grad school, every dollar went on trying to get my parents naturalized."

"Did you manage it?" asked Caroline.

"No. At least, not until Mer-Corp." Dame Eleanor dragged her eyes from the ashtray on her desk and stared gloomily above Mary's head. She cleared her throat.

"There was gossip in the Student Union of special assistance for students like me — those with perfect grades who

289

had financial *and* immigration problems. You had to apply to a box address, very discreet. I didn't understand at the time why I had to send a photograph and a family history, going back as far as possible."

"History," said Mary. "Let me guess. The box address was for The European History Foundation."

"Yes." Dame Eleanor dropped her head to her antique desk. Wearily she raised it and swept Mary and Caroline with her bleak expression.

"A Mer-Corp rep wrote back and directed me to the EHF. They said it was the educational arm of their community outreach. I got a big grant, no strings attached. As well as paying off all my debts with money to spare, they passed my papers to an excellent immigration lawyer. Mer-Corp picked up his bill."

Caroline looked confused. "But I thought the European History Foundation hates immigrants. They're racists. White supremacists."

"*European* history," said Mary, grimly. "They wanted to know that you are of Spanish descent."

Dame Eleanor would not look at her. "I thought the fact they helped me, born of Mexican immigrants, proved the EHF were not racists. Now I realize Mer-Corp has a bigger game. They were after the Alchemy Scroll, or manuscripts like it, all that time. The EHF cared about my heritage, but they were working for Mer-Corp, who'd picked up that my research would attract colleges like St. Julian's."

"How do you mean?" that was Caroline. Mary concentrated on every muscle in Dame Eleanor's jaw, every flicker of her eyes. Even now, she did not trust her to tell the whole truth. The Dame had paused on Caroline's question.

"The EHF suggested that I focus on medieval feminist theology in actual manuscripts. Julian of Norwich had been a chapter in my thesis. First, they backed me for a research fellowship in the States. When the position of Principal of St. Julian's came up — well, it made sense to apply. Big-name scholars were suddenly keen to recommend me. The EHF even paid for me to come over to England and lobby the dons."

Mary cut in. "St. Julian's was delighted to hook an academic with a limitless source of funding. You were perfect."

Dame Eleanor swallowed. "As soon as I was in position, they er... suggested they could help the college with its debts. They offered to endow a chair in Biochemistry and provide studentships."

She glanced at Mary and flushed. "Don't look at me like that. It happens all the time, Miss Wandwalker. Governments don't pay for education anymore. Colleges are told to rely on fees that students can't afford without building up a ton of debt. The alternative is sponsorship."

"They wanted the Alchemy Scroll as collateral," said Mary witheringly. Caroline looked horrified.

"Yes," said Dame Eleanor sadly. "They expected us to offer it on loan. I knew the college governors would never agree. With some fancy footwork, we got the loan signed without handing over the Alchemy Scroll. Unfortunately, Mer-Corp still held the mortgages."

"I thought the Alchemy Scroll was safe. Mother Julian's deed insists that the Scroll never leaves the premises. Then Mer-Corp announced they were sending an expert to authenticate it. It only took a couple of tests before Godric confirmed that our Scroll, the one in St. Julian's possession, is a seventeenth-century copy. The rest you know."

"Not quite," pounced Mary. "This isn't only about St. Julian's. You've told us that Mer-Corp had something scandalous they could hold over you."

Dame Eleanor scowled. "You're right. You don't need to spell out what they are holding over me. Thanks to their manipulations, my career is funded by fascists." She stopped and shook her head as if she could wash away the words she'd spoken. Then continued sorrowfully.

"Godric said he'd heard rumors about the EHF. So, I told him I'd make enquiries."

She hesitated. "I realized then I didn't want to know. St. Julian's didn't want to know, could not afford to know the truth about the EHF." Her expression became bleak. "A scholar who takes money from white supremacists is finished. Look at Cookie Mac. He began as Mer-Corp's reputable expert. Now, thanks to his work for the EHF, getting kicked out of the Symposium is just the beginning."

"Where is he?"

"He's been removed to the secure psychiatric wing of the John Whitcliffe, for evaluation. Didn't the police tell you?"

Mary frowned. She thought Caroline was still trying to understand the implications of the Dame's story when the other woman spoke.

"You were naive," she said, "and in an impossible position. Come on, Mary. You can see that."

Mary sniffed. Dame Eleanor's feelings were not her priority. "Perhaps you didn't know what you were getting into," she conceded. "Not at first."

Caroline winced as Mary went on.

"You were vulnerable, and you were targeted. But there was a point, wasn't there, Dame Eleanor, when you got comfortable with all that lovely money? You stopped caring about where the money was coming from, or if there would be strings." Mary crossed her arms and waited.

Dame Eleanor opened her mouth as if to retort, then closed it again.

"I did what I had to," she muttered.

"A man is dead." Mary's voice burned. "A young man. He did not sell his soul."

"Mary, that's enough," expostulated Caroline.

No, it's not, thought Mary, but her tongue stubbed on her own failings, her own unconscious racism that she had shown to the thoughtful D.P. back in Los Angeles. Yes, all right she did feel guilty. But right now, her job was to lever Dame Eleanor and St. Julian's away from harm. Therefore, she was about to say more when they were interrupted by a chime from Dame Eleanor's laptop. They'd forgotten that international call.

CHAPTER 43
PRESIDENT OF THE
ALCHEMY SCHOOL

"Wait please, wait while I set this up," said the Dame, pressing keys and plugging in speakers. The large screen on a wall glowed and warmed into halves. Scrambled American voices got louder. To Mary, one had an eerie familiarity.

"Director Oldcastle," she exclaimed, as that impeccably groomed woman came into focus. "The Los Angeles Museum Director," Mary explained to Caroline in an undertone. The other half of the screen showed a shaven-headed man with Native American features. He was sitting at a desk with a wall of print journals behind him.

"Good afternoon, English colleagues," he boomed, beaming at the camera. "And my long-lost cousin, Melissa." Mary caught his amused tone while noticing signs of discomfort. Could he be in pain?

"President Wiseman," acknowledged Melissa Oldcastle, who seemed be in some sort of grand bedroom in a blue satin robe. What time could it be over there? wondered Caroline.

"Jez, please," said the deep male voice. "After all, we've just discovered we're related over the St. Julian's Alchemy Scroll."

"Can somebody please explain what's going on?" Mary spoke loudly. She could not see any microphones attached to the enormous screen.

"Miss Wandwalker, I presume?" Wiseman grinned. "And perhaps the lady next to you is Mrs. Jones? President, sorry,

293

Principal Eleanor I know from the college website. We've been emailing. Miss Wandwalker. Do consult the text you've just received from an old friend of mine. We go way back to my Army Intelligence days."

Mary took out her phone automatically and stared at the text. It couldn't be. It was.

"I see," she said.

"What?" whispered Caroline. Mary passed her the phone. The text was laconic, even for Mr. Jeffreys. 'Wiseman trustworthy,' it read.

"Like your Dr. Watson, I could say I left part of myself in Afghanistan." Mary looked up. Now she could see that Wiseman, probably in his forties, was tapping the oddly shaped back of his chair by his shoulder.

"He's in a wheelchair," murmured Caroline.

"You enjoy English detective fiction?" Mary said awkwardly. Wiseman laughed again.

"Ah yes, we have an English mystery here, do we not? The whereabouts of the famous St. Julian's Alchemy Scroll, the medieval manuscript that never leaves your College. Except, it did. Well, I know where the original is."

"What? Where? You didn't tell me *that*." All the women spoke at once. Mary held up her hand. She heard herself croak: "Where *is* the Scroll, President Wiseman?"

Jez Wiseman smiled broadly. Mary was reminded of some of Mr. Jeffreys's expressions, too self-satisfied for her comfort.

"I believe the true St. Julian's Scroll to be somewhere safe, close to our Alchemy School. We're a hundred miles north of LA, you know. I had a phone message from a young Englishwoman, plus a touch of Romanian, if I am not mistaken. She said she would arrive shortly with a rare Alchemy Scroll from Europe. Given the wildfires in the mountains, I got back to her at once. She's storing it in a fireproof vault until she can get here."

Caroline leant over her chair and hugged Mary.

"It's Anna."

"Yes, of course, it's Anna," said Mary, impatiently. "We're going to meet her. Erm, Mr., er, Dr. Wiseman..."

"Call me Jez, like Cousin Melissa," he said. Mary detected a mischievous tone in his reference to the blond woman. "I got my doctorate here in Jungian and Archetypal Psychology. The army paid for my education after I was invalided out. Depth Psychology inspired me to do some genealogy; get to those roots, so to speak. You can tell that my ancestors are Native American."

"Genealogy, that's how he found me," chipped in Melissa Oldcastle, looking self-conscious. And she's embarrassed, realized Mary. There's something more.

The President was enjoying himself. "You see, Miss Wandwalker, I haven't told you my full name: it's Jez Robert Ransome Wiseman. Seems I'm descended from..."

"Francis Andrew Ransome," exclaimed Dame Eleanor. "Our seventeenth-century thief."

"Roberta Le More." That was Mary and Caroline.

"Robert and Ransome," added Mary.

"Just so," grinned Wiseman again. "Ms. Le More was Ransome's second wife. I'm descended from their daughter. The names Robert, Roberta, and Ransome remained in the family. My grandfather was Ransome Wiseman, for example."

He grinned. "We didn't know about the other children of Francis Andrew Ransome, our Connecticut alchemist. It appears that those born of the first wife were none too keen on an African in the family. After Ransome's death, they pushed Roberta Le More out of the colony."

"That's my side," said Melissa with a strained smile. "President... er Jez, showed me that I'm descended from the family of the first wife, an heiress from Wales named Isabel."

"We know Roberta moved to live with Native Americans," said Caroline. "She took the name Roberta Africanus."

"That's right, Mrs. Jones. They respected her as a healer. Eventually, she married again and practiced as a medicine woman. Her daughter married into the tribe. Later they were

295

forcefully relocated by the American Government to Wisconsin. Some got to helping plantation slaves run away, I'm proud to say."

The President tapped his wheelchair's arm and surveyed his rapt audience. He was relaxed, yet watchful. What did he want? Mary wondered.

"What do you want?" she said.

"Reputation," he replied unexpectedly.

"And I, that is we, at The Los Angeles Museum, want to know who killed our curator," added Melissa Oldcastle.

"You appreciated D.P.?" queried Mary. "You liked his dedication to the Museum?"

"Yes, I did," said Melissa, stiffly. "Although he was only briefly our Intern, he was my protégé, was Dennis Patrick Murphy. A good, hardworking intelligent young man with a smile for everyone. Now it seems his death — and my museum — is mixed up with racists. I wish I'd never heard of The European History Foundation."

"What is the EHF to you?" Mary queried and to her surprise, Wiseman answered.

"When they offered to sponsor the Alchemy Symposium and include the magnificent Scroll, we had no clue what they were. That is, I asked my assistant to check them out, and she said they were simply an educational charity set up by Mer-Corp, a respectable pharmaceutical business."

Caroline coughed. Pharma was a dirty word to her, Mary recalled.

"I still don't see *your* reputation problem," she said, looking directly at Wiseman. She knew the answer yet wanted his reaction.

"Perhaps I'm being oversensitive since the EHF is only briefly mentioned on the pre-publicity for the Symposium. That event has been well and truly canceled."

Wiseman smoothed his scalp where his hair would have been if he'd had any.

"You don't know us, Miss Wandwalker. Our Alchemy School is small, founded by a visionary educator in Depth Psychology, the science of the unconscious. We train clinicians, foster creativity in an incredible Humanities program for arts practitioners, plus doctorates in Jungian psychology, social justice psychology, myth, and alchemy. Ours is the most distinguished Counseling program in the state."

He paused and screwed up his mouth. "The EHF is inimical to everything we stand for. I don't ever want their name in this building."

"I'm glad to know it," said Mary. "I don't believe that the EHF is able to do any damage, not to your school, anyway, nor to the Los Angeles Museum of Early Manuscripts. But Director Oldcastle is right. D.P. was murdered for the Alchemy Scroll. This isn't over until we know who did it."

Melissa Oldcastle looked shocked. "Surely Professor Macdonald..."

"...is sick and in the John Whitcliffe hospital," continued Mary. "We think from handling the real Alchemy Scroll without gloves. He stole it from you, all right. But he claims that D.P. was dead when he arrived in the museum attic. He *said* he took the Scroll to keep it safe."

Dame Eleanor broke in. "They've arrested Professor Macdonald for attacking Godric St. John in his St. Julian's study. Both want the Alchemy Scroll for themselves." She paused. "He denies it, I understand. As for the Los Angeles murder, your police say they require more evidence before making an arrest."

This was news to Mary. She looked thoughtfully at Caroline, who nodded.

"Ladies, now we three institutions are in contact," began Wiseman. "I want to hire you, Miss Wandwalker and Mrs. Jones, to protect our Alchemy School's reputation by finding the killer of Melissa's curator. An unsolved murder means notoriety. We cannot afford the stink emanating from the EHF."

Mary jumped. Relief flamed in her. There was no credit in any of her cards, nor Caroline's. Too dangerous to get Anna

297

to steal their tickets to California, she told Caroline. The more Anna hacked into airlines' computers, the greater the likelihood of her getting caught. An official investigation of Anna did not bear thinking of. However, Dame Eleanor had other ideas.

"Miss Wandwalker's Agency is retained by St. Julian's College. Exclusively."

Mary coughed. She did not remember signing on to this.

"Are you saying our interests are different?" countered Wiseman.

"We all want D.P.'s killer found." That was Melissa. Her frown was directed, Mary presumed, at Dame Eleanor.

"And we mean to find him," said Mary, "or her. Dr. Wiseman, let us discuss business in person. Mrs. Jones and I will be traveling to California shortly. We plan to meet our associate and collect the Alchemy Scroll for St. Julian's. That *was* our task, was it not?" Mary challenged.

The Dame nodded unhappily.

A strange gurgling interrupted Mary. No, not her stomach. Caroline in the next chair swayed. Something wasn't right. Mary turned hastily to the screen.

"Director Oldcastle, I suggest that you, Dr. Wiseman and I speak again when I'm in California. I'd like to ask about visitors to the museum around the time of D.P.'s death."

"So do the police," said Melissa. "They want to talk to you too. I think we might hire you as well." She paused. "We owe D.P."

"We'll discuss this later," said Mary too quickly. She grabbed the remote from the astonished Dame and closed the screen. "Okay," she said to the St. Julian's principal, "time for partial payment. Give me a card so I can book our flights to California and other expenses. Otherwise, I'm taking Wiseman's offer right now. We will no longer be acting for St. Julian's."

Dame Eleanor goggled at her. Then she noticed Caroline shaking.

"What's the matter with Mrs. Jones? Is she sick?"

298

"Yes. It happens." Mary did not take her eye off Dame Eleanor.

"Have this card." It was gold and bore the stamp of Mer-Corp. Mary liked the irony. She pocketed it.

"I need to take Caroline home. Or back to Holywell."

"The airport," whispered Caroline.

"No, you can't fly like this. You know you can't, Caroline."

"I have an idea. Something that might help Mrs. Jones. Come with me, both of you." Dame Eleanor was recovering her dignity.

"Where are we going?" That was Mary.

"You've seen it, but let me take Mrs. Jones to our Alchemy Scroll. The one made by Roberta Le More. The Key Keeper came to visit it. I didn't tell you before. She said it had good magic; that it, too, could... help."

"Caroline..." began Mary.

"I want to see this Scroll. It's Roberta's book. Mary, please don't leave me."

CHAPTER 44
ROBERTA LE MORE'S SCROLL

Outside the Principal's office, Mary was surprised to see Ravi Patel huddled with Dame Eleanor's pale secretary. Absorbed in a laptop screen, neither man looked up. Mary frowned at Godric's well-traveled research assistant.

Caroline tugged Mary's arm to follow Dame Eleanor striding out of the room. Mary gave the shaking woman her most encouraging smile. Still wondering what she might have asked Ravi, Mary and Caroline followed Dame Eleanor down spiral staircases and corridors to the special Scroll Room.

Appropriately, the Scroll dwelled in the oldest part of St. Julian's. Fragments from the story of the medieval Hall of Residence floated back to Mary as she followed Dame Eleanor's straight back. Caroline trembled, even her fingers digging into Mary's arm were shuddering.

They came to where only cream paint covered stone walls; worn slabs made up the floor. With no heating, Caroline's teeth started chattering. Here there were only simple benches that might have come from the six-hundred-year-old chapel.

An incongruously large key emerged from Dame Eleanor's handbag. She opened the simple wooden door and beckoned Mary and Caroline, careful to lock the door from the inside. The room was unpainted stone, apart from the huge oak beams that crossed the ceiling. Mary flashed on an image of Druids in an old forest and shook her head. Caroline was sick; there was no time for daydreaming.

"They reproduced Mother Julian's cell," said Dame Eleanor, quietly. "Twelve feet square with a window into the chapel, now blocked off. Another opened to outside, for food, slops, and laundry. We think that window, looking onto the street, was where she did her teaching. Today it would be called counseling. Of course, nothing like that happened here at St. Julian's; the cell was constructed for the Scroll and its rare visitors."

"I thought anchorites were shut away from the world," said Mary. She sat Caroline down on the bench next to the glass case. Peering in, they could see a bundle of rust-colored cloth that must be protecting the Scroll.

"Shut away, yes," said Dame Eleanor, recovering her confidence by teaching. "From the world, no. Anchorites were an active part of their parish community. They chose to isolate themselves to pray and struggle spiritually *for* those living hard lives around them. As a result, they would be consulted about — well, you can guess the sorts of religious and moral problems."

She sat on the opposite bench and smiled at her captive audience. "Mother Julian also wrote letters. Unfortunately, as far as we know, none survived. However, contemporary wills record that she was contacted by the devout in spiritual distress. We think that's how she came to know Master Giles. It was he who built the original Hall. They funded it together."

"She was... a kind... of spiritual private detective." Caroline's whisper came out in bites. It meant the depression had gotten worse; Mary knew. She squeezed Caroline's hand. Dame Eleanor rose and went to the glass case. She opened it with a small silver key.

Through the arched window, Mary glimpsed a couple of students in gowns, heading for a tutorial, no doubt. The Alchemy Scroll case had a drawer built below the glass display panel. From this, Dame Eleanor took out soft leather gloves that looked handstitched to Mary. The Dame took great care in sliding them over each finger. Carefully, she lifted the glass lid and grasped the bundle.

As the wrappings came off, the smell began to permeate: spicy, like cinnamon or cloves, and rosemary, sage, maybe a hint of mint? It felt... medicinal. Mary gave up trying to decode the scents. The Alchemy Scroll wasn't for her, after all.

Caroline sat very still: her whole being concentrated on the Scroll partly revealed on the table next to the case. She reminded Mary of a hunting dog woven into a medieval tapestry. Slowly her shivering lessened. Mary wanted to talk. She should be organizing, doing something. She smiled wryly, then sat back, watching.

"There you go, Mrs. Jones," said the Dame. She, too, had eyes only for the Scroll. "I can let you use these gloves. They're specially made."

"No," whispered Caroline, stepping to the table. Talking was difficult, facing questions worse. Mary never understood that. She liked making decisions: They made her feel alive, not powerless. Looking at Caroline's intense frown, Mary signaled to Dame Eleanor to let her be.

Caroline sniffed the fragrant odor. She put her hands together as if she were praying. Mary heard some sounds that could be words — but in what language?

She was intrigued. Caroline had no other languages. Also, this was not the real Scroll of Mother Julian, but that of Roberta Le More, artist and alchemist. Mary tried to recall things Caroline had said. How she'd had long talks with Janet in the motel; how the witch needed to be relieved of her burden. Mary suddenly thought: Was Caroline going to be the next Key Keeper? *Caroline*?

With both hands, Caroline unrolled the Scroll a little further.

"The gloves," exclaimed Dame Eleanor, jumping to Caroline's side.

"No," said Caroline again. "I must use my bare hands. The Key Keeper said so; for the first time I touch it"

Mary stood to peer over Caroline's shoulder. Her previous time with the Scroll had concentrated on vellum, paper, and authenticity. Today, Le More's art released her sense of awe.

Gold-leafed creatures emerged from green fields. A few tiny flecks of gold seemed to rise into the lamplight.

Stunned into stillness, Mary stared at the dreamlike happenings on the page. Human figures faced each other; the man's head was a golden ball with rays reaching up to huge stars and out to the distant mountains; the woman's silver head was sickle-shaped and surrounded by birds like eagles with white beaks. Some of the black letters glowed because they had tips like tiny flames.

"At the conjunction of the sun and the moon there will be a great conflagration," came Caroline's strained voice. Mary saw that the new section showed fire spreading everywhere; it seemed to be advancing up a distant mountain. Flames swirled serpentlike in all directions. The three women were transfixed. The fire flickered and writhed; it burned rose red, bloody scarlet, and gold. Ash, Mary tasted ash.

Stepping back from the book, Caroline bumped into Dame Eleanor. Ignoring the Dame, Caroline's wet eyes found Mary. "Anna, the fire," she gasped.

Before Mary could speak, Caroline collapsed on the floor in a dead faint.

CHAPTER 45
LAND OF THE FIRE

The wildfire Jez Wiseman had mentioned changed that very night. It became a raging monster with limitless form and gargantuan appetite. Lightning ignited bleached hillsides in Los Angeles and Ventura counties. A range of mountains separated the coastal cities from the dry scrub of the interior. Los Angelenos rejoiced that the winds blew away from them to the drier north. There, flames jumped from tree to tree, until they nearly attained the ferocity of a nuclear blast.

Fire ate everything in its path, even vegetation damp from sprinkles of rain. The State Governor suspended flights to and from Southern California because of the smoke driven by high winds. For a hundred square miles, the earth melted into flames.

At Holywell, Caroline was sluggish. She slept for long stretches. Nothing came from Anna, despite their efforts to connect with her. When they realized that the wildfire on the TV news must be closing in on The Alchemy School, Anna's last known destination, Caroline became frantic. Even Mary decided that they could not wait. With Mr. Jeffreys's help, she arranged a flight to a private runway fifty miles to the east.

Sam begged to accompany them. He wanted to bring Leni too — to meet his parents. Too many complications, Mary said, looking at Caroline's haunted expression. Her current problem was Caroline. She remained trapped in some dark place, waiting for news that Anna was safe.

"Listen, Sam. We've got to get to Anna — and the real Scroll *fast*. The wind direction in California could change any

305

moment and burn down The Alchemy School. Fire already threatens Santa Emilia on the coast," Mary told him.

"I'm not delaying. Your parents insist you stay here in the UK. Yes, I know Dorothy's getting the charges dropped against Leni, but paperwork takes days, and Leni doesn't have a passport. It is all too complicated for this emergency. Wait here."

"But…but," Sam stammered. Mary reached for her backup argument.

"Besides, we need you to protect Leni and the witches. Remember, we don't know who took Janet. *Someone* stuck her in The Old Hospital to get the key to the Scroll. That person is out there and is dangerous."

"But…"

"We don't know for sure it's Cookie Mac." That was Caroline. Mary jumped. She is paying attention after all, thought Mary with relief. Sam was outraged.

"That racist scum killed my brother, I know it."

"He's sick, I know," said Mary wearily. "He handled the Scroll without gloves. We *think* it's Cookie Mac; I'm not so sure."

Caroline spoke again, more animated. "Don't you want to make sure Professor St. John sticks to his retraction? To support Leni until the charges are dropped?" Caroline began to shake; her hands were moon white.

Sam stopped protesting. He leaned over the breakfast table and dragged the big teapot to him. Then he grabbed a clean cup and the milk carton.

"I'm sure your friend's okay," Sam said. "She's quite a lady. I could tell that when we met at the airport."

Mary coughed, smiled, and patted Caroline's arm. They had to leave in twenty minutes for the flight booked on Dame Eleanor's Mer-Corp credit card. She nodded at the young man.

"Thanks, Sam. Keep working with Holywell's lawyers. Just being there for Leni is what she needs. I promise we'll be back as soon as we can."

"With Anna," whispered Caroline.

"With Anna," confirmed Mary. "Plus, the real Alchemy Scroll," she added. It would not escape her again.

*****

It took several changes of planes before Caroline and Mary landed in a remote airstrip. The smoke writhed thick as fog. Neither had slept on the eighteen-hour journey. Mary formulated plans to wring Anna's neck; Caroline was exhausted by despair.

As the plane wheels bumped along the tarmac, Mary heard a ping. This time it was no dream. She leaned forward to grab her purse. Yes, it was a text from Anna. That bare fact proved enough to revive Caroline. In Anna's laconic way, she directed them to La Luna, a valley near The Alchemy School.

"Come now. Booked house for us in grove of sacred healing."

Gazing in the direction where Anna waited, they saw the sky blaze red. The only thing to do was to rent a car. They drove west in the late California afternoon. Although the heat had increased, light dimmed behind bronze mist. The air inside the car began to taste of charcoal. Not fog; smoke, acknowledged Mary. Rounding a turn several miles into a valley, Mary and Caroline gasped.

It was an apocalyptic vista. Spiraling towers of smoke wound into the sky as if several volcanos had erupted. Now dark red, the ragged sun sank into a bloody sea on the right. To their left and as far as the eye could see, the black bones of trees littered the slopes interspersed with ash. Patches of ground still smoked.

This was the area where the fire had been tamed, not extinguished. Watching excerpts from California TV, Mary had learned that fire might linger in tree roots underground. Smoldering embers could reignite days after the fire crews moved on.

Beyond the corpses of trees was their destination: straight into a black curtain of sky with flaming edges. This was the mountain range between them and La Luna Valley, where Anna was waiting. All they could see of it was smoke rising like dragons.

Mary wanted to shut her eyes. Just in time, she remembered that she was driving. Those dragons had feet of fire; the horizon glowing below their scaly clouds of ash. She steered the car to the side of the road. Time for an informed decision, she decided.

Without speaking Caroline pointed to notices that proclaimed the highway officially closed, even to Emergency Services. They were still twenty miles from La Luna valley. The route rose steeply on a twisty narrow road. Yes, on those mountains where the fire is, Mary imagined explaining to Mr. Jeffreys. Yes, the only reason no one is stopping us is that the authorities consider it too hazardous to require a roadblock.

"They're calling in fire crews from other states," said Caroline. "Nevada, Oregon, Washington... I thought that's where the White House and Senate are?"

"Washington is also a state," replied Mary, straining to make out the darkening road. "Way up north, I believe. Anything more about the road to La Luna?"

"No, nothing about roads. Um... Mary, they say the fire is advancing toward La Luna township. Oh, see this post from the town before the internet cut off."

Don't worry about folks in La Luna valley was the reassuring message. Anyone not evacuated to Los Angeles is sheltering in La Luna High School. A whole division of firefighters is here to protect them. They were digging fire breaks right now.

Mary didn't know what a fire break was. She didn't need Caroline to spell out her conviction that wherever Anna was, it was not on a camp bed in La Luna High School. What *was* she playing at? Anna knew that they knew that she had stolen the Scroll from Cookie Mac. Was this part of a bigger plan?

Mary banged the steering wheel in frustration. Caroline silently offered the thermos that contained the airport coffee Mary had rejected earlier.

"Still can't stand that burnt taste," she murmured. "Okay, Caroline, if we take this road called Foothill, I think it will connect to the 150, the mountain road to La Luna. If the fire... well anyway. What's the address of Anna's rented house?"

"Oakgrove, one word; a grove of California Oaks. The land was won in a card game in the nineteenth century. In the 1940s, they built workers' houses under the oak trees. Apparently, the shade helps with summer heat. Um."

Caroline was reading from the Wikipedia entry on her iPad to keep calm. To show her appreciation, Mary restarted the car and headed up Foothill toward the burning mountains. Impossible to make it to La Luna, but they had to try. Anything to put off telling Caroline that they could not reach Anna.

In companionable silence, they drove through oak and sycamore woodland. Daylight began to die, and not because of the whirlpools of smoke. Soon Mary switched on the windscreen wipers to flick away falling ash. They were entirely alone on the road.

Entering the 150, they came to a deserted barricade. Caroline got out of the car to drag it aside. She was back slotting in her seatbelt before the older woman found words of sense and caution. Mary sighed, easing off the brake.

The thin road wound between mountains with their peaks on fire. After half an hour of thicker smoke and a redder sky, they swung around almost 360 degrees and reached a hilltop. Caroline gasped; Mary was too stunned for sound.

"It's the end of the world." For a moment Caroline was awed out of her anxiety.

Mary gulped. She had no memory of stopping the car. They gazed in silence. Fire poured over the mountains in expanding rivers of flame. Everywhere black peaks were tipped with red gold as if some cosmic artist was painting the world in flames.

"It's California, they have wildfires. It's the way the land works," Mary whispered.

She wasn't convinced. This is not a usual fire season; it's global warming, the news said. Mary agreed. Caroline did too.

"We have to go back." Mary said it because she had to. It was her role: the responsible one. Anna, where was bloody Anna? It was her fault that they were here, dodging sparks and choking on smoke.

"There's no cellphone service. No news. We're cut off," Caroline's voice was low. Was that roaring they could hear from the valley below? The fire bounded like a thousand lions. Mary coughed. Caroline strained not to. The younger woman had that despairing look.

"We'll try a bit further," said Mary, and restarted the car. If the world is ending in fire, then it's okay to go crazy, she said to herself.

Mary never could explain the rest of that journey. Her memory played tricks as she tried to recall the car skipping between trees burning ever closer to the liquefying tarmac. Patches of flaming vegetation expanded in all directions. The wind whipped them into animal shapes. It was a dream, those burning crags and precipices, *a dream*, she would repeat.

Falling ash started to carry tiny sparks. Once they saw the fire lunge across the road ahead. Again, the car decided to slow down. Blazing sticks bounced off the windscreen while their tires crunched on clumps of soil seeded with tiny flames.

Caroline shut her eyes; Mary stared through a blind windscreen. Slamming her foot on the gas pedal, the car shot ahead and out into the dark. Caroline opened her eyes and turned her head as a wall of fire was consuming the road behind.

There was no going back now. Rubber and metal could only take so much. The car could shatter and send its passengers into an elemental distillation of rock, flesh, blood, and ash.

Alchemy, thought Mary, grimly. Too much bloody alchemy. Even the lake down on their right was no barrier to the claws of flame. Fortunately, the road toward La Luna was mercifully dark, even if the fire was in pursuit of the town. Behind them, trees exploded into incandescent columns.

"The wind's trapped in the valley," said Mary. "It's beating the fire around the mountains above the lake. At least, that would be my guess."

"How far...?"

"Not far. I think we're close."

Arriving in La Luna valley, they were greeted by ghostly tissues of ash. So far, the town was fire-free, although surrounded by flaming summits. Worse still, Mary and Caroline could see ridges of fire advancing down the hillsides. Driving into Oakgrove, they saw fire trucks heading into the River Preserve, dry from several years of drought. (Caroline had checked her iPad earlier). Fire crews were fighting to save the town, as well as protect the shelter where the remaining inhabitants slept on cots.

They drove slowly through empty streets. Oakgrove's streetlamps glowed through the blizzard of ash including large embers. Finally, Mary halted the car at the address texted by Anna. Through the smoke, they glimpsed a ranch-style dwelling that was painted... was that purple?

After the unhealthy screech on the brakes, both women threw themselves out of the car. Caroline stumbled toward the house. Mary glanced back at the car and shuddered. All four wheels were running on partly melted rubber, and the windows had cracked. She could not remember what color the car had been at LAX; now it was coated with charcoal. The house before them was intact, yet shuttered and dark.

"Wait, wait, Caroline," she called. "We don't know if Anna's in there."

"Someone's in. I can see a crack in the curtains. Could be a lamp," she called out. "No one's answering. Let me find my picklocks." A birthday gift from Anna, Mary remembered. She had a bad feeling about this.

Caroline applied levers to the lock with trembling hands. Mary wanted to go back for a torch, then thought she should stick with Caroline. The sky flickered orange above the roof. White ash and glowing flakes were beginning to pile up everywhere. Mary thought it was a matter of time before the roof caught fire.

"Caroline, we've got to go. This house isn't safe." Caroline looked up at the sky.

"It's like snow."

"It may look like snow, but the roof could go any minute," said Mary, crossly.

In fact, she guessed they had longer. However, detaching Caroline from where Anna might be heading could take some doing. Beyond the street, Mary could see a glow from the hillside getting brighter. The true extent of the danger was hidden behind tall trees, some of them smoking ominously.

"We can't stay," said Mary. "We'll check if Anna is here, then head for that shelter in the La Luna High School."

Caroline rattled the door. "Nearly, nearly. Yes, now *ow*."

Falling through the door, Caroline was steadied by Mary at her heels. The room was occupied, but not by Anna. Mary and Caroline stood aghast at the figure lounging in a big armchair chair facing them. In the lamplight, it was easy to make out the gun.

CHAPTER 46
CONFRONTING DEMONS

Mary said to herself: Do not forget that rain of burning ash eating the roof. Time is not on the side of drama. Never mind the man pointing a gun at two women.

"This house could catch fire any minute," she said pleasantly. "We should leave."

There was a strangled sound from the man. The gun wobbled dangerously in his hand. I should have done a course about guns, thought Mary feverishly. I should know if the safety is off.

Caroline clutched her arm. "Get his attention," she whispered. "He'll put the gun down."

"It had to be you," said Mary, with more assurance than she felt. "There's no one left but you."

The young man twitched his lips. With the weapon, he waved to a shabby sofa adjacent the door.

Caroline sank down, knees visibly trembling. Mary never took her eyes off Ravi Patel, whose eyes were red-rimmed as if he had not slept for days. When the gun wavered, Mary saw his hand dripped sweat. Oh, not good.

"Where's Anna?" whispered Caroline, as if afraid of the answer. "What have you done with her?"

Mary managed to scan the room without moving her head. Whenever Ravi waved the gun, shadows danced across the white ceiling. She could see no sign of Anna.

"I've been waiting for five hours," said the young man hoarsely. The gun trembled again. He rested the elbow of his

313

gun hand on the chair's arm to steady himself. His other fist scrunched on his lap. Mary could see he was frightened as well as angry.

"Why don't you put the gun down," she said. "It must be heavy. You'll tire yourself out." Ravi swallowed. Mary added helpfully, "Anna could be hours."

Ravi shook his head. He had several days of beard. Even with the apocalyptic taste of flame and ash, Mary smelt unwashed male spiked with adrenalin. Ravi was close to losing control. Caroline was shaking.

"The gun," Mary said slowly, hypnotically. "The gun, Ravi. Put it down on that coffee table. We can't take it from you. See, we're too far away."

"We won't move, promise," squeaked Caroline. Mary dug her fingers into Caroline's arm. She was trying to reduce the energy in the room. Caroline was too anxious. The older woman fixed Ravi with the best smile she could produce.

"Ravi," she began, friendly (copied from Caroline). "If you put the gun down, we can help you. I presume you're here for the Alchemy Scroll?"

At that potent word, Ravi met Mary's eyes. With painful slowness, he forced his arm down. With his left hand, he peeled his fingers from the gun and rested it on the small table, pushing it closer to his right knee.

Mary could now make out that he had spilled egg down his sweater. She noticed the jacket she had first seen him wearing — was it two weeks ago? — tossed into the wooden floor's shadows.

"I'll kill you both if you move," he said defiantly. "The gun is loaded." His left knee started jiggling up and down.

"Where did you get it?" said Mary, interested as if they had just met in a pub (copied from Anna). She could hear Caroline trying to breathe more quietly.

Ravi made a harsh noise. It could have been laughter. "This is America! I went to the local gun shop and showed a driving license. Shop owner showed me how to load and shoot."

314

"How thoughtful," said Mary. Now Caroline thrust an elbow into her. No sarcasm, Mary, it said. "You don't *want* to kill us," added Mary, quickly. "All you want is the Alchemy Scroll to give to Godric St. John. So that he forgives what you did to him."

This sound was a sob. Ravi turned it into a vicious pout. He picked up the gun to show that he could, then put it down again. His hands continued sweating.

"Godric's going to be all right," Ravi said, looking down. "He knows I didn't mean to hurt him. And when that witch comes back, she'll give me the Alchemy Scroll. Or I'll kill you all."

"She's been here." Caroline's relief was heartfelt. It brought an unwelcome charge to the room. Mary flinched. Fortunately, Ravi was prepared to go on talking.

"The bitch wasn't here when I arrived. The firemen asked about her, the tenant, when they came round to check the houses. She refused to go to the high school shelter, they said. Today is the last chance. They don't know if they can stop the fire at the river bottom."

"You will have searched the house for the Alchemy Scroll," said Mary, just as if they were not in the room with a killer — the killer of D.P. Something glittered for a split second, just out of Mary's sightline. Don't let Ravi notice a shape that moved silently across the window, she prayed. A microtremor on Mary's arm meant Caroline saw it too. The shape had been human, hadn't it? I've got to distract him — for Anna. If it is Anna.

"Tell me about D.P.," she said. Bad choice. Damn.

"What the fuck?" Ravi gripped the gun, his mouth open.

"The boy who... er died. In the Los Angeles Museum," said Mary, wishing desperately she had not begun this incendiary topic. Fortunately, it seemed to tire Ravi.

"After you left, I banged on the door while he was in earshot. Because I told him I came from St. Julian's, he agreed to show me the Alchemy Scroll too. Then we both heard a noise."

Ravi stopped, but something forced him to continue. "He... was putting it back when I hit him. I *had* to. It was the only way to get the Alchemy Scroll in secret. So that Dame Eleanor wouldn't find out. Professor St. John told me to do whatever it took."

"But you didn't get it."

Ravi coughed. The smell of smoke was getting stronger.

"No." He paused. "I heard footsteps and hid. Couldn't believe it when I recognized Professor Macdonald, otherwise known as that racist troll, Cookie Mac."

He began stroking the gun with his right hand. Mary's marrow froze. "Cookie Mac took the Scroll," Ravi continued. "I'd dodged behind one of those big chests. He didn't even look at Murphy. He just grabbed the Alchemy Scroll and tiptoed round the... pool of blood and disappeared."

Mary remembered the blood. "What...did you do next?" she managed to say.

"The guy was dead. No pulse, I checked, so I knew for sure." Ravi stroked the gun again. "I don't remember much more of that night. The obvious thing was to follow Cookie Mac. I made it to the next street before I threw up." Ravi raised his head to Mary defiantly. "I thought Godric would be on my side. He promised to *understand*."

"You mean he didn't."

"Bastard said he was going to the police — when he finally got the whole story out of me. I'd done *everything* for him. For years he'd made me work like a dog. And then, when I'd risked everything, he... was going to make out it was all *my* fault."

"You didn't do it just for him," piped up Caroline, unexpectedly. "You did it for Mer-Corp, as well. They were paying you, not just by funding Professor St. John. Were you their spy at St. Julian's?"

Mary stared at Caroline. Where had this come from?

"Okay, so I send reports to Mer-Corp," muttered Ravi. "But I was going to give the Scroll to Professor Godric. He promised we'd work on it together; I'd get my doctorate at last. Maybe even a fellowship."

Mary wanted to ask more when Caroline gave a sort of gasp. "It was you, wasn't it? You put Janet Swinford in The Old Hospital."

Ah, Janet, realized Mary. Janet and Caroline's stay at The Old Hospital: She's been brooding on it. The connection with Ravi was confirmed by his expression. Resentment kept his lips clamped shut. Mary squeezed Caroline's arm again. *Be careful with the fuse that was an explosive Ravi Patel.*

"That was really clever of you," Caroline said. Ravi let out a breath. "You could visit the Key Keeper whenever you wanted."

Good girl, said Mary to herself. So hypocritical Godric had refused to take any responsibility for events getting out of hand. Ravi went on to explain that Godric didn't care if St. Julian's survived, because Mer-Corp had promised him a lucrative position in the States. So, after testing the Alchemy Scroll with chemical solvents (Mary winced), he'd pass the treasure to Mer-Corp. They'd pay a huge reward to keep it locked away so that no other pharma corporation could examine it.

Mary felt sickened. Godric's obsession and Ravi's slavish devotion had been paid for in blood by D.P. Ravi's lashing out at Godric was fueled by horror at what he'd done. His idol had abandoned him to face the murder charge alone.

Ravi must care for Godric to get in so deep, Mary surmised. She was trying to think like Caroline.

"I expect Professor St John really underestimated you," she added. "After everything you'd done for him."

Ravi's tone was bleak.

"He didn't want to know the details. 'Find the Alchemy Scroll; get that woman to reveal the Key,' he said. 'I don't care how.'"

There was something broken in Ravi. "I *revered* Godric. All he wanted was the real Alchemy Scroll — for himself."

Ravi's eyes flicked around the room. "So where is it? Where's that witch bitch? *Where is she?*" His voice cracked hysterically.

317

"No," yelled Mary, Caroline screamed. Instantly, the room went black. Mary pulled Caroline to the floor as two shots exploded above them like flashes of lightning. Something heavy fell over with a crash.

"Anna," called Caroline.

"No, no," shouted Mary. "Make for the door."

They could hear a struggle, another crash, then a man grunted incomprehensible words. The sound of breaking glass was followed by a big thump, a bang, and then a body falling hard.

Mary pulled Caroline into her arms. At least she hoped it was Caroline. She could see nothing at all. Yes, that had to be Caroline's scratchy jumper across her mouth. All they could do was crouch and wait. She listened. Surely the noises were lessening.

In the dark, Mary felt colder. Yes, air was moving like outside; there was a taste of fire. Ash must be blowing in from the broken window. She opened her eyes. A copper glow streamed from the streetlight.

"Stay still," came a woman's voice. Caroline let out a sob. It was Anna. "I'll get the light." A low moaning began; that must be Ravi.

As if by magic, a yellow light erupted from an overhead bulb. There was no sign of Anna, just an open doorway. The lamp lay smashed in the corner. Ravi Patel was crouched in front of the bookcase with blood on his jaw; he was clutching an arm, moaning: "She hit me. She broke my arm."

"Where's the gun, Anna?" shouted Mary.

"Here." Anna materialized from what they later learned was the kitchen. She was clad entirely in black and held a black ski mask in one hand. The gun rested in the other. Nonchalantly, she approached Ravi.

Mary feared Anna wanted to kick the moaning man. She coughed. At the second cough, Anna handed the gun to Mary. Taking a small roll of duct tape from a pocket, she gave that to Caroline.

318

"Tie his feet and hands, love," Anna said. "We don't want him going anywhere."

"Did you really break his arm?" Caroline looked impressed; then shamefaced.

Mary sighed. "We'll take him to the High School Evac Center. I think the car can make it. They'll have medics there." Mary was flicking ashes from her clothes.

"Is it over, Mary?" That was Caroline.

"It had better be."

Anna shook her hair out of her collar. Mary glimpsed tiny sparks leap and die. Caroline wrapped the tape around Ravi's wrists while avoiding Anna's eyes. Mary tried to work out how to remove bullets from the gun.

"Here, I'll show you," Anna said, holding out her hand. Mary hesitated, then said, firmly,

"We three have unfinished business." She handed the gun to Anna.

PART ELEVEN
IMAGINATIO

CHAPTER 47
FIRE IN THE VALLEY

In the path of the approaching fire, Mary, Caroline, and Anna gathered their wits and their prisoner. Leaving the purple house in Oakgrove was essential, yet far from straightforward.

Outside they paused under the covered porch. Fire ringed the valley of La Luna. All the mountains burned. Like furnaces, thought Mary, mesmerized. They are like furnaces of the old alchemists without the protective container.

It was Anna who jerked her back to current problems. Shaking ash off her hair, she explained she'd deposited the real Alchemy Scroll in a bank in Santa Emilia.

"I tried to imagine what you would do," she said to Mary.

The older woman tried to smile. There would be no discussions about the future until the real Scroll was back at St. Julian's, she'd decided. Anna's arson at The Old Hospital and theft of the Alchemy Scroll would be the headache of another day.

"Mary, the car's melted," came the voice of Caroline from the gate.

Staring at the black metal shape glued to the road by the remains of the tires, Mary realized she'd been optimistic about whisking them to the shelter. Caroline mumbled under her breath about the death of Janet's horse, Mercurius. She could hear the voice of her new friend in her head, she explained.

Falling ash did not make the empty street inviting. Mary opened her mouth. Perhaps she could scout out a more

323

serviceable vehicle. Before she could speak, a siren blared. A fire truck was trawling the neighborhood again.

Mary and Caroline ran into the street, Anna dragged Ravi behind. When the blue lights reached Mary's coat, she managed a wave. Three exhausted women plus a bound and gagged man arrived at the Evacuation Center in the back of the fire truck. The shelter had food, makeshift beds, and relative safety. It also had people asking a lot of questions.

Explaining duct-taped Ravi became too much for Anna and Caroline, who collapsed on adjacent camp beds. Mary stayed awake long enough to provide names to the Fire Chief. He held the only communication device still operating in the valley: a satellite phone. After a couple of calls, he ordered Ravi locked into the ambulance where he was receiving treatment.

Mary let her jaw relax. Her head was ready to roll onto the floor. Despite the noise, the lights, the coughing, and snores of around seventy evacuees, she, Caroline, and Anna fell deeply and soundlessly asleep.

CHAPTER 48
YOUR HOST, JEZ WISEMAN

It took a further two weeks to contain the Southern California wildfire. Oakgrove and much of the La Luna valley had been saved by fire crews who for several days went without sleep. On the day they were escorted out, Mary, Anna, and Caroline saw a chain of helicopters scooping water out of the reservoir.

La Luna's miracle, some said. After all, converging fires had been tearing through the valley like a marauding army. Somehow, beyond any analysis, the great wall of flames had been halted.

Meanwhile, Ravi was delivered to the police in Santa Emilia. Dame Eleanor informed Mary in a terse phone call that the geographical wandering of the Alchemy Scroll no longer required discretion. Their investigative work had enabled Mr. Jeffreys to put pressure on Mer-Corp to hold off on those pesky mortgages. He even got them to reduce the interest payments to something of a bargain. There would be a celebration when the Alchemy Scroll arrived back at St. Julian's. A chastened convalescent Godric St. John would attend.

However, the three women didn't return to Oxford for a couple of days. There was a newer establishment solicitous of their attention. The Agency was invited to visit The Alchemy School President, Jez Robert Ransome Wiseman. He continued to surprise.

"Thank you for coming, brave investigators. First, let me say that I didn't ask you here because I want to see the Alchemy Scroll," he said with a broad smile.

325

Waving away Mary's assistance, he maneuvered his wheelchair to help himself to coffee on a side table. It was a big office with a view of the Pacific on one side, blackened mountains on another, and sofas arranged around a functioning fireplace. Mary was glad to see it unlit.

They all clutched huge mugs of dark brew. Anna added extra sugar and frowned. Mary sipped the tolerable roast, the first drinkable beverage since the nasty brew in the Evacuation Center. She gave the shaven-headed man one of her appraising stares. He grinned back.

It struck Mary that President Wiseman was the first person since their quest began *not* to want to get his hands on the Alchemy Scroll. Her curiosity stirred. Before she could frame a question, he spoke with more seriousness.

"I mean it: Don't bring the Alchemy Scroll here before you take it back to Oxford."

"Why not?" said Caroline, astonished. "That's what this has all been about, hasn't it? The *real* Scroll?"

"Ah yes, the *real* Alchemy Scroll. Which one is that, do you think?" A teacher now, Jez mischievously surveyed all three of them. An impromptu class, they were lined up in chairs, silent, pondering.

"You mean," said Mary, taking her time, "that Roberta Le More's Scroll has been at St. Julian's for centuries. Everyone believed it to be Mother Julian's."

She recalled how Caroline had been affected by the seventeenth-century copy. Her voice strengthened. "The Le More Scroll has been doing the work, the alchemical opus. We could say it's as real as Mother Julian's Scroll is real."

Jez nodded.

"It's real," Caroline announced, her face shining. "I *know* the Le More Scroll is real. Of course, it is."

Mary cast her mind back to Caroline touching the book. On the plane over, Caroline had told her more about her talks with Janet. The Key Keeper would train Caroline to take over as the Key Keeper *when the time came.*

"Don't you have to be a witch?" Mary had whispered. Her elbow almost struck Caroline's jaw as she held the tiny cup of white wine.

"Not, not… for us. Not with chronic dep…"

"Okay, I got it," Mary said hastily. She knew Caroline hated naming her illness. I guess that's a sort of spell, she realized. Naming makes it real.

Today, with the backdrop of still smoking mountains, Mary wanted to understand her host.

"President Wiseman, why not see the real Alchemy Scroll, the one from Mother Julian?" Mary's crisp authority drew another grin from Jez.

"My reluctance is all about Mother Julian," he said. "Plus, the wildfire. And, at the other extreme, I'm thinking of Cookie Mac. By the way, where is that disgrace to the history profession?"

Wildfire? Mary homed into what she could answer. "Cookie Mac's still in hospital, the John Whitcliffe in Oxford. Doctors say he has mercury poisoning. Probably from handling the re… *first* Scroll, improperly. He'll get better eventually." She sniffed.

"Dame Eleanor tells me that Mer-Corp wants him transferred to a research facility in Washington, DC. Naturally, we expect the Los Angeles police to have something to say about that. Either way, he'll be repatriated."

"Macdonald in a Mer-Corp lab? There's justice in that."

"Irony," said Mary. She liked irony. "So, what about the original Scroll, President Wiseman?"

"Jez, please."

"Is it because Mother Julian said the Scroll should never leave the College?" Caroline piped up.

"Precisely, Mrs. Jones. The Scroll should never leave the College for the health of the 'pore scholars.' Given that wise precept, look where we are now."

He spun his wheelchair in a full circle of indignation. "In the twenty-first century, an obscenely wealthy corporation funded a white supremacy group to get it *out* of Mother Julian's

College." He paused. "My Alchemy School wants no part of that. Ever, period."

He fixed his serious face on all three women. "One day I'll call on Mother's Julian's Scroll in its proper place. I'll go to her anchorite cell at St. Julian's."

"The fire on the mountain." That was Anna. "Alchemy," she said. "I feel it singing in my bones."

"Singing?" Mary would never understand Anna. The young woman turned away.

Wiseman's reply was tinged with respect.

"That great pair of alchemists, Francis Ransome and Roberta Le More, believed the work they did affected the world's spirit, the *anima mundi*. The Native Americans they met believed they too could and *should* interact with the Great Spirit. They lived with reverence for the land and all its peoples, the ancestors, the animals, the rocks, the trees, mountains."

Mary's jaw dropped; Caroline glowed; Anna pretended not to listen. Wiseman nodded, then continued.

"You mean...?" began Mary.

"Yes, it could have been so different, a meeting of like-minded earth-based spiritualities. Just imagine, *what could have been*?" There was a pause before Wiseman continued.

"It changed, of course. True alchemists were never powerful in Europe, merely tolerated by the Church. Those countries settled for the false alchemy of making gold for profit. In America the immigrants exploited the land and enslaved its peoples. Exploitation and capitalism are not alchemy, which was always in partnership with wild nature. The result is what you see."

Wiseman swung his chair to point directly at the ash piles and blackened trees out of the window. "That which has been split must be conjoined," he said.

Sparks ignited up Mary's spine. "Climate change," she said, slowly.

"Climate *emergency*," retorted Caroline.

328

Anna got up and left the room. Mary's gaze followed her until she caught a sound from Wiseman. He shook his head to say, don't go after her. To Mary's surprise, Caroline didn't either.

Changing his tone, Wiseman cocked a finger at Mary. "My old buddy Jeffreys called. As well as proper oversight for the appalling mental hospital that Mrs. Jones so bravely entered," here he smiled beatifically at Caroline who spluttered. "Jeffreys says that St. Julian's is bringing in researchers from your National Health Service. He thinks there's an arrangement to be made with the NHS for studentships for St. Julian's. He told me you'd proposed a sweet deal with Mer-Corp."

Mary flushed with pleasure; her plans were coming to fruition. While stuck in La Luna valley with only her notebook, she'd used the time to draft emails to Jeffreys and Dame Eleanor. After forthright suggestions about The Old Hospital, she tackled the shadowy role of Mer-Corp. Given insufficient evidence to indict Mer-Corp, perhaps they could try to broker a resolution for those College mortgages?

Mr. Jeffreys promised to contact Holywell's long-suffering lawyer. Mary also let slip that a St. Julian's graduate student was about to be charged with murder in Los Angeles. She could just imagine Jeffreys's reaction to that headache. She added that a long-established *Oxford* firm must have contacts in the States. What about a deal in which Ravi pleads guilty to the second-degree murder of D.P. and is allowed to serve his sentence in England? After all, he was also wanted in Oxford to answer for his battery of Godric St. John.

"Yes," said Mary, primly, to Jez. "Our representative is in talks with Mer-Corp. And if there really is a new antibiotic in the… in Mother Julian's Alchemy Scroll, then the NHS will get the benefit. If it can license a new drug, then the revenue will be considerable."

"So, you see, I'm honoring her, Mother Julian," said Jez, earnestly. "She wrote that awesome book on how her God never told anyone to rape the earth in His name. He was also a She, loving and maternal. Julian had heart enough to see that an Arab and African Scroll could heal the poor in England; at least those who wanted to be educated."

Jez's large hands waved. "That's a rare act in any day. Too rare in our day. Here at The Alchemy School, we want to give scholarships to poor students too. I've got something interesting for your Dame Eleanor. And I'm having another chat with my long-lost cousin Melissa in Los Angeles." His eyes twinkled. "She lives and breathes rich donors."

His enthusiasm stirred Mary. "What about that Symposium?" she said. "The European History Foundation is about to be exposed as a front for white supremacists — I have a historian friend who's following up what we discovered. The EHF is dead to academia. But you, President... Jez, um, The Alchemy School, could do it."

She was fired up. Caroline began to smile. Mary continued. "In fact, you could hold a joint event with St. Julian's. It's time to combine the scholarship in Oxford and California."

"On the African roots of alchemy," Jez nearly shouted. He almost fell out of his wheelchair with excitement. He leaned forward gipping both chair's arms.

"We could ask St. Julian's for a loan of Roberta Le More's Scroll. Just imagine, she's a genuine African American alchemist."

"The Agency could help," said Caroline.

"First condition of the Symposium," beamed Jez.

CHAPTER 49
LAST ACT IN OXFORD

The following day, three subdued women traveled from a bank in Santa Emilia to Heathrow, via a newly reopened Los Angeles Airport. Without debate they took turns carrying the suitcase containing the real Alchemy Scroll.

During the achingly long flight and drive that followed, Mary's stomach knotted over Anna and the fate of their Agency. Things are bad when Caroline won't look at Anna, she worried. In turn, the young woman avoided contact by scowling out of windows.

Steering through potholes that splashed mud on their battered car, Mary gulped as the wet roof of Holywell rose steaming in the sun.

Leni and Sam spotted the car first. They jumped up and down outside the main entrance with grins as wide as barns. Sam insisted on hugging all three exhausted travelers. He had news.

"Leni and I are engaged. Look, we got a ring at Oxford covered market," he crowed. "I'm going to enroll in a psychology degree. My mother's met Leni on Skype; she's over the moon."

"Fantastic, Sam," said Mary. She forced a smile through her sleep-deprived face. "We'll talk, I promise. Tomorrow for sure. Perhaps we can help pay for the course with some freelancing for the Agency? Right now, please take this to Janet's room. She's expecting it. The three of us must sleep. We've an appointment at St. Julian's tomorrow morning."

331

"You look like ghosts, happy ghosts," said Dorothy, smiling at the foot of the stairs. "The girls have made your beds. Amazingly, no one moaned. They're so happy to see you. And thankful for Leni. She's a different person since the charges were dropped. Did you know Godric St. John sent a bouquet of flowers?"

Mary looked unconvinced by Godric St. John's change of heart. Anna scowled.

*****

The next day required them to rise early. All three grouched as they stumbled to breakfast. Dame Eleanor spoke vaguely of the College's gratitude. *Needs to be accompanied by a cheque*, Mary said to herself, grimly. Today, however, the Agency and the St. Julian's principal would return the manuscript to the (reinforced) glass case. Three hundred and sixty years after the theft, the Alchemy Scroll had come home.

The jetlagged trio spoke little in the jarring sunshine of an unseasonably warm spring day. A surprise awaited them at the college. With each taking turns lugging the suitcase from the Oxford multistory car park, they entered the first quad to an eerie emptiness.

Even traffic noise ceased. A blackbird bounded along the damp lawn to trills of its mate from the gargoyle over the Chapel door. Mary was about to enquire of the porter when a grinning face appeared. An arm in a black gown waved frantically. The Organ Scholar, Michaela Agbabi, was inviting them in.

The Chapel was dark after the bright sun outside. As their eyes adjusted, Mary heard only murmuring voices. Apart from radiant stained-glass windows, illumination came from candles everywhere: all over the altar, the choir stalls, at the end of every pew. The warm fug was echoed by jars of yellow daffodils on the altar, a stand of iridescent narcissi by the pulpit.

The Chapel was packed, Mary realized. Most present were young, staring at the three women with curious sleepy eyes.

332

The students of St. Julian's turned out to welcome home their Alchemy Scroll. At a signal from Dame Eleanor, they all stood up in honor of The Depth Enquiry Agency. Mary felt her throat tighten.

Anna stuck her chin in the air and made off down the aisle. She could lug the Scroll suitcase using only one hand, unlike the other two. Mary linked arms with Caroline and followed. Dame Eleanor reverently opened the suitcase in front of the altar; the perfume from the blooms nearly choked Caroline. The principal tenderly unrolled the cloth bundle.

When she stood up, the Scroll's vellum skin was visible, cradled on a bed of wool in the open case. There was a collective intake of breath as several hundred students leaned forward to catch a glimpse.

Directed into the vacant front pew, Mary and Caroline took the opportunity to take in the assembly. Anna scuttled into a corner. Yes, that was Mr. Jeffreys slipping into a back pew next to… Oh, so that was why breakfast at Holywell had been so sparsely attended. The witches must have eaten earlier. They'd brought all the resident women, including Leni and Sam. He was waving. The engaged pair held up their clasped hands. For a split second, a spark flamed in the rose light from the back window.

Mary never cried. She wasn't going to now. Caroline glanced longingly at Anna, who moved with the grace of a leopard when they were directed to open the hymnbooks. Caroline and Mary stood ramrod straight as a choir began to sing "Ave Maria."

PART TWELVE
SUBLIMATIO

CHAPTER 50
A QUESTION OF TRUST

Two hours later Mary, Caroline and Anna gathered in the Queen's Lane Coffeehouse. Thank goodness for English coffee, thought Mary, as she stirred her cappuccino. They could no longer put off a difficult conversation. Mary had no idea how to begin.

Anna was demolishing a huge pastry, every so often breaking off bits as if she meant to offer them around. Caroline tried to ignore temptation by clamping hands and eyes on her black coffee. Anna also took sips from a glass of black tea with a lot of sugar.

"Russian," she once said when asked how she liked the traditional British brew.

The silence grew thick as they avoided each other's eyes. Mary's lavender suit needed dry cleaning, Caroline's orange jumper and jeans had a musty smell. Only Anna was superbly attired. Her blue cashmere sweater gave her olive skin a warm tint. Her black jeans were designer. Mary was sure of it — not that she knew clothes; she just knew Anna. Or thought she did. Did Caroline? Did she really know her lover?

Awkwardness shifted to gloom. It wasn't right, especially after the unexpectedly joyful ceremony for the Alchemy Scroll. Dame Eleanor handed them new contract along with a cheque. It included a retainer; this was to be an ongoing relationship with St. Julian's. They had hopes of a similar arrangement with The Alchemy School in California. After all they'd suffered, they should be celebrating that their Agency now had a future.

"Um, financially...the Agency is..."

337

"You can't set fires, Anna. Never again. Promise."

So fierce was Caroline that Anna choked on the pastry: crumbs tumbled from her mouth. Her hand shook. Swallowing more tea, she avoided Caroline's eyes. Instead, she aimed her defiance at Mary.

"And you? What's your reason to hate me?"

Mary sighed. "No one hates you."

"We love you," Caroline again. "Okay, Mary loves you differently from me. Yet even she loves you. Don't you, Mary?"

"Um." Mary coughed under the two pairs of eyes. She stepped up. "Of course. But what Caroline means is that the problem isn't love, it's trust. How can we trust you when you set fires and steal priceless scrolls. How can we trust you *when you don't trust yourself?*"

A gasp from Caroline led to silence. Mary could hear the old-fashioned clock on the wall ticking beneath the hum of conversation.

Eventually, Anna snorted in disbelief. That ignited something in Mary. It was now or never.

"Stop this, Anna. We drove through fire for you. The car *melted*. Don't you dare turn your nose up at our family."

In her expression, Anna's dark ashes stirred. Mary was not done.

"You stole the Alchemy Scroll. Yes, we know about the blackmail. Maybe you thought you were helping Leni; maybe yourself. Either way, you didn't inform us. You set a trap for a killer — a killer, Anna. Yet you *still* did not tell us. Ravi almost shot us. Are you sensing a theme yet?"

Caroline spoke quietly. "We nearly died — in the fire in those mountains and at the house when Ravi had a gun pointed at us." Her eyes were full of tears. "The fire you set at The Old Hospital could have killed me as well as Janet and Agnes."

Anna muttered into the syrupy dregs of her tea. "Fire, you're firing me?"

Mary grimaced. There had been too much fire. Too much even now, between them.

338

"The problem, Anna, is you're not sorry. You'd do it again. Maybe not the same things, but something just as reckless."

"Dangerous," said Caroline more gently. Anna moved a hand toward her, then snaked it back to her side. Mary had one last fear.

"You're a lone wolf, Anna. Not like us."

She hadn't wanted to say it, because she did not want to believe it — that Anna would never be like other people. The formerly trafficked cyberwitch would always be explosive and unpredictable.

Jeffreys had warned her. Anna never had a childhood. She had lived — no, *existed*, from one trauma to the next. She was a wildfire who could never really be contained. Even now, she wasn't denying it. No protests of reform came from the young woman kicking the table leg.

"I don't know what more to say," said Mary.

She really didn't. She never got depressed, but this case made her depressed. She'd been at rock bottom in the John Whitcliffe when Caroline found her. Now, at the height of their success Mary was stuck. She who always found a plan had no plan.

They sat silent for five terrible minutes. Tears coursed down Caroline's face. She reached out and grabbed Anna's second pastry. With a wail, she began to devour it.

"Don't overeat, Caroline," said Mary. She removed a large portion from Caroline's clutch. "Don't do this. You've eaten nothing today. Eat the rest slowly."

She stuck the crumbling remains in her handbag, repressing a shudder. "Caroline, slow bites. Chew, chew."

A harassed mother glanced from the next table. She was trying to get her child to eat a piece of toast, rather than using it to smear jam all over his face.

"Choo choo," called the little boy, momentarily angelic. "Choo choo." He put the jammy bread onto his curls like a hat. Seizing it, the mother gave an embarrassed smile to Mary.

Caroline offered a gallant wave. Then she put down the last lump of pastry.

"Choo, choo," said Mary, humor returning.

"Choo, choo," came another voice. Caroline and Mary stared at Anna, who was grinning. Then her face became serious. She caught both with the effort of her next words.

"You know I… kept going… on the case. I didn't give up… on our plan."

"We know," said Mary, quietly.

"Even when I thought you both… hated me."

"Never…"

Mary held up her hand to stop Caroline. It was Anna's turn.

"Is that… love?"

Mary was startled. Caroline brushed away her tears. She looked questioningly at Mary. Love? To carry on without hope, all alone. Was it enough? Was it a start?

Mary thought furiously. No, thinking won't do it. How did she feel, about these two women — because they were a pair, however you put it. Incurable, extraordinary, and needing her.

"If I try to *imagine* where we've been on this case…" she couldn't believe what she was about to say, "then we've been… well, I suppose, *connected*. Perhaps there's a kind of trust that goes on even if there is… a lack of…consultation."

Mary continued. "Perhaps it is togetherness… of a sort. I don't know if it's enough."

"We'll try, won't we?" Caroline echoed Mary's uncertainty. So did Anna's answering nod. Uncertainty linked them, as well as whatever it was that had drawn them safely through the fire. Welcome to the twenty-first century, thought Mary.

The Agency had begun to find its depth. Even in the darkness of incurable pain, they could reach out to each other. Mary bought another round of tea. This time the silence was affectionate.

"You know," said Caroline, eventually, "what Mother Julian famously said: "All shall be well, and all manner of things shall be well."

Anna twisted her lips. "That's not the world we live in."

Mary thought of the Anchorite sending the valuable Alchemy Scroll to help "pore scholers."

"Plenty of work ahead for the Agency," she said.

THE END

CPSIA information can be obtained
at www.ICGtesting.com
Printed in the USA
JSHW021046020423
39736JS00001B/2

9 781685 031299